Thank you for picking up my book. Your support means a lot, and I hope you find the read both enjoyable and insightful. Beyond being an author, my work extends into research and consultancy within organizational behavior and leadership. I engage with a broad spectrum of clients, from individuals to larger teams and organizations, offering guidance in leadership development.

For a deeper dive into my professional background and consulting philosophy, several websites are available. There, you'll also find my contact details. I'm eager to hear your thoughts on the book or discuss potential collaboration in leadership coaching.

Discover more about my work and other publications related to leadership and organizational behavior at my personal website, https://thomaspatrickhuber.com.

Learn about my specific approach to leadership coaching and consulting at https://elevateus.ch, the official website of my company.

Lastly, in case you want to reach out to me directly please send me an email at thomaspatrick@mac.com.

I appreciate your support in purchasing this book and look forward to connecting with you.

Wishing you an enlightening journey,

Thomas P Huber, PhD, MS ECS

Dedication

This book is dedicated to the resilient leaders across the globe who have navigated uncharted waters during the COVID-19 pandemic. To those who adapted swiftly, led with empathy, and showed unwavering strength in the face of uncertainty.

To the mentors and coaches who have tirelessly worked to shape the leaders of tomorrow, imparting wisdom and fostering growth amidst tumultuous times.

To every aspiring leader who stands at the threshold of this new era, ready to embrace change and forge a path of innovation and resilience.

May this book serve as a beacon, guiding you towards effective and compassionate leadership in a world that continues to evolve and challenge us in unprecedented ways.

Foreword

In "Navigating the New Normal: Leadership Strategies for a Post-Pandemic World," we embarked on this journey to explore and understand the transformative impact of the COVID-19 pandemic on the landscape of leadership. This book is born out of a deep-seated belief that the challenges we have faced during these times are not just obstacles but opportunities – opportunities to redefine, reshape, and rejuvenate the way we lead and manage in our businesses, governments, and communities.

Throughout the pandemic, leaders across various sectors have been thrust into a vortex of unprecedented challenges. We've witnessed a seismic shift in leadership dynamics, demanding a new set of skills and competencies. In writing this book, my aim was to investigate these emerging paradigms and offer a guide that resonates with both current leaders and those aspiring to lead in this new era.

In Section 1, the book explores the essential skills and competencies that have become indispensable in the post-pandemic world. This part of the book is a synthesis of research, interviews, and personal insights, focusing on adaptability, digital literacy, emotional intelligence, and crisis management. It is designed to offer you, the reader, not just theoretical knowledge but practical strategies to develop and enhance these skills.

Section 2 reflects on one of the most significant leadership transformations in recent history – the shift to managing remote and hybrid teams. Here, I share insights from leaders who have successfully adapted to this change, offering you a compilation of strategies, best practices, and lessons learned. It's a section close to my heart, as it echoes the resilience and ingenuity I've seen in so many leaders during these times.

In Section 3, the focus turns to the future – preparing and nurturing a pipeline of resilient leaders. This section is born out of a conviction that leadership is about foresight and preparation. It discusses how we can mentor and coach the next generation of leaders to be agile, adaptable, and ready for the unforeseen challenges that the future might hold.

Writing this book has been a journey of discovery, learning, and reflection. I have been humbled by the stories of resilience and innovation I've encountered and inspired by the adaptability and strength of leaders around the globe. This book is a tribute to all those who have led through these challenging times and a guide for those who aspire to lead in the future.

As you turn these pages, I invite you to reflect on your leadership journey and consider how the insights and strategies shared here can be woven into your personal and professional narrative. The path ahead may be laden with uncertainties, but with the right tools and mindset, I believe we can navigate it with confidence and purpose.

Thank you for joining me on this journey, and I hope this book serves as a valuable companion as you navigate the complexities and opportunities of leadership in a post-pandemic world.

Thomas P Huber, PhD, MS ECS

January 2024

Section 1: Essential Skills and Competencies for Post-Pandemic Leadership

In this pivotal section of "Navigating the New Normal: Leadership Strategies for a Post-Pandemic World," we turn our focus to the essential skills and competencies that have emerged as crucial for effective leadership in the aftermath of the COVID-19 pandemic. The landscape of leadership has been irreversibly altered, and with it, the skill set required to navigate this new terrain.

The pandemic was more than a global health crisis; it was a catalyst for profound change in organizational dynamics, team management, and leadership approaches. Leaders found themselves at the forefront of unprecedented challenges, from transitioning to remote work environments to managing the well-being of their teams amidst uncertainty. This section is dedicated to unraveling these complexities and laying out a clear path for developing the skills necessary to thrive in this changed world.

We begin by identifying the key skills and competencies that have become indispensable in the post-COVID era. These include adaptability, a skill that has taken on new significance as leaders navigate fast-changing scenarios; digital literacy, crucial in an increasingly digital world; emotional intelligence, which underpins the ability to lead with empathy and understanding; and crisis management, a skill that has been tested like never before during the pandemic.

Each chapter in this section is not just a discussion but a practical guide. We explore why these skills are essential, how they have evolved in the face of the pandemic, and, most importantly, how you can develop and enhance them. This section is designed to be interactive and introspective, encouraging you to assess your current skillset and identify areas for growth.

We explore the concept of continuous learning and upskilling, a critical aspect of post-pandemic leadership. The world is evolving rapidly, and staying abreast of these changes is vital for any leader. This section provides insights into how you can foster a mindset of continuous improvement and lifelong learning, ensuring that you are always prepared to meet the challenges and seize the opportunities that lie ahead.

As you embark on this journey through Section 1, I invite you to engage with an open mind and a willingness to grow. The skills and competencies discussed here are more than just requisites for professional success; they are tools that will empower you to lead with confidence, resilience, and foresight in a world forever changed by the events of the past few years.

Introduction

As we step into the realm of this book, it is crucial to first paint the backdrop against which modern leadership is evolving. The COVID-19 pandemic, a global crisis unprecedented in modern times, has not only impacted societies and economies across the world but has also fundamentally reshaped the landscape of business and leadership. This introduction aims to provide a brief overview of these profound changes and set the stage for the in-depth exploration of leadership in the chapters that follow.

When the pandemic swept across the globe, it brought with it a tidal wave of challenges. Businesses faced sudden disruptions, from supply chain breakdowns to mandatory closures. The economic impact was colossal, with industries struggling to adapt to rapidly changing market conditions. But beyond these operational and financial hurdles, the pandemic brought about a seismic shift in organizational dynamics and the very essence of workplace interaction.

Remote work, once a privilege offered by a few forward-thinking organizations, became a necessity overnight. Leaders were tasked with steering their teams through the murky waters of virtual collaboration, often without a playbook to guide them. This abrupt transition tested the adaptability and resilience of leaders and their teams to their limits.

The crisis highlighted the critical importance of emotional intelligence in leadership. The pandemic's toll on mental health and well-being demanded a leadership approach that was not just efficient but also empathetic and understanding. Leaders had to balance business objectives with the genuine human needs of their team members, navigating uncharted territory in employee engagement and support.

In this new landscape, the traditional, hierarchical models of leadership were quickly overshadowed by more agile, inclusive, and collaborative approaches. The pandemic underscored the need for leaders who could not only adapt to rapid changes but also foresee and navigate future uncertainties. It called for a reevaluation of what effective leadership looks like and the skills and qualities it entails.

As we dive deeper into this book, we will explore these shifts in detail, examining the new skills and competencies that leaders must possess in this post-pandemic era. We will look at how leaders can adapt their styles to meet the demands of a changing world, manage remote and hybrid teams effectively, and build resilience and innovation within their organizations. This journey is not just about understanding the changes but also about equipping current and aspiring leaders with the tools and insights to thrive in this new normal.

The post-COVID-19 world presents both formidable challenges and unique opportunities for leadership. As we navigate through the chapters of this book, we invite you to reflect, learn, and prepare to lead in this transformed landscape, where adaptability, empathy, and resilience are not just desirable but essential qualities for success.

In the wake of the COVID-19 pandemic, the very essence of leadership has undergone a significant transformation. This shift, necessitated by a global crisis, has rewritten the roles and expectations of leaders in almost every sector. As we explore this new paradigm, it is essential to understand how these changes manifest in the daily responsibilities of leaders and the broader impact on organizational culture.

One of the most evident changes has been the rapid shift to remote work. This transition has not only altered where work is conducted but also how leaders engage with their teams. The physical distance has necessitated a greater emphasis on clear, concise communication and trust-based management. Leaders are now expected to navigate the delicate balance of overseeing work without micromanaging, fostering a sense of autonomy among their teams while ensuring alignment with organizational goals.

The pandemic has highlighted the importance of emotional intelligence in leadership. Leaders are now expected to demonstrate heightened empathy, understanding, and support for their team members' mental and emotional well-being. This shift marks a move away from a solely performance-driven focus to a more holistic view of team management, recognizing that employee well-being directly impacts productivity and satisfaction.

Another significant change has been in crisis management and adaptability. Leaders are now expected to be more agile, capable of quickly adjusting strategies and plans in response to rapidly changing circumstances. This agility extends beyond crisis management to encompass broader strategic thinking, with leaders needing to anticipate future trends and prepare their organizations accordingly.

The pandemic has also presented new opportunities for innovation. With change being a constant, leaders are finding novel ways to drive business growth and adaptation. This has involved exploring new markets, embracing digital transformation, and rethinking traditional business models. Leaders are now at the forefront of fostering a culture of innovation, encouraging their teams to think creatively and take calculated risks.

The focus on sustainability and social responsibility has intensified. Leaders are increasingly expected to prioritize not just profit but also the impact of their decisions on the environment and society. This shift towards a more conscious form of leadership aligns with growing stakeholder expectations for businesses to contribute positively to global challenges.

The role of leadership in the new normal is characterized by a greater emphasis on flexibility, empathy, strategic agility, innovation, and social responsibility. Leaders who embrace these changes and adapt their styles accordingly are better positioned to navigate the complexities of the post-pandemic world, turning challenges into opportunities for growth and success. As we move forward, these evolving roles and expectations will continue to shape the trajectory of effective leadership.

The COVID-19 pandemic has not only been a disruptor but also a catalyst for a significant transformation in leadership skills. This transformation reflects a shift from traditional leadership paradigms, which often emphasized hierarchical, command-and-control models, to a more agile, empathetic, and adaptive approach. Understanding this shift involves analyzing traditional leadership skills against the backdrop of the new requirements that have emerged in the post-pandemic world, and identifying gaps that the pandemic has brought to light.

Traditional Leadership Skills

- Command and Control: Pre-pandemic leadership often valued decisiveness and authority, with a strong focus on command-and-control structures.

- Consistency and Uniformity: Leaders were expected to maintain consistency in processes and policies, valuing uniformity over flexibility.

- Long-term Planning: Emphasis was on long-term strategic planning, with rigid roadmaps and fixed objectives.

- In-Person Management: Leadership skills were largely exercised in a physical workspace, relying heavily on face-to-face interactions.

Post-Pandemic Leadership Requirements

- Adaptability and Agility: The ability to quickly pivot and adapt strategies in response to rapid changes has become crucial.

- Digital Proficiency: Skills in managing virtual teams and leveraging technology for communication and operations are essential.

- Emotional Intelligence: A greater emphasis on empathy, understanding, and supporting the mental well-being of team members.

- Crisis Management: Competence in navigating through uncertainty and making swift decisions under pressure.

- Inclusivity and Diversity: A heightened focus on leading diverse teams with inclusivity and cultural sensitivity.

Identifying Gaps in Leadership Skillsets

- From Stability to Agility: Many leaders who excelled in stable environments found themselves challenged by the need for rapid adaptation and flexibility.

- Remote Leadership Challenges: The shift to remote work exposed gaps in digital skills and the ability to manage teams effectively from a distance.

- Emotional and Mental Health Awareness: The pandemic highlighted a lack of training in addressing mental health issues and providing emotional support to employees.

- Short-term Reactive Planning: The need for short-term, reactive planning revealed a gap for leaders accustomed to long-term, predictable strategies.

- Crisis Preparedness: Many leaders were unprepared for the scale and immediacy of the crisis, indicating a gap in crisis management and resilience skills.

The pandemic has thus prompted a reevaluation of what effective leadership looks like, pushing leaders to develop skills that cater to a more dynamic, uncertain, and digitally connected world. The transformation of these skills is not just a response to a temporary crisis but a long-term evolution that sets the foundation for resilient, empathetic, and adaptive leadership in the future.

The necessity for new skills and competencies in the aftermath of the pandemic is rooted in the profound changes that have occurred in the business landscape. These changes have redefined the qualities that constitute effective leadership. In this new paradigm, certain skills have emerged as more critical than ever, reflecting the evolving challenges and expectations that leaders face today.

Adaptability stands out as a pivotal skill in this new era. The pandemic's sudden onset and the ongoing fluctuations in the business environment have shown that the ability to adapt quickly and effectively to change is not just an asset but a necessity. Leaders who demonstrate adaptability are better equipped to navigate uncertainties, pivot strategies in response to evolving circumstances, and guide their teams through transitions smoothly.

Digital proficiency has also become increasingly important. With the shift to remote work and the accelerated digital transformation of businesses, leaders must be comfortable and competent in leveraging digital tools and platforms. This proficiency goes beyond basic technological know-how; it encompasses the ability to lead teams remotely, engage employees through digital channels, and utilize technology to drive innovation and efficiency.

Emotional intelligence, which includes skills such as empathy, self-awareness, and social awareness, has taken center stage. The pandemic has placed unprecedented stress on individuals and organizations, making the human aspect of leadership more important than ever. Leaders who possess high emotional intelligence can better understand and respond to the needs and concerns of their team members, fostering a supportive and cohesive work environment. This ability to connect on a human level helps in building trust, enhancing communication, and maintaining morale during challenging times.

Crisis management is another competency that has gained prominence. The pandemic was a clear demonstration of how quickly crises can arise and how deeply they can impact organizations. Leaders must now be adept at managing crises, which involves making rapid decisions under pressure, communicating effectively during emergencies, and steering the organization through periods of instability. This skill is crucial not only for navigating the immediate challenges of a crisis but also for positioning the organization for post-crisis recovery and growth.

The post-pandemic world demands a new set of leadership skills and competencies. These skills are essential for leaders to effectively address the unique challenges of this era and to guide their organizations toward sustained success and resilience. As the business landscape continues to evolve, the importance of adaptability, digital proficiency, emotional intelligence, and crisis management will likely become even more pronounced, defining the new standard for effective leadership.

The emergence and widespread adoption of remote and hybrid work models have significantly altered traditional leadership approaches. This shift, largely accelerated by the COVID-19 pandemic, has introduced new dynamics into the workplace, compelling leaders to rethink how they manage and interact with their teams.

One of the most fundamental changes brought about by remote and hybrid work models is the physical separation of teams. This distance challenges leaders to maintain team cohesion, communication, and a sense of shared purpose without the benefit of face-to-face interactions. It necessitates a more deliberate and structured approach to communication, ensuring that all team members, regardless of their location, feel connected and informed. Leaders have had to become more proficient in using digital communication tools, not just for task delegation and progress checks, but also for maintaining team morale and a sense of community.

These work models have underscored the need for trust and autonomy in the leader-team member relationship. With employees working remotely or in a hybrid setting, leaders can no longer rely on direct oversight as a management technique. Instead, they are required to set clear expectations and trust their team members to carry out their responsibilities. This shift calls for a more results-oriented approach, where the focus is on the outcomes rather than the process.

The remote and hybrid models have also highlighted the importance of flexibility. Leaders must accommodate diverse working hours and conditions, recognizing that a one-size-fits-all approach is less effective. This flexibility extends to understanding individual team members' situations, such as balancing home responsibilities and work, which can vary significantly across the team.

Adapting to managing distributed teams effectively also involves a renewed focus on mental health and well-being. Remote work can blur the lines between professional and personal life, leading to burnout and isolation. Leaders need to be attuned to these risks and proactive in offering support, be it through flexible working arrangements, regular check-ins, or resources for mental health support.

Leaders must hone their skills in managing team dynamics and conflict resolution from a distance. The lack of informal, in-person interactions means that misunderstandings and conflicts might not be as readily apparent. Leaders must be vigilant and proactive in identifying and addressing such issues before they escalate.

The impact of remote and hybrid work models on leadership is profound and multifaceted. It requires leaders to develop new skills and approaches, particularly in the areas of communication, trust-building, flexibility, and mental health awareness. Adapting to these models is not just a temporary adjustment but a long-term transformation in the way leadership is practiced in the modern workplace. As organizations continue to embrace these models, the ability to effectively manage distributed teams will become an increasingly vital component of successful leadership.

In a digitally accelerated world, the significance of digital literacy and technology adoption in leadership cannot be overstated. The rapid pace of digital transformation, further expedited by the COVID-19 pandemic, has fundamentally reshaped not only organizational strategies but also the very roles and expectations of leaders. This evolution calls for a deep dive into how leaders can navigate and lead effectively in an increasingly digital landscape.

The first critical aspect of this digital acceleration is the need for leaders to possess robust digital literacy. This goes beyond basic technological competence; it encompasses a comprehensive understanding of digital trends, tools, and their implications for the business. Leaders must be adept at leveraging digital resources to enhance operational efficiency, drive innovation, and create competitive advantages. This literacy enables them to make informed decisions that align with the evolving digital landscape and the organization's strategic objectives.

The role of technology in shaping organizational strategies has become more pronounced. Digital tools and platforms are no longer just facilitators of operations; they are integral drivers of business growth and transformation. Leaders are now expected to not only understand these technologies but to be proactive in their adoption and implementation. This might involve exploring new digital business models, integrating advanced technologies like artificial intelligence and big data analytics into decision-making processes, or redefining customer engagement through digital channels.

Another dimension of leadership in a digitally accelerated world is the emphasis on data-driven decision-making. The abundance of data available through digital means provides leaders with insights that were previously inaccessible. However, the ability to harness this data effectively – to analyze, interpret, and apply it to business strategies – is a critical skill that modern leaders must possess.

Digital transformation has also led to changes in the workforce and workplace dynamics. The rise of remote work, digital collaboration tools, and virtual project management has necessitated a shift in leadership styles. Leaders are required to manage and motivate teams in a virtual environment, maintain productivity, and foster a collaborative culture, all through digital means. This requires not only technical skills but also a high degree of adaptability and emotional intelligence to engage and inspire teams remotely. Cybersecurity also becomes a paramount concern. Leaders must be knowledgeable about the risks associated with digital operations and ensure that robust cybersecurity measures are in place. This involves understanding the landscape of digital threats and working closely with IT and cybersecurity teams to safeguard organizational data and systems.

Leadership in a digitally accelerated world demands a multifaceted approach. It requires leaders to be digitally literate, embrace technology in strategic decision-making, leverage data effectively, adapt to new digital work environments, and prioritize cybersecurity. As digital transformation continues to reshape the business landscape, these skills and competencies will become increasingly crucial for leaders seeking to drive their organizations forward successfully.

In today's fast-evolving and often unpredictable business environment, underscored by challenges like the COVID-19 pandemic, the significance of leading with empathy and emotional intelligence (EI) has been magnified. These attributes have become indispensable in steering teams through times of uncertainty and maintaining a sense of cohesion and morale within organizations.

Emotional intelligence in leadership encompasses the ability to understand and manage one's emotions and those of others. This skill set, which includes self-awareness, self-regulation, motivation, empathy, and social skills, is particularly crucial during uncertain times. It enables leaders to navigate complex emotional dynamics, ensuring decisions and interactions are not adversely affected by heightened stress or anxiety.

Self-awareness and self-regulation allow leaders to remain composed and clear-headed, crucial qualities when guiding teams through uncharted territories. A leader's ability to stay motivated and convey optimism is infectious, fostering a similar spirit of perseverance and focus among team members. Additionally, EI encompasses adeptness in managing relationships and social complexities, vital for maintaining unity and collaboration, especially when traditional working norms are disrupted.

The role of empathy in leadership extends beyond understanding and resonating with the feelings of team members. It is about maintaining team cohesion. Empathetic leaders can effectively address concerns and conflicts, ensuring that every team member feels heard and valued. This empathetic approach boosts morale, particularly in challenging times when anxieties run high and the future seems uncertain.

Empathy also contributes significantly to building and maintaining trust within a team. When team members feel genuinely cared for, their trust in leadership strengthens, fostering a more open and collaborative environment. Empathetic leaders not only recognize the emotional needs of their team members but also address these needs, thus enhancing the overall team spirit and commitment.

Leading with empathy and emotional intelligence is a strategic approach to leadership. It goes beyond the realm of soft skills and has tangible implications for team performance, especially during periods of change and uncertainty. An empathetic and emotionally intelligent leader is equipped to handle the complexities of human emotions, fostering a supportive team environment and guiding the organization through challenges with unity and resilience. As the business landscape continues to evolve, these qualities are essential for any leader aiming to inspire and effectively guide their team.

The importance of preparing leaders for future crises has been starkly highlighted by the COVID-19 pandemic. This global event has underscored the need for robust crisis management skills, not only to navigate current challenges but also to fortify organizations against future unforeseen events. The experiences gleaned from the pandemic provide a valuable framework for building more resilient leadership practices, ensuring leaders are better equipped to handle similar situations in the future.

Crisis management skills have emerged as a critical component of effective leadership. The ability to quickly assess situations, make decisive actions, and communicate effectively under pressure are essential in managing any crisis. Future leaders must be adept in these areas, understanding that the unpredictable nature of crises requires flexibility and the capacity to adapt strategies rapidly.

The COVID-19 pandemic has been a profound learning experience for leaders worldwide. It has tested their ability to respond to rapidly changing scenarios, manage teams under stress, and make critical decisions amidst uncertainty. This experience has highlighted several key areas for development in crisis leadership, including the importance of contingency planning, the value of clear and empathetic communication, and the need for swift yet calculated decision-making.

Building more resilient leadership practices involves incorporating these learnings into ongoing leadership development programs. It means training leaders to anticipate and prepare for crisis scenarios, even those that seem unlikely. Leaders should be encouraged to think critically about risk assessment, business continuity planning, and scenario planning. These skills are not just for senior executives but should be integrated throughout the organizational hierarchy, creating a culture of preparedness and resilience.

The pandemic has shown the importance of emotional resilience in leadership. The human element of crises – managing one's own stress and anxiety while supporting the emotional well-being of team members – has been as crucial as operational management. Future leadership training should thus emphasize the development of emotional intelligence and stress management skills, alongside traditional crisis management competencies.

Another vital lesson from the pandemic is the need for adaptability in leadership styles. Crises often require a departure from standard operating procedures, calling for leaders who can innovate and think outside the box. This adaptability also extends to embracing new technologies and digital tools, which have proven invaluable in maintaining operations and communication during the pandemic.

Preparing leaders for future crises is a multifaceted endeavor. It involves not only equipping them with traditional crisis management skills but also fostering emotional resilience, adaptability, and innovative thinking. The COVID-19 pandemic, while challenging, offers a blueprint for building these resilient leadership practices, ensuring that future leaders are better prepared to navigate and manage any crisis they may face.

The imperative for leaders to evolve and adapt their skills in the face of an ever-changing global landscape has never been more apparent. The COVID-19 pandemic, with its far-reaching impacts, has served as a crucial catalyst for this transformation, shedding light on the deficiencies of traditional leadership models while simultaneously unveiling the competencies necessary for effective leadership in the new normal.

The chapters that follow are dedicated to a deep dive into the development of these essential skills. Each chapter has been meticulously crafted to guide current and aspiring leaders through the nuances of this new leadership paradigm. From enhancing adaptability and digital literacy to fostering emotional intelligence and honing crisis management abilities, the forthcoming sections offer a comprehensive exploration of the skills that are indispensable in today's world.

This journey of skill development is not just about professional growth; it is about preparing leaders to navigate complexities with confidence and lead their organizations towards a future that, though uncertain, is replete with opportunities. The emphasis is on building a repertoire of skills that are robust, versatile, and aligned with the demands of a rapidly evolving global environment.

The importance of continuous learning and adaptation cannot be overstated. The ability to learn, unlearn, and relearn is fundamental in this era of constant change. As such, the chapters ahead do not merely present information; they encourage introspection, application, and continuous personal and professional development.

The journey through these chapters is an invitation to leaders to embark on a transformative path. It is an opportunity to acquire new perspectives, sharpen existing skills, and develop new competencies that are critical for success in the post-pandemic era. As you dive into the following chapters, be prepared to challenge your assumptions, broaden your horizons, and embrace the journey of becoming a leader who is not only equipped to face the challenges of today but also poised to seize the opportunities of tomorrow.

Identifying Key Skills and Competencies

As we transition into a world profoundly altered by the COVID-19 pandemic, it becomes imperative to identify and understand the key skills and competencies necessary for effective leadership in the post-COVID era. This chapter aims to dissect and explain how the skillset required for successful leadership has evolved in response to the changes and challenges brought about by the pandemic.

The onset of COVID-19 has not just been a health and economic crisis; it has fundamentally altered the way businesses operate and how leaders need to interact with their teams and stakeholders. With these changes come new demands on leaders – demands that require a different set of skills and competencies than those that were prioritized in the pre-pandemic world.

One of the most significant shifts has been the movement towards a more digital, remote, and fluid working environment. This shift has elevated the importance of digital literacy, not just as a technical skill but as a vital component of leadership. Leaders are now required to manage teams remotely, utilize digital tools for collaboration and decision-making, and lead digital transformation initiatives within their organizations.

Another critical aspect that has come to the forefront is emotional intelligence. The pandemic has placed unprecedented stress on employees, and leaders must now be adept at navigating these emotional landscapes. This involves a greater focus on empathy, understanding, and the ability to connect with team members at a deeper level. Leaders need to foster a supportive environment, one where the mental well-being of their team is as important as their physical health.

Adaptability and resilience have become cornerstone competencies. The rapidly changing business landscape, marked by uncertainty and volatility, requires leaders who can pivot strategies quickly, embrace change, and guide their teams through uncharted waters with confidence and assurance. Crisis management, too, has taken on new dimensions. Leaders must now be prepared not just for typical business crises but also for large-scale disruptions that can impact their entire operation. This requires an ability to think critically and strategically, manage risk effectively, and make swift decisions under pressure.

Viewing the landscape of leadership in the post-COVID era, it becomes increasingly clear that certain skills have risen in prominence, becoming essential for effective leadership. These skills – adaptability, digital literacy, emotional intelligence, and crisis management – form the cornerstone of what it takes to lead successfully in this transformed world. This chapter provides a brief introduction to each of these four essential skills, setting the stage for a deeper exploration in the subsequent sections.

Adaptability has emerged as a key skill in a world where change is the only constant. The ability of a leader to pivot strategies, embrace new methodologies, and lead teams through transitions has become critical. Adaptability is not just about reacting to changes but proactively anticipating them and being prepared to evolve accordingly.

Digital Literacy goes beyond basic technological know-how. In the wake of widespread remote work and the acceleration of digital transformation, leaders must be adept at using technology to enhance operations, communication, and collaboration. Digital literacy in leadership involves understanding the strategic implications of digital technologies and being able to leverage them effectively to achieve organizational goals.

Emotional Intelligence has taken center stage as leaders navigate the complexities of managing teams through uncertain and stressful times. This skill involves understanding and managing one's own emotions as well as recognizing and appropriately responding to the emotions of others. Emotional intelligence is crucial for fostering a supportive work environment, maintaining team morale, and ensuring effective communication.

Crisis Management, always a critical skill for leaders, has gained new dimensions in the post-pandemic world. The global crisis has underscored the need for leaders to be able to manage and respond to emergencies effectively. This involves swift decision-making, clear communication, and the ability to keep teams focused and calm under pressure.

In the following sections, we will review each of these skills in detail, examining why they are necessary, how they can be developed, and their practical application in the current leadership context. Understanding and mastering these skills will be instrumental for leaders who aspire to navigate the challenges of the post-pandemic world successfully and lead their organizations toward a thriving future.

Adaptability, often hailed as the cornerstone of post-pandemic leadership, has taken on a pivotal role in defining how leaders navigate the current business landscape. In the context of leadership, adaptability refers to the ability of a leader to quickly adjust to new circumstances, rethink strategies, and embrace change, not just as a challenge but as an opportunity for growth and innovation. This quality has become indispensable in the fast-evolving business environment shaped by the COVID-19 pandemic.

The pandemic has thrust the world into a state of flux, with rapid shifts in market demands, work arrangements, and consumer behaviors. Leaders who have demonstrated adaptability have been able to pivot their operations, explore new business models, and maintain team cohesion in the face of these challenges. This agility has allowed them not only to survive but often to thrive, finding new avenues for growth and efficiency.

Examples of adaptability in action during the pandemic are numerous and varied. One notable instance is how businesses shifted to remote working models. Leaders who adapted quickly implemented new technologies and work practices to ensure continuity. Another example is seen in the retail and hospitality sectors, where businesses pivoted to online platforms or reimagined their services to meet changing customer needs, such as offering home deliveries or virtual experiences.

To develop and enhance adaptability in leadership roles, several strategies can be employed:

1. Fostering a Growth Mindset: Encourage a culture of learning and experimentation. Leaders with a growth mindset view challenges as opportunities to learn rather than obstacles to success.

2. Embracing Change: Cultivate an attitude that is open to change. This involves staying informed about industry trends, being receptive to new ideas, and willing to discard outdated practices.

3. Building Flexible Strategies: Develop business strategies that are flexible and can be adjusted as circumstances change. This might involve scenario planning and creating contingency plans.

4. Encouraging Team Agility: Promote agility within the team by encouraging cross-functional skills and empowering team members to take initiative and make decisions.

5. Practicing Resilience: Develop resilience to handle setbacks and failures. Resilient leaders are better equipped to bounce back from challenges and use their experiences to grow.

Adaptability in leadership is more than a skill; it's a mindset that embraces change, seeks out opportunities in challenges, and constantly strives for improvement. In the post-pandemic world, this adaptability will continue to be a key determinant of successful leadership, enabling leaders and their organizations to navigate an ever-changing business landscape with agility and confidence.

The expanded role of digital technology in business and leadership has been one of the most significant shifts in the modern workplace, particularly highlighted by the pandemic's challenges. Digital literacy for leaders is no longer a nice-to-have skill but a fundamental requirement. It encompasses a broad understanding and effective utilization of digital technologies to enhance business operations, communication, decision-making, and innovation.

The importance of digital literacy in leadership manifests in various aspects. First, in the realm of communication, digital proficiency enables leaders to leverage various platforms and tools to connect with their teams, stakeholders, and customers effectively. In a world where remote work has become commonplace, being adept at using these tools is essential for maintaining clear and consistent communication.

In terms of decision-making, digital literacy plays a crucial role in accessing, analyzing, and interpreting data. The abundance of data available through digital means can inform more nuanced and strategic decisions if leaders are skilled in data analysis. Furthermore, an understanding of digital tools and platforms can help leaders identify trends and insights that might otherwise be overlooked.

Regarding innovation, digital literacy opens up new avenues for business growth and development. Leaders who are digitally literate can spearhead initiatives that leverage technology to create new products, services, or business models, thus staying ahead in a competitive market.

For leaders looking to improve their digital skills and integrate technology into their leadership practices, several practical steps can be taken:

1. Continuous Learning: Engage in ongoing learning to stay updated with the latest digital trends and technologies. This can be through formal courses, online workshops, webinars, or self-guided learning.

2. Collaboration with IT Teams: Work closely with IT and digital teams to gain insights into the latest technologies and how they can be applied within the organization.

3. Experimentation: Encourage and participate in experimenting with new technologies within the team or department. This could involve pilot projects or small-scale implementations.

4. Leveraging Digital Tools for Collaboration: Actively use digital tools for team collaboration, project management, and communication to set an example for the team and understand the practical applications of these tools.

5. Seeking Feedback: Regularly solicit feedback from team members on the effectiveness of digital tools and practices being used, and be open to making adjustments based on this feedback.

Digital literacy for leaders in the current business environment is about more than just understanding technology; it's about leveraging it to drive strategic objectives, foster innovation, and lead teams effectively in a digitally transformed world. As digital technologies continue to evolve, so too must the capabilities of leaders in harnessing these tools for the growth and success of their organizations.

Emotional intelligence has emerged as a critical component in the repertoire of modern leadership, especially underlined during times of crisis and uncertainty, such as those experienced during the COVID-19 pandemic. This form of intelligence transcends the conventional understanding of cognitive abilities, emphasizing the profound impact of empathy, understanding, and emotional awareness in leading teams.

At the core of emotional intelligence lies the concept of self-awareness. This is the ability of a leader to understand and recognize their own emotions and how these emotions can affect their thoughts and behaviors. This awareness is crucial as it lays the foundation for effective self-regulation – the ability to control or redirect disruptive emotions and impulses and adapt to changing circumstances.

Alongside these, motivation is another key component of emotional intelligence. It is not just about personal drive but also about the ability to inspire and motivate others. Leaders with high emotional intelligence harness their passion to guide their teams towards achieving goals, especially in challenging times when morale may be low.

Empathy, perhaps the most talked-about aspect of emotional intelligence in recent times, is the ability to understand and share the feelings of others. In leadership, empathy translates to a genuine concern for team members' well-being and an understanding of the emotional undercurrents within the team. This understanding is pivotal in managing teams effectively, as it fosters a supportive and open environment where individuals feel valued and understood.

Social skills in emotional intelligence refer to the ability to manage relationships and build networks. Leaders with strong social skills are adept at finding common ground, building rapport, and managing and influencing others effectively. These skills are vital in creating a collaborative and cohesive team environment.

Enhancing emotional intelligence involves a combination of self-reflection, feedback, and deliberate practice. Leaders can work on their emotional intelligence by seeking regular feedback from peers and team members, engaging in active listening, and being open to understanding different perspectives. Practices such as mindfulness and empathy exercises can also help leaders become more attuned to their own emotions and those of others.

Incorporating emotional intelligence into leadership is not just about applying these skills in isolation. It's about integrating them into everyday interactions and decision-making processes. It involves leading with a sense of compassion and understanding, taking into account the emotional needs of team members, and recognizing the human aspect of business operations.

Leading with emotional intelligence is crucial in today's fast-paced and often unpredictable business environment. It empowers leaders to create a work culture that values and nurtures emotional well-being, ultimately leading to more effective, resilient, and cohesive teams.

Crisis management has always been a critical aspect of leadership, but its significance has been magnified in the post-pandemic world. Defined broadly, crisis management is the process by which an organization deals with a disruptive and unexpected event that threatens to harm the organization or its stakeholders. The COVID-19 pandemic, a crisis of unprecedented scale and impact, has brought to light the vital need for effective crisis management skills in leadership.

The pandemic has been a real-time, global case study in crisis response and management. It has shown that the traditional approach to crisis management, often reactive and focused on specific, predictable scenarios, is no longer sufficient. Instead, the emphasis has shifted towards a more proactive, adaptive approach. The lessons learned from COVID-19 in terms of crisis response include the importance of swift decision-making, the need for clear and transparent communication, and the ability to pivot strategies in response to rapidly evolving situations.

One of the key learnings from the pandemic is the necessity of having a robust crisis management plan in place. Such a plan should not only outline the steps to take in various crisis scenarios but also include mechanisms for quick decision-making and adaptability to unforeseen circumstances. Regular reviews and updates of this plan are crucial, as they ensure that the organization remains prepared for a range of potential crises.

Effective communication is another critical component of crisis management. During a crisis, leaders must communicate with clarity, transparency, and empathy to maintain trust and calm among stakeholders. This involves not only disseminating information about the crisis and its impacts but also providing clear guidance on the organization's response and what is expected of employees and other stakeholders.

Problem-solving skills are also tested during crises. Leaders must be able to think critically and creatively to navigate challenges, often with limited information and time. This requires a balance of analytical thinking to understand the situation and creative thinking to find solutions.

Resilience is a key aspect of crisis management. This encompasses not just the ability to withstand a crisis but also to learn from it and emerge stronger. Resilient leaders are able to maintain a sense of perspective during crises, provide support to their teams, and use the experience as an opportunity for organizational learning and improvement.

Crisis management in the post-pandemic world requires leaders to be prepared, adaptable, communicative, problem-solving, and resilient. Building these skills enables leaders to not only navigate the unpredictability of crises but also to lead their organizations through such challenging times with confidence and foresight.

Integrating adaptability, digital literacy, emotional intelligence, and crisis management into leadership practice is not just about developing these skills in isolation; it's about understanding how they interconnect and support one another. Successful leaders recognize that these competencies are interwoven and that their combined application can lead to more robust and effective leadership.

Adaptability and digital literacy, for instance, go hand in hand. In today's fast-paced and technology-driven business environment, being adaptable often means being digitally savvy. Leaders who quickly adapted to remote working during the pandemic did so by leveraging digital tools and platforms, demonstrating how adaptability in mindset is complemented by digital skills.

Emotional intelligence plays a crucial role in all aspects of leadership, including crisis management. Leaders who excel in crisis situations are often those who can empathize with their team members, understand their concerns, and communicate effectively. This emotional connection helps in maintaining team morale and cohesion, especially during challenging times.

Numerous case studies from the pandemic era illustrate how leaders have successfully integrated these skills. For instance, CEOs who navigated their companies through the initial shock of the pandemic did so by quickly adapting their business models, using digital platforms to maintain operations, empathizing with both employees and customers, and managing the crisis through clear communication and strategic decision-making.

For leaders looking to self-assess and continuously improve these competencies, reflection and feedback are key. Regular self-reflection on leadership practices and decisions, especially in challenging situations, can provide valuable insights. Seeking feedback from peers, mentors, and team members is also crucial in understanding the impact of one's leadership style and identifying areas for improvement.

Another tip for continuous improvement is to engage in lifelong learning. This could involve taking courses on digital literacy, attending workshops on emotional intelligence, or participating in leadership development programs that focus on adaptability and crisis management. Staying informed about the latest trends and challenges in the business world can also help leaders apply their skills more effectively.

Integrating adaptability, digital literacy, emotional intelligence, and crisis management into leadership practice requires a holistic approach. It involves not only developing these skills but also understanding how they complement each other and applying them in a coordinated manner. Leaders who master this integration are better equipped to lead effectively, especially in a business environment that continues to be shaped by rapid change and uncertainty.

As we reach the conclusion of this exploration into the key skills essential for leadership in the post-COVID era, it becomes clear that adaptability, digital literacy, emotional intelligence, and crisis management are not just isolated competencies but fundamental pillars of modern leadership. The pandemic has accelerated changes in the business landscape, necessitating a leadership approach that is dynamic, empathetic, technologically savvy, and resilient in the face of crises.

The importance of these skills has been repeatedly underscored in recent times. Adaptability has emerged as a crucial trait for navigating the constant flux of the business environment, while digital literacy has become imperative in a world where virtual interactions and digital operations are the norm. Emotional intelligence, with its focus on empathy and understanding, has proved vital in managing teams through the stresses and uncertainties of the pandemic. Lastly, crisis management skills have become essential in preparing for and navigating through unexpected challenges that can disrupt businesses.

As leaders, the journey of developing and honing these skills is ongoing. The post-COVID world is characterized by continuous change and unpredictability, making it crucial for leaders to not only possess these skills but to continually refine and apply them in various scenarios. This involves staying curious and committed to lifelong learning, being open to feedback, and being willing to adapt one's leadership style as circumstances evolve.

Leaders who successfully integrate these skills into their practice are better equipped to lead their organizations through the complexities of the current era and beyond. They are capable of fostering innovation, driving growth, and creating resilient and agile teams. The encouragement for every leader, therefore, is to embrace this journey of continuous development, recognizing that the evolution of their skills is integral to their effectiveness and success in an ever-evolving world.

The post-COVID era presents both challenges and opportunities for leaders. By embracing adaptability, enhancing digital literacy, cultivating emotional intelligence, and developing robust crisis management skills, leaders can not only navigate these challenges successfully but also emerge as visionary guides, steering their organizations towards a thriving future.

Developing Adaptability and Flexibility

As we transition into the next crucial chapter, 'Developing Adaptability and Flexibility,' we dive into the heart of what makes a leader truly effective in today's ever-changing business environment. This chapter is dedicated to understanding and enhancing two intertwined and pivotal skills: adaptability and flexibility.

Adaptability and flexibility are often spoken of together because they represent two sides of the same coin in the realm of effective leadership. Adaptability refers to the ability of a leader to change or modify their approach in response to new information, changing conditions, or unexpected obstacles. It's about being able to pivot strategies, embrace new methodologies, and lead teams through transitions with ease and confidence. Flexibility, on the other hand, is about the capacity to bend without breaking. It's the skill of being open to new ideas, different viewpoints, and alternative ways of working. It requires a certain level of comfort with uncertainty and the unknown.

In the context of the post-pandemic world, where businesses are continually facing unprecedented challenges and disruptions, the value of adaptability and flexibility cannot be overstated. Leaders who exhibit these skills are better positioned to navigate the complexities of an ever-evolving landscape. They are the ones who can lead their teams to not just survive but thrive amidst change.

This chapter will provide a comprehensive exploration of how to develop these critical skills. From understanding the psychological underpinnings of adaptability and flexibility to practical strategies for cultivating these qualities in yourself and your team, the chapter aims to equip leaders with the necessary tools to excel in a world where change is the only constant.

Emphasizing real-life examples, practical exercises, and reflective questions, the chapter will guide leaders through the process of transforming challenges into opportunities for growth and innovation. The goal is to create leaders who are not just capable of handling change but who can anticipate and drive it, ensuring their organizations are agile, resilient, and prepared for the future.

In the context of leadership, adaptability and flexibility are traits that have gained extraordinary significance, especially in the rapidly evolving business environment of today. Adaptability in leadership refers to the capacity of leaders to adjust their strategies, approaches, and behaviors in response to changing circumstances, new information, or unforeseen challenges. It is about being agile in decision-making, open to new ideas, and ready to pivot when the situation demands. Flexibility, a closely related trait, involves the willingness and ability to modify plans and approaches, accommodate different perspectives, and embrace change with a positive attitude.

These traits have become increasingly crucial in the current business landscape, which is characterized by volatility, uncertainty, complexity, and ambiguity (VUCA). The rapid pace of technological advancements, shifting market dynamics, and unexpected global events like the COVID-19 pandemic have underscored the need for leaders who are not just capable of navigating through changes but can also thrive in such environments.

Adaptable and flexible leaders are able to lead their organizations through transitions smoothly, minimizing disruptions while maximizing opportunities that arise from new situations. They can quickly reassess and realign their strategies to fit the new context, ensuring their organizations remain relevant and competitive. Additionally, such leaders are adept at managing the anxiety and resistance that often accompany change, helping their teams to embrace new directions and approaches.

Adaptability and flexibility in leadership are about more than survival; they're about fostering a culture of continuous improvement, innovation, and resilience. Leaders who embody these traits inspire their teams to be more agile and responsive, creating organizations that are better equipped to face the challenges and capitalize on the opportunities presented by a rapidly changing world.

The role of adaptability in modern leadership has become increasingly critical, particularly in the post-pandemic era. This era, marked by continuous change and uncertainty, has catapulted adaptability from a desirable trait to an essential skill for effective leadership. Understanding why adaptability is so vital and how it links to successful leadership outcomes is key to comprehending the nuances of modern leadership.

Adaptability in leadership refers to the ability to quickly respond to changing circumstances, adjust strategies and tactics, and remain effective in a variety of situations. In the post-pandemic world, this skill has become indispensable due to several factors:

1. Rapid Change: The pace of change in the current business environment is unprecedented. Leaders must be able to pivot quickly in response to new technologies, market shifts, evolving customer demands, and other external factors. The pandemic, for instance, forced many businesses to rethink their operations almost overnight – a change that required immense adaptability from leaders.

2. Increased Complexity: Modern leadership involves navigating a complex landscape of global interconnectivity, diverse workforces, and intricate market dynamics. Adaptability enables leaders to understand and manage this complexity effectively, allowing them to make informed decisions in a multifaceted context.

3. Innovation and Growth: Adaptability is closely linked to innovation. Leaders who are adaptable are more open to exploring new ideas, experimenting with different approaches,

and taking calculated risks – all of which are essential for innovation and growth.

4. Team Engagement and Morale: Adaptable leaders are often better at managing their teams through change. They can adjust their leadership style to meet the needs of their team members, foster a positive work environment, and maintain morale even during challenging times.

The link between adaptability and successful leadership outcomes is evident across various dimensions. Adaptability contributes to better decision-making, as leaders who are adaptable are more likely to consider a wider range of options and perspectives before making decisions. It also enhances problem-solving capabilities, as adaptable leaders can think creatively and are not bound by traditional ways of thinking. These kinds of leaders are often more resilient. They view challenges as opportunities for learning and growth rather than as setbacks. This resilience not only benefits them personally but also inspires it within their teams, creating a culture where challenges are approached with a positive mindset and a focus on solutions.

Adaptability is not just a skill for managing change; it is a multifaceted capability that impacts all areas of leadership, from strategic planning to team management. In the post-pandemic era, where change is the only constant, adaptability stands as a cornerstone of effective leadership, enabling leaders to guide their organizations successfully through an ever-evolving landscape.

Adaptable leaders possess a unique set of characteristics that enable them to navigate through the complexities and uncertainties of the modern business world. These traits go beyond mere flexibility and encompass a broader mindset and approach to leadership.

Resilience is a hallmark of an adaptable leader. It's the ability to withstand adversity and bounce back from challenges. Resilient leaders are not deterred by setbacks; instead, they view them as opportunities for learning and growth. This quality ensures that they remain steadfast and focused, even under pressure or in the face of failure.

Openness to change is another critical trait of adaptable leaders. They understand that change is inevitable and approach it with a positive and proactive attitude. These leaders are not wedded to the status quo but are always looking for better ways to do things. Their openness extends to seeking out new ideas, listening to feedback, and being willing to alter their course of action based on new information or shifting circumstances.

Innovative thinking is closely tied to adaptability. Adaptable leaders are creative problem-solvers. They think outside the box and are not afraid to challenge conventional wisdom. Their innovative approach is not just about coming up with new ideas but also about fostering a culture of innovation within their teams. They encourage experimentation and are open to taking calculated risks.

Another aspect of adaptable leaders is their ability to manage uncertainty. They are comfortable operating in situations where not all variables are known and can make decisions with incomplete information. This capability is crucial in a rapidly changing business environment where delay can mean missing out on opportunities.

Effective communication is also a key characteristic of adaptable leaders. They understand that in times of change, clear and consistent communication is vital. They are skilled at articulating their vision and plans in a way that is easy to understand and rallying their teams around shared goals. Finally, adaptable leaders are empathetic. They recognize the human element in business and understand that change can be difficult for people. They are skilled at empathizing with their team members, addressing their concerns, and helping them navigate through transitions. They are resilient, open to change, innovative, comfortable with uncertainty, effective communicators, and empathetic. These traits allow them to lead effectively in a dynamic and often unpredictable business environment.

Adaptable leadership is characterized by flexibility, openness to new ideas, and a willingness to modify plans and strategies in response to changing circumstances. These leaders thrive on change and see it as an opportunity for growth and innovation. They are comfortable with ambiguity and can make decisions even when not all the information is available. Adaptable leaders are also excellent communicators, able to articulate the reasons behind changes and bring their teams along with them. They place a high value on feedback, using it to adjust their strategies and approaches as needed. Empathy is also a significant trait; they understand the impact of change on their teams and work to address concerns and support their members through transitions.

In contrast, more rigid leadership styles often adhere to established methods and procedures, even when they may no longer be effective. These leaders may prefer predictability and control, and as a result, might struggle with rapid or unexpected changes. Decision-making in a rigid leadership style can be slower, as these leaders might wait for complete information before taking action. Communication in more rigid structures tends to be top-down, with less emphasis on feedback and team input. These leaders may also be less inclined to consider the emotional and human aspects of change, focusing more on maintaining processes and systems.

The impact of these differing styles becomes especially apparent in times of crisis or significant change, like the COVID-19 pandemic. Adaptable leaders were often able to pivot quickly, changing business models or work arrangements to cope with new realities. They could innovate and find new opportunities amidst the crisis. On the other hand, more rigid leaders might have found these times particularly challenging, struggling to move away from established practices and quickly implement necessary changes.

In today's fast-paced and ever-evolving business environment, the limitations of a rigid leadership approach become increasingly evident. While stability and consistency are important, the ability to adapt quickly and effectively is what often differentiates successful organizations from the rest. Adaptable leadership, therefore, is not just a preferable style; it's become essential for navigating the complexities and uncertainties of the modern business world.

Overcoming barriers to adaptability is a crucial step for leaders who wish to enhance their ability to navigate the rapidly changing business environment. Several common challenges can hinder adaptability, but with targeted solutions and approaches, these obstacles can be surmounted.

One significant barrier to adaptability is resistance to change. This resistance can stem from a variety of sources, including fear of the unknown, comfort with the status quo, or perceived threats to power or competence. To overcome this resistance, leaders can focus on creating a culture that values and encourages flexibility and change. This involves clear and transparent communication about the reasons for change, the benefits it will bring, and addressing any concerns or fears that team members may have. Encouraging participation in the change process and providing support throughout can also help mitigate resistance.

Another challenge is a lack of necessary skills or resources to adapt effectively. This can be particularly evident in the context of digital transformation or when new skills are required to meet changing market demands. To address this, leaders can invest in training and development programs for themselves and their teams. They can also ensure that the necessary resources, such as technology or external expertise, are available to facilitate adaptation.

Fixed mindsets can also be a barrier to adaptability. Leaders and team members who hold a fixed mindset may believe that abilities and talents are static, which can limit their willingness to take on new challenges or learn new skills. Promoting a growth mindset, where abilities and intelligence can be developed through dedication and hard work, can encourage a more adaptable approach. This can be achieved through modeling learning and development, celebrating efforts and progress, and reframing challenges as opportunities to learn.

Inertia or organizational bureaucracy can also hinder adaptability. In some organizations, established processes and hierarchies can slow down decision-making and impede the ability to respond swiftly to changes. Streamlining processes, empowering teams to make decisions, and reducing unnecessary bureaucratic hurdles can enhance the organization's overall agility.

Finally, a lack of strategic vision or alignment can make it difficult to adapt effectively. Without a clear understanding of the organization's goals and how they might shift in response to external changes, efforts to adapt can be misguided or inconsistent. Leaders can overcome this by developing a clear, flexible strategic vision, one that can guide decision-making and priorities even as external circumstances change.

While there are challenges to becoming more adaptable, these can be overcome with targeted strategies. By addressing resistance to change, investing in skills and resources, fostering a growth mindset, streamlining organizational processes, and ensuring strategic clarity, leaders can enhance their adaptability and guide their organizations more effectively through the uncertainties of the modern business landscape.

The concept of adaptability in leadership can be best understood through real-world examples where leaders have successfully navigated their organizations through challenging times by demonstrating remarkable adaptability. These case studies not only illustrate the effectiveness of adaptability in various business scenarios but also provide insights into how this key trait can lead to positive outcomes, especially during crises like the COVID-19 pandemic.

One notable example of adaptability is seen in the retail industry. During the COVID-19 pandemic, many traditional brick-and-mortar retailers faced unprecedented challenges due to lockdowns and social distancing measures. A prominent global retailer, however, quickly adapted by ramping up its e-commerce capabilities. This swift transition included enhancing their online platform, improving logistic operations for faster home deliveries, and expanding the range of products available online. This adaptability not only allowed the retailer to sustain operations during the lockdown but also led to a significant increase in online sales, helping them reach new customers and markets.

Another example comes from the food service industry. With restaurants facing closures due to pandemic restrictions, a well-known fast-food chain adapted by focusing on drive-thru and contactless delivery services. They also implemented digital ordering and payment systems to streamline operations and improve customer experience. This adaptability not only helped them maintain revenue streams during a challenging period but also improved their overall service efficiency, garnering positive customer feedback.

In the corporate sector, a tech company demonstrated adaptability by swiftly transitioning to remote work at the onset of the pandemic. Recognizing the challenges this could pose to employee collaboration and productivity, the company's leadership quickly implemented a range of digital tools and platforms for virtual collaboration. They also initiated regular virtual check-ins and adapted their HR policies to support employee well-being in a remote work environment. This adaptability not only ensured business continuity but also enhanced the company's reputation as a flexible and employee-centric workplace.

The healthcare sector provides another compelling example. Faced with an overwhelming influx of patients during the pandemic, a hospital's management team showcased adaptability by quickly converting sections of their facility into COVID-19 units and reallocating staff and resources to these areas. They also adopted telehealth services to continue providing non-emergency care, ensuring patient needs were met without compromising safety. This adaptability not only helped the hospital manage the crisis effectively but also highlighted the importance of flexible resource management in healthcare.

These examples underline the critical role of adaptability in navigating business challenges. Whether it's pivoting to new business models, adopting technological innovations, or rethinking operational strategies, adaptability proves to be a key determinant of success in various scenarios. These case studies also illustrate that adaptability is not just about survival during crises; it can also lead to discovering new opportunities, enhancing customer experiences, and improving organizational resilience.

Developing adaptability, both at an individual and team level, is essential for navigating the ever-changing business landscape. This skill can be cultivated through various strategies and techniques, focusing on mindset, behaviors, and organizational culture.

For Individual Leaders

- Embrace Continuous Learning: Stay curious and open to new knowledge. This can involve taking courses, attending workshops, or simply staying informed about industry trends.

- Cultivate a Growth Mindset: See challenges as opportunities to grow rather than insurmountable obstacles. Embrace mistakes and failures as learning opportunities.

- Practice Flexibility: Regularly step out of your comfort zone. This could mean taking on different types of projects, working with new teams, or experimenting with new ways of working.

- Seek Diverse Perspectives: Actively seek out opinions and ideas different from your own. This can broaden your thinking and open you up to new possibilities.

For Teams

- Encourage Experimentation: Create a safe space for team members to try new approaches and ideas without fear of criticism or failure.

- Promote Cross-Functional Collaboration: Encourage team members to work with different departments or on varied projects. This exposes them to new ideas and ways of thinking.

- Provide Regular Feedback: Offer constructive feedback that focuses not just on outcomes but also on the learning and adaptation process.

- Celebrate Adaptive Behaviors: Acknowledge and reward behaviors that demonstrate flexibility and adaptability. This reinforces their value to the team and organization.

For Organizational Culture

- Embed Adaptability in Organizational Values: Make adaptability a core part of the company's values and mission. This sets the tone for its importance throughout the organization.

- Lead by Example: Leadership should model adaptability. When leaders demonstrate flexible thinking and behavior, it sets a precedent for the rest of the organization.

- Develop Adaptive Policies and Processes: Ensure that organizational policies and processes are not overly rigid. Flexibility in work arrangements, for example, can contribute to a culture of adaptability.

- Foster an Environment of Open Communication: Encourage open dialogue about changes and challenges. An environment where employees feel their voices are heard can enhance collective adaptability.

Developing adaptability involves a combination of personal development, team dynamics, and organizational culture. By focusing on these areas, leaders can foster a more adaptable mindset in themselves and their teams, creating an environment where flexibility and responsiveness to change are part of the organizational DNA.

Adaptable leadership styles and more rigid approaches to leadership present a stark contrast, especially in how they navigate change and uncertainty in the business environment. Understanding this contrast helps in appreciating why adaptability has become so crucial in modern leadership.

Flexibility in decision-making and problem-solving is increasingly crucial in the modern business environment, where leaders often face complex challenges and rapidly changing circumstances. This flexibility allows for more dynamic and responsive leadership, which is key to navigating uncertainty and fostering innovation.

The importance of flexibility in decision-making lies in its ability to accommodate shifting realities and diverse perspectives. Flexible decision-making enables leaders to adjust their strategies and approaches as new information emerges, preventing them from being locked into one course of action when it may no longer be viable. This adaptability is especially valuable in crisis situations or when dealing with ambiguous problems where the variables and potential outcomes are continually evolving.

To develop flexible problem-solving skills, leaders can adopt several techniques:

1. Embrace Diverse Thinking: Encourage a range of perspectives in the decision-making process. Diverse viewpoints can lead to more innovative solutions and help avoid groupthink. This might involve consulting team members from different departments, backgrounds, or levels of expertise.

2. Practice Scenario Planning: Engage in exercises that explore various potential scenarios and outcomes. This not only prepares leaders for different possibilities but also enhances their ability to think flexibly and consider a broader range of strategies.

3. Cultivate an Agile Mindset: Develop an agile approach to problem-solving, where plans and decisions are viewed as flexible and adjustable. This mindset can be fostered through training in agile methodologies or by adopting practices like iterative development and continuous feedback.

4. Encourage Experimentation: Create an environment where experimentation is valued. This might mean allowing team members to test new ideas on a small scale, learning from both successes and failures, and iterating on these experiences.

5. Develop Emotional Intelligence: Emotional intelligence, particularly self-awareness and self-regulation, can enhance decision-making flexibility. Being aware of one's biases and emotional responses can help leaders remain objective and open to changing their approach as needed.

6. Stay Informed and Curious: Keeping abreast of industry trends, new technologies, and emerging business models can provide fresh insights and ideas, fueling more flexible and innovative problem-solving.

7. Learn from Other Industries: Sometimes, the most flexible and creative solutions come from looking outside one's own industry. Exploring how other sectors solve problems can inspire new ways of thinking and approaches.

Flexibility in decision-making and problem-solving is essential for effective leadership in today's fast-paced and uncertain business world. By developing this flexibility, leaders can ensure that their decision-making processes are as dynamic and responsive as the environments in which they operate.

Adaptability in action, particularly when leading teams through change, involves a blend of strategic planning, effective communication, and empathetic leadership. This approach not only helps in navigating the team through the change but also in maintaining morale and productivity during such periods of uncertainty.

Practical examples of applying adaptability in leading teams through change are manifold. A common scenario is when a company undergoes a significant shift in strategy or operational processes. In such cases, adaptable leaders proactively engage with their teams, explaining the reasons for the change and how it aligns with the broader organizational goals. They also remain open to feedback, acknowledging the concerns of team members and addressing them thoughtfully.

Another instance where adaptability plays a crucial role is during organizational restructuring. Here, leaders can demonstrate adaptability by being transparent about the changes, actively listening to and addressing the concerns of team members and ensuring that everyone understands their new roles and responsibilities. They might also need to reallocate resources or shift project timelines to accommodate the new structure.

In terms of maintaining team morale and productivity, adaptable leaders focus on clear and consistent communication. They provide regular updates about the changes and how they're impacting the organization, ensuring that no team member feels left in the dark. This transparency helps in building trust and mitigating uncertainty.

Creating a sense of stability within the team is another strategy. While the external environment might be changing, ensuring that some elements of the team's routine or culture remain constant can provide a sense of normalcy. This could be anything from maintaining regular team meetings to upholding certain team traditions or rituals.

Adaptable leaders also pay close attention to the well-being of their team members. They understand that change can be stressful and make efforts to support their teams emotionally. This might involve one-on-one check-ins, providing access to resources for stress management, or simply creating an open environment where team members feel comfortable sharing their concerns.

Encouraging team participation in the change process can also enhance adaptability. When team members are involved in planning and implementing changes, they are more likely to buy into the new direction. This participation can take many forms, from brainstorming sessions to task forces focused on different aspects of the change.

Leading through change with adaptability means being proactive, communicative, empathetic, and supportive. It involves not just managing the practical aspects of change but also addressing the human side, ensuring that the team remains cohesive, motivated, and productive even in the face of uncertainty.

Continuous learning is an indispensable tool for adaptability in the ever-evolving business landscape. Emphasizing this role involves recognizing that learning is a continuous, dynamic process integral to professional life. Leaders who prioritize ongoing learning and development foster an environment where adaptability flourishes, understanding that staying informed and current with industry developments, emerging technologies, and new management practices is crucial for navigating modern business complexities.

Various avenues facilitate this culture of continuous learning. Professional development programs offered by many organizations include workshops, courses, seminars, and conferences, providing structured opportunities to learn about a wide range of leadership and management topics. Online learning platforms like Coursera, LinkedIn Learning, and Udemy offer extensive courses covering different business and leadership aspects, allowing for flexible learning tailored to individual needs and schedules.

Engaging in mentorship and coaching provides personalized guidance and learning. These relationships offer valuable insights, share experiences, and help identify development areas. Participation in industry associations and networking groups also presents opportunities to learn from peers, with regular meetings, webinars, and discussions on current business challenges and trends.

A simple yet effective avenue is keeping up with relevant books, journals, and articles. Many leaders dedicate part of their daily routine to reading, ensuring they remain informed. Involvement in cross-functional projects allows exposure to different business areas, fostering a broader understanding and diverse skill set.

Implementing regular feedback mechanisms is another powerful learning tool. Whether it's from peers, superiors, or subordinates, feedback can provide insights into strengths and improvement areas.

Incorporating continuous learning into everyday work life demands commitment and a proactive approach. Making learning an ongoing activity ensures that leaders and their teams are constantly evolving, adapting, and staying ahead in an ever-changing business environment. This commitment to ongoing self-improvement and development fuels adaptability and long-term success.

The exploration of adaptability and flexibility in this context underscores their critical importance in modern leadership. These are not just desirable traits but essential skills in today's business world, marked by rapid change, uncertainty, and continuous evolution. Adaptability, the ability to adjust and change course swiftly in response to shifting circumstances, and flexibility, the capacity to modify approaches and embrace new methods, are indispensable in navigating the complexities of the current business landscape.

The significance of these skills has been particularly highlighted in the face of challenges such as the COVID-19 pandemic. Leaders who have demonstrated adaptability and flexibility have been able to guide their organizations through unprecedented times, seizing opportunities amidst adversity and maintaining resilience in the face of disruption. These traits have proven to be key in ensuring not just the survival but the thriving of organizations in periods of uncertainty.

Embracing and cultivating adaptability and flexibility is an ongoing journey for leaders. It involves a mindset that welcomes change, a willingness to learn continuously, and an openness to new perspectives. Leaders must actively seek opportunities to develop these skills, whether through formal training, experiential learning, or reflective practice. Encouraging and fostering these traits within their teams and broader organizations is equally important, creating a culture that values agility and responsiveness.

In conclusion, adaptability and flexibility are foundational elements of effective leadership in the 21st century. Leaders who embrace these qualities and commit to their continuous development are well-positioned to lead with confidence and competence, regardless of what the future holds. The call to action for today's leaders is clear: cultivate these skills, embed them in your leadership practice, and nurture an environment where adaptability and flexibility are at the forefront of navigating the path to success.

Enhancing Digital Literacy

As we move into the next critical chapter of our exploration, "Enhancing Digital Literacy in Leadership," we explore a skill set that has become increasingly vital in the modern era: digital literacy. This chapter is dedicated to understanding the importance of digital literacy in leadership and how it can be effectively integrated into a leader's skill set.

In today's rapidly evolving digital world, where technology plays a pivotal role in every aspect of business, digital literacy transcends basic familiarity with technology. For leaders, it encompasses a deep understanding of digital trends, tools, and strategies and how they can be harnessed to drive organizational success. Digital literacy in leadership involves not just leveraging technology for operational efficiency but also using it to innovate, engage, and inspire.

This chapter will provide insights into the various facets of digital literacy, highlighting why it is crucial for leaders to be technologically adept in a business landscape characterized by digital transformation. The focus will be on how leaders can stay abreast of technological advancements and incorporate them into their strategic thinking and decision-making processes.

As we navigate through this chapter, we will explore practical steps and strategies for leaders to enhance their digital literacy. From understanding the latest digital platforms and tools to leveraging technology for effective team management and organizational growth, the chapter aims to equip leaders with the knowledge and skills necessary to thrive in a digitally connected world.

The goal is to build leaders who are not only proficient in the use of technology but who also possess a strategic understanding of how digital innovation can be a key driver of success in their organizations. Embracing digital literacy is no longer optional; it is a fundamental aspect of effective, forward-thinking leadership.

In the context of leadership, digital literacy extends beyond basic familiarity with technology; it encompasses a comprehensive understanding and strategic utilization of digital tools and trends to enhance organizational goals. This involves not just the technical capability to use digital platforms but also the strategic insight to harness them for innovation, communication, efficiency, and competitive advantage.

The importance of digital skills in the modern business environment has been significantly accelerated by post-pandemic changes. The COVID-19 pandemic has catalyzed a monumental shift towards digital operations, making digital literacy an indispensable facet of effective leadership. This shift is evident in several key areas:

1. Remote Work and Virtual Collaboration: The pandemic has made remote work a norm for many organizations. Leaders must be adept at using digital tools to manage teams, collaborate on projects, and maintain productivity remotely.

2. Digital Communication: With the increase in virtual interactions, leaders need to effectively communicate through digital means. This includes not just emails and messaging but also video conferencing, social media, and other digital communication platforms.

3. Data-Driven Decision Making: The digital age has brought an abundance of data. Leaders must have the skills to interpret this data and use it to make informed decisions, whether it's about market trends, customer behavior, or operational efficiency.

4. Cybersecurity Awareness: As reliance on digital technologies increases, so does the risk of cyber threats. Leaders must understand the basics of cybersecurity to safeguard their organization's data and digital assets.

5. Digital Transformation and Innovation: Leaders are often at the helm of driving digital transformation initiatives. This requires not only an understanding of the current digital landscape but also the ability to foresee how emerging technologies can be leveraged for organizational growth and innovation.

Digital literacy in the leadership context is about strategically integrating technology into every facet of organizational operations. It's a skill set that enables leaders to navigate the complexities of the digital world and to guide their organizations through the challenges and opportunities it presents. The current digital landscape is a complex and ever-evolving terrain that has a profound impact on business operations and leadership. This landscape is characterized by rapid technological advancements, digital transformation, and the integration of digital technologies into nearly every aspect of business.

One of the most significant aspects of the evolving digital landscape is the ubiquitous use of data. The vast amounts of data generated by online interactions and transactions have become a goldmine for businesses, offering insights into customer behavior, market trends, and operational efficiencies. Leaders now need to understand how to harness this data effectively to drive decision-making and strategy.

The proliferation of digital tools and platforms has also transformed how businesses operate. Cloud computing, for instance, has allowed for more flexible and scalable operations, while technologies like AI and machine learning are enabling more sophisticated analysis and automation. E-commerce and digital marketing have become critical components of business strategy, with online presence and digital engagement playing key roles in customer acquisition and retention.

Another key aspect is the shift to remote and hybrid work models, accelerated by the COVID-19 pandemic. This shift has required leaders to not only manage teams and projects remotely but also to maintain productivity and team cohesion without the traditional in-person interactions. It has also highlighted the need for robust cybersecurity measures as businesses become more reliant on digital infrastructures.

The digital landscape has also given rise to new business models and opportunities. For example, the gig economy and platform-based business models have changed the traditional employment and service delivery paradigms. Leaders need to understand these models to leverage them effectively and stay competitive.

Social media and digital communication channels have become vital tools for brand building, customer engagement, and even internal communication. Leaders must be adept at using these channels not just for marketing but also for reputation management and stakeholder engagement.

In this rapidly changing digital landscape, leaders must be able to navigate technological complexities, integrate digital strategies into business operations, and lead teams in a digitally connected environment. The ability to adapt to and leverage these digital changes is crucial for any leader looking to drive their organization forward in the modern business world.

Assessing digital literacy levels is a critical step for leaders in understanding their current proficiency and identifying areas for improvement. This assessment helps in setting targeted goals for enhancing digital skills, which is essential for effective leadership in the digitally-driven business world. There are various tools and methods that leaders can use to gauge their digital literacy:

1. Self-Assessment Questionnaires: These are structured questionnaires that help leaders reflect on their own digital skills. They typically cover various aspects of digital literacy, such as knowledge of digital tools, data analysis capabilities, familiarity with digital trends, and understanding of cybersecurity basics. These self-assessments can highlight areas of strength and those needing improvement.
2. Feedback from Colleagues and Team Members: Getting feedback from peers, supervisors, and team members can

provide valuable insights into a leader's digital capabilities. This feedback can be collected through formal surveys or informal discussions, focusing on areas like the leader's effectiveness in using digital tools for communication, decision-making, and team management.

3. Performance Reviews: Regular performance reviews can include an assessment of digital skills. These reviews can be used to evaluate how effectively a leader has integrated digital tools and strategies into their work and the impact of their digital literacy on team performance and business outcomes.

4. Digital Literacy Workshops and Training: Participating in digital literacy workshops or training programs can be an eye-opener for leaders. These sessions often include assessments that help participants understand their current level of digital proficiency.

5. Benchmarking against Industry Standards: Comparing one's digital skills with industry benchmarks can provide a clear picture of where a leader stands in relation to their peers. This could involve researching the digital competencies required in similar roles or industries and evaluating oneself against these standards.

6. Online Courses and Certifications: Many online courses include assessments or tests as part of their curriculum. Leaders can enroll in these courses not just to improve their skills but also to gauge their current level of digital literacy.

Once the assessment is complete, leaders should identify specific areas for improvement and set concrete goals for enhancing their digital skills. This might involve undertaking specific training programs, dedicating time to learning about new digital tools, or engaging in projects that require the application of digital skills. Regularly revisiting and updating these goals ensures that the leader's digital literacy keeps pace with the rapidly changing digital landscape.

Digital literacy for leaders in the modern business environment is a multifaceted skill set essential for effective management and decision-making in our digitally driven world. These core components of digital literacy are critical for leaders to understand and master as they significantly impact organizational operations, strategy, and competitiveness.

Data literacy is a crucial aspect, involving the ability to read, analyze, and derive meaningful information from data. Leaders must understand how to interpret data trends, draw insights, and make data-driven decisions. This encompasses understanding key metrics, using data analytics tools, and effectively communicating data insights to inform strategy and business choices.

Cybersecurity awareness is increasingly important as organizations rely more on digital platforms and data. Leaders need to be aware of potential cyber threats, understand the importance of data protection, and know the best practices for safeguarding digital assets. This awareness is vital not only for protecting the organization's data but also for ensuring compliance with data security and privacy regulations.

Proficiency in digital communication tools is also key. Effective communication in a digital world requires familiarity with various tools and platforms, including email, messaging apps, video conferencing tools, social media, and collaboration platforms like Slack or Microsoft Teams. Leaders must be adept at using these tools for both internal team communication and external stakeholder engagement.

Understanding digital platforms and ecosystems relevant to their industry is another important component. This includes everything from e-commerce platforms and customer relationship management (CRM) systems to cloud computing services and enterprise resource planning (ERP) systems. Leaders should have a good grasp of how these platforms work and how they can be leveraged for business advantage.

Staying abreast of emerging technologies such as artificial intelligence (AI), blockchain, and the Internet of Things (IoT) is also vital. Leaders don't need to be technical experts but should have a foundational understanding of how these technologies can impact their business, which is essential for strategic planning and innovation.

Adapting to new digital workflows and processes is part of digital literacy. This involves understanding how digital tools can optimize workflows, enhance productivity, and transform business processes, and leading digital transformation initiatives within the organization.

Developing these components of digital literacy enables leaders to guide their organizations effectively in a technology-driven landscape, equipping them with the necessary skills to make informed decisions, drive digital initiatives, and lead teams in a digital environment.

The role of technology in decision-making and strategy in the modern business environment is increasingly significant, fundamentally transforming how leaders approach and execute business strategies. Technology is not merely a tool for operational efficiency; it has become a critical factor in shaping strategic decision-making, offering new insights, driving innovation, and creating competitive advantages.

One key aspect is data-driven decision-making. With advancements in technology, organizations have access to vast amounts of data that can provide deep insights into customer behavior, market trends, operational efficiency, and more. Leaders who effectively use technology to gather, analyze, and interpret this data can make more informed, evidence-based decisions. For instance, predictive analytics can help anticipate market shifts, customer analytics can inform product development, and real-time data can drive agile responses to changing circumstances.

Technology also plays a pivotal role in strategic planning. Tools like digital modeling and simulation can help leaders visualize potential outcomes and make strategic choices in a virtual, risk-free environment. This ability to simulate various scenarios aids in understanding the potential impacts of different strategies, making it easier to choose the most effective course of action.

Moreover, technology enables greater agility in strategy execution. Cloud computing and other digital tools allow organizations to be more flexible, adapting quickly to new opportunities or challenges. This agility is crucial in a fast-paced business world where the ability to pivot swiftly can be a key differentiator.

In terms of innovation, technology is a driving force. Digital platforms can facilitate the exploration of new business models, and emerging technologies like AI, IoT, and blockchain can lead to groundbreaking products and services. Leaders need to understand these technologies' strategic implications and how they can be harnessed to drive growth and innovation.

Technology has reshaped competitive landscapes, making it essential for strategic decisions to consider the digital context. For example, e-commerce and social media have changed how businesses reach and interact with customers, requiring leaders to integrate digital marketing and online customer engagement into their strategies.

The role of technology in decision-making and strategy is multifaceted and profound. It empowers leaders to make better decisions, plan strategically with more accurate information, respond quickly to market changes, drive innovation, and compete effectively in a digital world. For modern leaders, embracing the strategic role of technology is not just beneficial; it's imperative for success.

Improving digital communication skills is crucial for leaders in an era where much of the interaction and collaboration happens through digital means. Effective digital communication involves more than just sending and receiving messages; it requires an understanding of how to best leverage digital platforms for clear, concise, and impactful communication. This is especially important for virtual team management and online collaboration, where nuances of face-to-face interactions are absent.

To enhance digital communication skills, leaders can adopt several strategies:

- Understanding the Medium: Each digital platform has its own set of norms and best uses. For instance, email is suitable for formal communication, while instant messaging apps are better for quick, informal conversations. Video conferencing tools are ideal for meetings that require visual engagement. Understanding the strengths and limitations of each platform can help leaders choose the most effective one for their communication needs.

- Clear and Concise Messaging: Digital communication often requires brevity and clarity. Leaders should aim to convey their messages clearly and concisely, avoiding unnecessary jargon or complexity that could lead to misunderstandings. This is particularly important in written communication, where tone and intent are harder to discern.

- Regular Check-ins and Updates: When managing virtual teams, regular check-ins are vital to maintain connection and ensure everyone is aligned with their tasks and objectives. These can be done through video calls, emails, or collaborative project management tools.

- Fostering Engagement and Participation: Encouraging team members to participate and share their thoughts in virtual meetings can enhance collaboration. This can involve asking open-ended questions, conducting polls, or having team members lead parts of the discussion.

- Adapting to Different Communication Styles: Recognize that team members may have different communication preferences and styles. Some may be more responsive to visual presentations, while others prefer detailed written communication. Adapting your communication approach to suit these preferences can improve understanding and engagement.

- Setting Communication Guidelines: Establish clear guidelines for digital communication within the team. This can include expectations around response times, appropriate platforms for different types of communication, and guidelines for video conferencing etiquette.

- Emphasizing the Human Element: Despite the digital medium, it's important to maintain a personal touch. This can involve acknowledging team members' achievements, celebrating milestones virtually, or simply checking in on their well-being.

- Securing Sensitive Information: When communicating digitally, especially in leadership roles, it's essential to ensure the security and confidentiality of sensitive information. Understanding and utilizing secure communication channels is key.

By honing these digital communication skills, leaders can effectively manage virtual teams, foster collaborative online environments, and leverage digital platforms to enhance their leadership communication. In doing so, they not only improve their team's efficiency and cohesion but also model the communication standards and practices suited for the digital age.

Data literacy has become a critical component of informed decision-making in the modern business landscape. It involves the ability to understand, interpret, and use data effectively to make business decisions. For leaders, data literacy is not just about having access to data; it's about deriving actionable insights from that data to inform strategy and drive business outcomes.

The importance of data literacy lies in its power to provide a factual basis for decision-making. In a world where intuition and experience alone are no longer sufficient to navigate the complexities of the business environment, data offers objective insights that can validate or challenge assumptions and hypotheses. Leaders who are data literate can make more informed decisions, anticipate market trends, understand customer behavior, and identify areas for improvement and growth within their organization.

To effectively interpret data and use it to drive business strategies, several techniques can be employed:

- Understanding the Basics of Data Analysis: This involves grasping fundamental concepts such as statistical significance, trends and patterns, and data visualization. Leaders don't need to be statisticians but should have a basic understanding of how to interpret graphs, charts, and reports.

- Asking the Right Questions: Good data analysis starts with asking the right questions. Leaders should be clear about what they want to know and why. This helps in focusing the data analysis on relevant areas and deriving meaningful insights.

- Utilizing Data Analytics Tools: There are numerous data analytics tools available that can help in processing and analyzing large datasets. Familiarity with these tools can enable leaders to extract, process, and visualize data more efficiently.

- Critical Evaluation of Data: Leaders should be able to critically evaluate the data sources, methodologies used in analysis, and the resulting conclusions. This critical approach ensures that decisions are not just based on data but on high-quality and relevant data.

- Incorporating Data into Strategic Planning: Data insights should be integrated into the strategic planning process. This might involve using data to identify market opportunities, assess risks, or evaluate the potential impact of strategic decisions.

- Developing a Data-driven Culture: Encouraging a data-driven culture within the organization can enhance collective data literacy. This involves promoting data usage in decision-making processes across all levels of the organization.

Data literacy is essential for leaders to make informed decisions and develop strategies that are aligned with the realities of their business environment. By enhancing their data literacy skills and encouraging a data-driven approach within their organization, leaders can ensure that their decisions are well-informed, strategic, and likely to lead to successful outcomes.

In the digital era, cybersecurity awareness has become a critical component of effective leadership. As organizations increasingly rely on digital technologies, leaders are tasked with understanding and managing cybersecurity risks to ensure data protection and mitigate digital threats. This responsibility extends beyond the IT department, becoming a strategic issue that impacts every facet of the organization.

Understanding the basics of cybersecurity involves recognizing various cyber threats such as malware, phishing attacks, ransomware, and data breaches. Leaders must be aware of how these threats can occur, the vulnerabilities within their organization, and the potential consequences, including financial loss, reputational damage, and legal implications. It's essential for leaders to grasp that cybersecurity is not just a technical issue but a critical business concern.

Ensuring data protection and managing digital risks require a comprehensive approach. Leaders should develop and enforce robust cybersecurity policies that guide password management, access controls, data encryption, and the use of secure networks. Additionally, conducting regular training and awareness programs is crucial in fostering a culture of cybersecurity awareness throughout the organization. These programs help ensure that all team members understand how to identify and appropriately respond to potential cyber threats.

Investing in advanced cybersecurity technologies and services, including firewalls, anti-virus software, intrusion detection systems, and secure cloud services, is another critical step. Regular risk assessments are necessary to proactively identify and address vulnerabilities within the organization's network and systems.

Having a clear incident response plan is vital for effectively managing and responding to cybersecurity incidents. This plan should outline the immediate steps to take in the event of a security breach, including communication strategies and actions to minimize damage.

Staying informed about the latest cybersecurity trends and threats is imperative for leaders. This can involve engaging with security bulletins, participating in cybersecurity conferences, or consulting with cybersecurity experts. Keeping abreast of the evolving cybersecurity landscape helps leaders make informed decisions to protect their organization's digital assets and maintain trust with customers, employees, and partners.

Cybersecurity awareness for leaders is about understanding the digital risks, integrating cybersecurity into strategic planning, and taking proactive measures to protect the organization. By prioritizing cybersecurity, leaders not only safeguard their organization's digital assets but also contribute to building a resilient and trustworthy business in the digital age.

Integrating digital tools into leadership practice involves practical guidance on selecting and utilizing various technologies to enhance leadership tasks. In today's business environment, a leader's ability to leverage digital tools effectively can greatly influence organizational success and team productivity.

When it comes to choosing digital tools, the key is to identify technologies that align with the organization's goals and the specific needs of the team. Leaders should evaluate tools based on their functionality, ease of use, compatibility with existing systems, and the ability to enhance communication, collaboration, and decision-making processes. For instance, project management tools like Asana or Trello can help in organizing tasks and tracking progress, while communication platforms like Slack or Microsoft Teams facilitate efficient team interactions.

The effective use of digital tools also extends to data analysis and management. Tools like Tableau or Microsoft Power BI can assist leaders in visualizing and interpreting data, aiding in more informed decision-making. Similarly, CRM systems can provide valuable insights into customer interactions and preferences, enabling leaders to tailor strategies for customer engagement and service.

The integration of digital tools should also consider cybersecurity and data protection. Leaders must ensure that the tools they choose comply with security standards and protect sensitive information. This aspect is crucial in maintaining trust and safeguarding the organization's digital assets.

Case studies of effective integration of digital tools in leadership provide valuable insights. For example, a CEO of a global marketing firm implemented a suite of collaborative tools to enhance communication and project management across geographically dispersed teams. This move not only improved team efficiency but also led to increased innovation as team members could collaborate more effectively.

Another case study involves a healthcare organization that integrated data analytics tools to improve patient care. The leadership used these tools to analyze patient data, leading to better-informed clinical decisions and improved patient outcomes. This integration of technology into their leadership practice not only enhanced operational efficiency but also provided significant value to their primary stakeholders - the patients.

The integration of digital tools into leadership practice requires careful consideration of the organization's needs, an understanding of available technologies, and a commitment to ongoing learning and adaptation. By effectively leveraging these digital tools, leaders can enhance decision-making, improve team collaboration, and drive organizational success in the digital age. Staying current with digital trends is a critical aspect of modern leadership, requiring proactive approaches and a commitment to continuous learning. In an era where digital technologies evolve rapidly, leaders must remain informed about the latest developments to maintain a competitive edge and lead their organizations effectively.

Approaches for keeping up-to-date with digital trends involve various strategies. Engaging with professional networks and industry groups is one way to stay informed. These networks often provide insights into emerging trends and best practices through conferences, webinars, and online forums. Participating in such events allows leaders to exchange ideas with peers and experts, keeping their knowledge fresh and relevant.

Subscribing to reputable tech and business publications is another effective strategy. Many online platforms, journals, and newsletters offer valuable content on the latest technological advancements and their impact on business. Regularly reading these publications can provide leaders with a broader perspective on how digital trends are shaping their industry. Online courses and training programs offer structured learning paths in digital literacy and related fields. Platforms like Coursera, edX, and LinkedIn Learning provide courses designed by industry experts, covering topics from data analytics and cybersecurity to digital marketing and AI. These courses not only offer in-depth knowledge but also often include practical case studies and hands-on projects.

Attending industry-specific training and workshops can also be beneficial. These sessions provide insights into how digital trends are specifically impacting one's industry and what strategies can be employed to leverage these changes.

Engaging with consultants or digital experts can provide tailored insights and recommendations. These professionals can offer guidance on the latest digital tools and strategies that are relevant to the leader's specific business context.

Building a culture of learning within the organization is equally important. Encouraging team members to stay informed about digital trends and share their knowledge can foster a collaborative learning environment. This might involve organizing regular knowledge-sharing sessions or creating internal discussion forums focused on digital innovations.

Staying current with digital trends requires a multifaceted approach, involving professional engagement, continuous education, and fostering a culture of learning. By employing these strategies, leaders can ensure they remain knowledgeable about evolving digital technologies and trends, positioning themselves and their organizations to take full advantage of the opportunities these advancements offer.

Building a digitally literate leadership team is essential in today's technology-driven business environment. It involves implementing strategies that foster digital literacy and creating a culture that values and encourages ongoing digital skill development. This approach ensures that the leadership team is equipped to handle the challenges and opportunities presented by the digital world.

The first step in fostering digital literacy within a team is to set a clear expectation of its importance. This involves communicating the vital role that digital skills play in the organization's success and ensuring that digital literacy is recognized as a key competency for leadership roles. Providing training and development opportunities is crucial. This can include workshops, seminars, and courses focused on digital trends, tools, and best practices. Encouraging team members to attend these training sessions not only improves their digital skills but also keeps them abreast of the latest digital advancements.

Encouraging collaborative learning can also enhance digital literacy. Leaders can initiate group projects that involve using new digital tools or methodologies, fostering a hands-on learning experience. Peer-to-peer learning sessions, where team members share knowledge and experiences related to digital technologies, can also be effective.

Integrating digital tools into everyday work processes is another effective strategy. When team members regularly use digital tools for communication, project management, and data analysis, their comfort and proficiency with these technologies naturally increase.

Creating a culture that values innovation and experimentation can further enhance digital literacy. Encouraging team members to experiment with new technologies and digital approaches in their work fosters a mindset of continuous improvement and adaptability.

Recognizing and rewarding digital initiatives and achievements is important in reinforcing the value of digital literacy. Whether it's successful implementation of a digital tool or an innovative digital strategy, acknowledging these successes can motivate the team and highlight the importance of digital skills.

Leaders should lead by example. Demonstrating a commitment to digital literacy through their actions and decisions, leaders can inspire their team to follow suit. This might involve the leader actively engaging with digital tools, participating in digital training, and staying informed about digital trends.

Building a digitally literate leadership team requires a multifaceted approach. It involves setting clear expectations, providing training and development opportunities, fostering collaborative learning, integrating digital tools into daily processes, creating an innovative culture, recognizing digital achievements, and leading by example. These strategies ensure that the leadership team is well-equipped to navigate the digital aspects of modern business.

As we conclude this chapter on "Building a Digitally Literate Leadership Team," it's clear that cultivating digital literacy within leadership is not just a one-time initiative but an ongoing process that requires dedication, strategic planning, and a culture that supports continuous learning and adaptation.

In today's rapidly evolving digital environment, the need for leaders who are not only familiar with but also proficient in digital technologies is paramount. This proficiency goes beyond the basic use of digital tools; it encompasses a comprehensive understanding of how these technologies can strategically benefit the organization, enhance communication, drive innovation, and lead to more informed decision-making.

The journey towards building a digitally literate leadership team involves a commitment to education and development, a willingness to adapt and embrace new technologies, and the creation of an organizational culture that values digital advancement and innovation. This journey is crucial for maintaining competitive edge and ensuring the long-term success of the organization in a digital world.

As leaders, the responsibility lies not only in self-development but also in nurturing these skills within the team. By fostering an environment that encourages exploration, learning, and the practical application of digital knowledge, leaders can create a team that is not only digitally savvy but also prepared to lead in the digital age.

Remember that digital literacy is an evolving competence. As technology continues to advance, so too must the digital skills of the leadership team. Staying current, adaptable, and forward-thinking are the keys to navigating the challenges and leveraging the opportunities presented by the digital revolution. With a committed approach to developing digital literacy, leaders can ensure that their teams are well-equipped to lead effectively and innovatively in the digital era.

Cultivating Emotional Intelligence

As we venture into the chapter on "Cultivating Emotional Intelligence," we explore a realm of leadership that has become increasingly recognized for its critical importance in the modern business world. This chapter explores the concept of emotional intelligence (EI) and its profound impact on effective leadership.

Emotional intelligence, at its core, is the ability to understand, use, and manage our own emotions in positive ways to relieve stress, communicate effectively, empathize with others, overcome challenges, and defuse conflict. In a leadership context, it goes beyond personal emotion management to include the ability to recognize and influence the emotions of others.

The significance of EI in leadership cannot be overstated. In today's dynamic and often challenging business environment, leaders are expected to navigate not only the complexities of the market and organizational goals but also the human dynamics of their teams. Emotional intelligence is crucial in this regard, as it empowers leaders to connect with their teams, understand their needs and motivations, and create a work environment that is conducive to high performance and job satisfaction.

This chapter will explore the various dimensions of emotional intelligence, including self-awareness, self-regulation, motivation, empathy, and social skills, and how these aspects can be cultivated and applied effectively in a leadership role. The goal is to provide insights into how leaders can enhance their emotional intelligence to lead more effectively, build stronger teams, and drive their organizations towards success.

Emotional Intelligence (EI), in the realm of leadership, encompasses a wide array of skills and abilities crucial for managing personal behavior, navigating social complexities, and making decisions that achieve positive results. It is broadly categorized into five key areas:

- Self-awareness: This is the ability to recognize and understand one's own emotions, strengths, weaknesses, values, and drivers, and understand their impact on others. Self-aware leaders are conscious of their emotional state and how it affects their decisions, behavior, and performance.

- Self-regulation: This involves controlling or redirecting one's disruptive emotions and adapting to changing circumstances. Leaders with strong self-regulation do not make rushed decisions, are not overly reactive, and do not compromise their values.

- Motivation: This aspect of EI is characterized by a passion to work for reasons beyond money or status. Leaders with high motivational levels are driven to achieve for the sake of achievement, display a high level of commitment, and are optimistic even in the face of failure.

- Empathy: This is the ability to understand the emotional makeup of other people. Empathetic leaders can build and retain talent, understand the dynamics of their organization, and increase their ability to give and receive constructive feedback.

- Social Skills: These are skills needed to manage relationships and build networks. Leaders with strong social skills are excellent communicators, good at managing change, and adept at persuading and leading others.

The impact of high EI on leadership effectiveness and team dynamics is profound. Leaders with high EI are better equipped to handle stress and conflict, understand and manage their own and others' emotions, and lead and motivate their teams effectively.

They are adept at fostering a positive work environment, which can lead to improved team morale and productivity.

In the context of team dynamics, a leader's high EI promotes a more collaborative and positive environment. Such leaders are skilled at recognizing the needs and values of their team members, facilitating open communication, and fostering trust and respect. This creates a climate where team members feel valued and understood, leading to higher engagement and commitment to the team's goals.

High EI in leaders also correlates with better decision-making. Understanding their own emotions helps leaders make more objective decisions. Empathy allows them to consider and understand the impact of their decisions on others, fostering a more inclusive and collaborative decision-making process.

Overall, emotional intelligence is a critical factor in enhancing a leader's effectiveness. It not only contributes to personal success but also enhances the way leaders interact with their teams, influences their approach to challenges, and shapes the overall culture and performance of their organization.

The components of Emotional Intelligence (EI) – self-awareness, self-regulation, motivation, empathy, and social skills – collectively form the bedrock of effective leadership. Each component plays a vital role in shaping a leader's ability to manage themselves and interact with others effectively.

Self-awareness is the foundation of EI. It involves understanding one's own emotions, strengths, weaknesses, and values, and recognizing their impact on others. A self-aware leader is able to reflect on their actions and decisions, understand how they are perceived by others, and adjust their behavior accordingly. This level of self-knowledge is crucial for leaders, as it allows them to lead with authenticity and confidence, make informed decisions, and foster genuine relationships with team members.

Self-regulation refers to the ability to control or redirect disruptive emotions and adapt to changing circumstances. Leaders who excel in self-regulation are not impulsive; they think before acting, remain calm and clear-headed under pressure, and handle stress and uncertainty gracefully. This ability to maintain control and composure is critical in a leadership role, as it sets a positive example for the team and creates a stable and predictable environment, even during challenging times.

Motivation in the context of EI is characterized by a leader's inner drive to achieve, commitment to their goals, and optimism even in the face of failure. A motivated leader is resilient and can inspire and energize their team. Their passion and commitment often translate into a high level of performance and an infectious enthusiasm that motivates others. This aspect of EI is particularly important for driving teams towards achieving organizational goals and overcoming obstacles.

Empathy is the ability to understand and share the feelings of others. It's an essential skill for leaders as it enables them to build deeper connections with their team members, understand their individual needs and concerns, and respond appropriately. Empathetic leaders are better equipped to manage workforce diversity, resolve conflicts, and make personnel decisions that are considerate of individual team members' perspectives.

Social skills encompass a leader's ability to manage relationships, communicate effectively, and build a network. Leaders with strong social skills are adept at finding common ground with others, building rapport, and managing team dynamics. They are effective communicators, capable of conveying their vision and inspiring their team. Their ability to manage change and resolve conflicts is enhanced by their social competencies.

Each component of EI contributes significantly to effective leadership. Self-awareness and self-regulation ensure leaders manage their own emotions and behavior effectively; motivation drives them to achieve and inspires others; empathy allows them to connect with and understand their team; and social skills enable them to communicate and interact effectively. Together, these components form a comprehensive framework that can guide leaders in developing their emotional intelligence to lead more effectively and foster a positive, productive workplace.

Self-awareness is a critical aspect of leadership, enabling leaders to understand their own emotions, strengths, weaknesses, and the ways in which their actions affect others. Enhancing self-awareness is not only about introspection but also about seeking external perspectives and engaging in practices that foster a deeper understanding of oneself.

Techniques for enhancing self-awareness often start with reflection. Leaders can set aside time for regular self-reflection, pondering their decisions, behaviors, and their outcomes. Reflective practices such as journaling can provide insights into patterns of behavior and thought, helping leaders identify areas for personal and professional growth.

Feedback is another powerful tool for developing self-awareness. Constructive feedback from peers, mentors, and team members can provide new perspectives and highlight blind spots that might not be apparent through self-reflection alone. Leaders can establish regular feedback mechanisms, such as 360-degree reviews, to gain a comprehensive understanding of how their actions and leadership style are perceived by others.

Mindfulness practices, such as meditation or focused breathing exercises, also play a significant role in enhancing self-awareness. These practices help in developing an ability to focus on the present moment and observe one's thoughts and feelings without judgment. This heightened state of awareness can lead to better emotional regulation and more thoughtful responses to challenging situations.

The role of self-awareness in understanding one's impact on others cannot be overstated. A self-aware leader is better equipped to recognize how their emotions and actions influence their team's morale, productivity, and overall dynamics. For instance, understanding one's own stress triggers and responses can help in managing stressful situations more effectively, thereby reducing the stress experienced by the team.

Self-awareness also contributes to more authentic leadership. Leaders who are aware of their values and beliefs are more likely to lead in a manner consistent with those values, fostering trust and respect within their team. This authenticity can create a more open and honest workplace culture, where team members feel valued and understood.

Enhancing self-awareness involves a combination of reflective practices, seeking and acting on feedback, and mindfulness. As leaders develop greater self-awareness, they gain a deeper understanding of their impact on others, leading to more effective, empathetic, and authentic leadership.

Developing self-regulation is a crucial aspect of emotional intelligence, particularly in leadership roles. Self-regulation involves managing one's emotions and impulses, especially in stressful situations, and maintaining control over one's actions. This skill is essential for leaders to make rational decisions, manage crises effectively, and maintain a positive work environment.

Strategies for improving self-regulation often begin with recognizing and understanding one's emotional triggers. Leaders need to be aware of the situations or stressors that elicit strong emotional responses and develop strategies to address them. This awareness allows for more deliberate and controlled responses, rather than reactive or emotional ones.

Stress management techniques are fundamental to self-regulation. This can include practices such as deep breathing exercises, mindfulness meditation, or physical activities like yoga or jogging. Such practices not only reduce stress but also enhance overall emotional control, contributing to better self-regulation.

Another effective strategy is to develop and practice emotional control techniques. This can involve taking a moment to pause and reflect before responding to a challenging situation, which allows for a more measured and less emotional response. Setting aside time for regular relaxation and disengagement from work can also help maintain emotional balance, preventing burnout and emotional exhaustion.

The importance of self-regulation in decision-making is particularly notable. Leaders with strong self-regulation can remain calm and clear-headed, enabling them to assess situations objectively and make decisions based on rational analysis rather than emotional reactions. This ability is crucial in high-stakes or high-pressure situations where emotional responses could cloud judgment.

In crisis management, self-regulation is equally critical. Crises often create high-stress environments and demand rapid responses. Leaders who can regulate their emotions during crises are better equipped to lead their teams effectively, communicate calmly and clearly, and navigate the organization through challenging periods.

Developing self-regulation involves understanding one's emotional triggers, employing stress management techniques, practicing emotional control, and maintaining a healthy work-life balance. By strengthening this aspect of emotional intelligence, leaders enhance their decision-making capabilities, improve their ability to manage crises, and set a positive example for their teams.

Motivation in leadership is a dynamic and influential factor that drives both personal and organizational success. It involves more than just the pursuit of external rewards; intrinsic motivation, or the drive to achieve for the sake of accomplishment, plays a crucial role in effective leadership. When personal values align with organizational goals, leaders are more likely to exhibit sustained motivation, which positively impacts their teams and the broader organization.

Aligning personal and organizational values starts with a clear understanding of one's own core values and beliefs. Leaders should take the time to reflect on what truly matters to them, what drives their passion, and what they consider meaningful in their work. This self-awareness enables them to seek out or create roles and responsibilities within their organization that resonate with these personal values.

Once personal values are clearly understood, the next step is to explore how they align with the organization's values and mission. This alignment creates a powerful synergy, boosting a leader's intrinsic motivation. Leaders who believe in what their organization stands for and see a connection between their personal goals and the organization's objectives are more committed, passionate, and effective.

To maintain high levels of motivation in challenging situations, several techniques can be employed:

- Setting Clear and Achievable Goals: Goals provide direction and a sense of purpose. By setting and working towards achievable goals, leaders can maintain focus and motivation, even when facing obstacles.

- Seeking Challenge and Variety: Engaging in challenging tasks and seeking variety in work can keep leaders stimulated and motivated. Tackling new and complex problems can be invigorating and provide a sense of accomplishment.

- Maintaining a Positive Attitude: A positive outlook can significantly impact a leader's ability to stay motivated. This involves focusing on solutions rather than problems and viewing challenges as opportunities for growth.

- Fostering a Supportive Network: Building and maintaining a network of supportive colleagues and mentors can provide encouragement and inspiration, especially during tough times.

- Self-Care and Balance: Ensuring a healthy balance between work and personal life is essential for sustained motivation. Regular physical activity, hobbies, and time with loved ones can rejuvenate a leader's energy and perspective.

- Continuous Learning and Development: Pursuing personal and professional development keeps leaders engaged and motivated. Learning new skills or gaining new knowledge can reignite a leader's passion and drive.

Motivation is a key element of successful leadership. Aligning personal values with organizational goals enhances intrinsic motivation, while employing strategies to maintain motivation in challenging situations ensures leaders remain effective and resilient. A motivated leader not only achieves personal success but also inspires and energizes their team, driving organizational performance.

Empathy, often described as the heart of emotional intelligence, is crucial in effective leadership. It's the ability to understand and share the feelings of others, essential for building strong relationships, encouraging team cohesion, and leading with compassion. Developing empathy in leadership goes beyond recognizing others' emotions; it also involves appropriately responding to these emotions.

Understanding empathy begins with its recognition as a vital workplace component. Leaders who demonstrate empathy can effectively handle diverse workforces, manage conflicts, and provide the necessary support to their team members. This approach fosters an environment where employees feel valued and understood, leading to increased satisfaction and engagement.

Active listening is a key skill for developing empathy. It involves paying full attention to the speaker, acknowledging their feelings, and responding thoughtfully. This practice allows leaders to genuinely understand their team members' perspectives and emotions.

Perspective-taking is another important exercise. By mentally placing themselves in their team members' situations, leaders can better understand their thoughts, feelings, and motivations. This exercise is especially useful when making decisions that affect the team.

Regular check-ins with team members also promote empathy. These interactions provide opportunities to understand personal challenges and concerns, leading to more empathetic leadership decisions and actions.

Enhancing emotional awareness, such as reflecting on one's emotional responses and recognizing emotional triggers, can also improve a leader's empathy. Being aware of one's emotions is a crucial step towards empathizing with others.

Seeking feedback about one's leadership style and interactions can offer valuable insights into how empathetically one is perceived. This feedback is an essential tool for continuous improvement in empathetic leadership.

Empathy is a fundamental aspect of emotional intelligence in leadership. Developing empathy through active listening, perspective-taking, regular check-ins, emotional awareness, and feedback can significantly enhance a leader's effectiveness. Empathetic leaders not only create a supportive work environment but also inspire loyalty and dedication from their team members.

Building social skills is an integral part of leadership, encompassing a range of techniques and practices that enhance a leader's ability to communicate effectively, resolve conflicts, and foster team cohesion. These skills are vital in creating a collaborative and inclusive work environment where every team member feels valued and engaged. Improving social skills starts with effective communication. This means not just conveying information clearly and concisely, but also being an attentive listener. Leaders must be able to engage in two-way communication, showing genuine interest in the ideas and concerns of their team members. This kind of open communication fosters trust and transparency within the team.

Conflict resolution is another critical aspect of social skills in leadership. Conflicts, if not managed properly, can lead to a negative atmosphere and decreased team performance. Leaders need to be adept at identifying and addressing conflicts early on. This involves being impartial, understanding different perspectives, and working collaboratively to find solutions that satisfy all parties involved.

Team building is also essential for developing social skills. Leaders can organize team-building activities that promote collaboration, strengthen relationships, and improve team dynamics. These activities can range from formal team-building exercises to informal social events. The goal is to create opportunities for team members to connect and work together, fostering a sense of unity and teamwork.

In addition to these practices, leaders can enhance their social skills by showing empathy and appreciation for their team's efforts. Recognizing and celebrating the achievements of team members can boost morale and reinforce a positive team culture.

The role of social skills in creating a collaborative and inclusive work environment cannot be overstated. Leaders with strong social skills can build and maintain effective teams, where open communication, mutual respect, and cooperation are the norms. These skills enable leaders to not just manage people but to inspire and motivate them, creating an environment where everyone can contribute to their fullest potential.

Building social skills is a continuous process that requires commitment and practice. By focusing on effective communication, conflict resolution, and team building, and by fostering empathy and appreciation, leaders can create a work environment that is not only productive but also supportive and inclusive.

Emotional intelligence in action can be best illustrated through real-life examples and case studies where leaders have effectively utilized their emotional intelligence skills to positively impact organizational outcomes. These examples offer valuable insights into how emotional intelligence contributes to leadership effectiveness and organizational success.

One notable example is a tech company CEO who led his organization through a significant transition period. Faced with declining market share, he utilized his high emotional intelligence to navigate the change. By actively listening to his employees' concerns and demonstrating empathy, he was able to maintain morale and foster a sense of unity among the workforce. His ability to manage his own emotions and remain optimistic in the face of challenges inspired confidence in his team. The result was not only a successful organizational turnaround but also an increase in employee engagement and loyalty.

Another case involves a hospital administrator who exhibited exceptional emotional intelligence during a crisis situation. When the hospital faced a severe staffing shortage, she employed her emotional intelligence skills to manage the situation effectively. Her empathetic approach to the staff's workload and well-being helped her to understand and address their concerns, leading to the implementation of new policies that improved work conditions and reduced turnover. Her effective communication and conflict resolution skills also played a key role in maintaining a collaborative environment during this stressful period.

In a different scenario, a sales team manager used his emotional intelligence to revitalize a demotivated sales team. Recognizing the low morale, he initiated one-on-one meetings with team members to understand their individual challenges and motivations. By applying his empathy and social skills, he was able to build trust and open communication channels within the team. He also demonstrated self-regulation by maintaining a positive and motivational attitude, despite initial setbacks. His approach led to increased motivation and performance within the team, resulting in improved sales figures.

These examples highlight the positive impact of emotional intelligence in various leadership contexts. Emotionally intelligent leaders are able to create a supportive and positive work environment, effectively navigate through changes and crises, and inspire and motivate their teams. The result is often enhanced organizational performance, improved employee satisfaction, and a strong organizational culture.

Emotional intelligence is a powerful tool in a leader's arsenal, one that has a profound impact on organizational outcomes. The ability to understand and manage emotions, both one's own and those of others, is essential for effective leadership and can be the difference between success and failure in today's complex and rapidly changing business environment.

Developing Emotional Intelligence (EI) can be challenging, as it requires not only an understanding of various complex emotional competencies but also the willingness and ability to modify deeply ingrained behaviors and attitudes. Identifying and addressing common barriers is crucial in enhancing EI.

One common barrier is a lack of self-awareness, which can prevent leaders from recognizing their emotional responses and understanding how these affect others. To overcome this, leaders can engage in reflective practices like journaling, seek honest feedback from peers and subordinates, and participate in self-awareness training or coaching.

Another challenge is managing emotional reactions, particularly in high-pressure situations. Leaders who struggle with this aspect of EI can benefit from stress management techniques such as mindfulness meditation, deep breathing exercises, or physical activity. These practices can help in gaining control over emotional responses and responding more thoughtfully in challenging situations.

For some, empathy might be a challenging area. This can be improved by actively practicing active listening, putting oneself in others' shoes, and making a conscious effort to understand and respond to the feelings and needs of others. Engaging in role-playing exercises or empathy training can also be beneficial.

Building effective social skills, especially in communication and conflict resolution, can also be challenging. Leaders can improve these skills through communication workshops, mentoring, and practical experience. Engaging in role-play scenarios and receiving constructive feedback can provide valuable insights into improving these skills.

For leaders who find it challenging to develop certain aspects of EI, setting specific, achievable goals can be an effective strategy. Focusing on one area at a time and gradually building competence can lead to significant improvements. Additionally, seeking support from mentors, coaches, or therapists can provide guidance and accountability.

Recognizing and embracing the value of EI in leadership is also crucial. Understanding how EI directly impacts their effectiveness as a leader can provide the motivation needed to overcome these challenges.

While developing EI can be challenging, it is a worthwhile endeavor for leaders. By identifying personal barriers to EI, utilizing various strategies to overcome these challenges, and recognizing the importance of EI in effective leadership, leaders can enhance their emotional intelligence, leading to more successful and fulfilling leadership experiences.

The journey to improve Emotional Intelligence (EI) is ongoing, and utilizing the right tools and resources is key for continuous development. Leaders can leverage various methods to enhance their EI, and fostering a culture that values emotional intelligence within the organization can have a widespread positive impact.

Coaching is a powerful tool for EI development. Professional coaches can provide personalized guidance, helping leaders to understand and work on their emotional competencies. Coaching sessions often involve setting specific EI goals, receiving feedback, and working through real-life scenarios to improve emotional skills.

Workshops and training programs focused on EI are also beneficial. These programs can cover various aspects of emotional intelligence, such as self-awareness, empathy, and effective communication. They often include interactive exercises that allow participants to practice EI skills in a safe environment.

Self-assessment tools, such as emotional intelligence questionnaires and 360-degree feedback surveys, are useful for understanding one's current EI level. These tools can help leaders identify their strengths and areas for improvement, providing a baseline for their EI development journey.

Reading books and consuming content related to EI can also aid in ongoing development. There are many books, articles, and online resources that offer insights into different aspects of emotional intelligence and provide practical advice for improving these skills.

To encourage a culture of emotional intelligence within the organization, leaders can lead by example. Demonstrating empathy, effective communication, and emotional regulation in their interactions sets a standard for others to follow.

Organizations can also incorporate EI into their training and development programs for all employees, not just leaders. This approach ensures that everyone in the organization understands the importance of EI and is equipped with the skills to interact effectively. Regular discussions and workshops on EI topics can keep the concept at the forefront of organizational culture. Creating open forums where employees can discuss EI experiences and challenges can foster a supportive environment for emotional growth.

Recognizing and rewarding emotionally intelligent behaviors in the workplace can further reinforce the value of EI. Acknowledging instances where employees demonstrate high EI, such as effectively managing a conflict or showing great empathy, can motivate others to develop these skills. Continuous improvement of emotional intelligence requires a combination of personal effort, leveraging the right tools and resources, and fostering an organizational culture that values and supports EI development. By committing to ongoing learning and practice, leaders can enhance their emotional intelligence, leading to more effective leadership and a more emotionally intelligent organization.

As we conclude this exploration of emotional intelligence (EI) in modern leadership, it's clear that EI is not just a desirable attribute but a fundamental component of effective leadership. The ability to understand and manage one's own emotions and those of others is crucial in today's complex and rapidly changing business environment.

This chapter has underscored the importance of EI in various aspects of leadership, from improving communication and building strong teams to making better decisions and managing stress. The competencies of EI, including self-awareness, self-regulation, motivation, empathy, and social skills, collectively enhance a leader's ability to navigate the intricacies of human dynamics effectively. Leaders who possess high EI are better equipped to create a positive work environment, inspire and motivate their teams, and lead with authenticity and integrity.

The journey to develop and apply EI in leadership is continuous and ever-evolving. It requires commitment, self-reflection, and a willingness to grow and change. Utilizing tools like coaching, workshops, and self-assessment can aid in this development, as can creating a culture within the organization that values and encourages the growth of emotional intelligence.

Incorporating EI into everyday leadership practice is both a challenge and an opportunity. It's a challenge because it demands ongoing effort and vigilance, but it's an opportunity because it leads to more fulfilling and effective leadership. Leaders who prioritize their emotional intelligence development can expect to see not only improved personal performance but also a positive impact on their teams and the overall organization.

In closing, emotional intelligence is an indispensable part of the leadership toolkit. Its relevance and significance will only continue to grow as the business world becomes more complex and interconnected. Leaders who embrace the journey of developing their EI will find themselves well-equipped to lead with confidence, empathy, and effectiveness in the diverse and dynamic landscape of modern business.

Effective Crisis Management

In the forthcoming chapter titled "Effective Crisis Management," we embark on a comprehensive exploration of the pivotal role that adept management of crises plays in leadership. This chapter explores the intricacies of crisis management within the leadership realm, offering insights into its definition, scope, and the nuanced challenges presented by various types of crises. Each type, be it financial, reputational, natural disasters, or technological, demands a unique approach and strategy for effective mitigation.

The discourse begins by emphasizing the critical importance of pre-crisis planning and preparedness. It underscores the necessity for leaders to adopt a proactive stance, developing comprehensive crisis management plans that encompass risk assessment and mitigation strategies. Such preparation is instrumental in arming organizations with the resilience needed to navigate potential crises.

Central to navigating crises is the cultivation of key leadership qualities and skills, including decisiveness, effective communication, and resilience. The chapter will elucidate how leaders can identify and develop these essential traits within themselves and their teams, thereby enhancing their capacity to steer their organizations through turbulent times.

A significant focus is placed on the art of decision-making in crisis situations, where leaders are often required to make swift yet accurate decisions under immense pressure. The chapter offers strategies to balance these imperatives, providing leaders with the tools to make informed decisions amidst uncertainty.

Communication during crises is another critical area of focus. Effective crisis communication principles, both within the organization and with external stakeholders, are dissected to reveal how clear, concise, and transparent messaging can serve as a beacon during tumultuous periods.

The management of teams and resources during crises is discussed, highlighting techniques for maintaining team morale and operational continuity. Efficient allocation and management of resources during high-stress periods are pivotal in ensuring the organization's resilience.

Post-crisis analysis and feedback are identified as invaluable processes for learning and growth. The chapter outlines how conducting thorough evaluations post-crisis can unveil lessons learned, guiding the implementation of changes based on insights gained.

The chapter addresses building organizational resilience and preparing for future crises. Continuous improvement of crisis management plans, informed by past experiences and evolving challenges, is presented as essential for fortifying organizations against future adversities.

Through a deep dive into these aspects, "Effective Crisis Management" aims to equip leaders with the knowledge and tools necessary for managing crises effectively, ensuring their organizations are not just prepared to face challenges but are also poised for growth and success in their aftermath.

Crisis management, within the leadership context, is a critical competency that involves preparing for, responding to, and recovering from events that threaten to harm an organization, its stakeholders, or the general public. It encompasses a wide range of activities including preemptive planning, immediate response actions, and post-crisis recovery efforts, all aimed at minimizing the negative impact of crises. Effective crisis management requires leaders to not only navigate the organization through the crisis but also to seize opportunities for improvement and growth that may arise from these challenging situations.

Leadership in crisis management involves more than just addressing the immediate threats. It includes maintaining clear communication, making decisive and informed decisions, and leading the organization's adaptation and resilience-building efforts. A leader's role in crisis management is to instill confidence, guide the organization through uncertainty, and emerge stronger on the other side.

Crises can vary widely in their nature and scope, each presenting unique challenges. Broadly, they can be categorized into:

- Natural Disasters: These include earthquakes, floods, hurricanes, and other events caused by natural forces. The challenges here involve logistical issues, safety of personnel, and continuity of operations.

- Technological Crises: These are caused by the failure of technology, such as data breaches, system hacks, or major software failures. The primary challenges include safeguarding data, maintaining operations, and restoring trust among users or customers.

- Financial Crises: Financial downturns, significant losses, or liquidity issues fall under this category. Leaders must address investor confidence, cash flow management, and strategic restructuring.

- Reputational Crises: Events that harm an organization's reputation, such as scandals or negative publicity, require careful management of public perception, stakeholder communication, and brand recovery strategies.

- Human-caused Events: These include accidents, acts of violence, or misconduct within an organization. The focus here is on ensuring safety, managing legal implications, and restoring morale.

Understanding the specific dynamics and potential impacts of each type of crisis is crucial for leaders. This knowledge enables them to develop tailored strategies that not only address the immediate challenges but also position the organization for successful recovery and future resilience. Effective crisis management is not a one-size-fits-all approach but a nuanced process that reflects the unique aspects of each crisis and the specific needs of the organization.

Proactive crisis planning and preparedness are paramount in leadership, serving as the foundation for an organization's resilience in the face of unforeseen events. The importance of this proactive approach lies in its ability to significantly reduce the potential impact of crises, ensuring that leaders and their organizations are not merely reactive but are strategically positioned to handle challenges effectively.

Developing a comprehensive crisis management plan is a critical step in proactive planning. This plan is a detailed blueprint that guides the organization through the stages of crisis management, from prevention and response to recovery. It starts with a thorough risk assessment, a process that identifies potential crises that could impact the organization. This assessment considers various types of crises, including natural disasters, technological failures, financial downturns, reputational threats, and human-caused events, and evaluates their likelihood and potential impact.

Following the risk assessment, the next step involves devising mitigation strategies tailored to the specific risks identified. These strategies aim to either prevent crises where possible or minimize their impact should they occur. Mitigation can involve a range of actions, such as implementing stronger cybersecurity measures to ward off data breaches, establishing financial reserves to buffer against economic downturns, or developing communication protocols to manage reputational threats effectively.

The crisis management plan also outlines the roles and responsibilities of key personnel during a crisis, ensuring that everyone knows what is expected of them when swift action is needed. This clarity is crucial in high-pressure situations where confusion can exacerbate the crisis.

The plan should include procedures for internal and external communication, ensuring that stakeholders are kept informed in a timely and accurate manner. It also outlines the process for mobilizing resources and coordinating with external agencies if necessary.

Regular training and drills are an essential part of the preparedness phase, helping to ensure that team members are familiar with the crisis management plan and can execute their roles effectively under stress. This training can also highlight areas where the plan may need refinement, ensuring that it remains effective and up-to-date.

Proactive crisis planning and preparedness equip leaders and their organizations with the tools and strategies needed to navigate crises successfully. By anticipating potential challenges and developing a comprehensive crisis management plan, organizations can not only survive crises but also emerge stronger and more resilient.

Effective crisis leadership is defined by a set of essential qualities and skills that enable leaders to navigate their organizations through turbulent times. Among these, decisiveness, communication, and resilience stand out as critical attributes for managing crises effectively. Cultivating these skills in oneself and in the leadership team is crucial for ensuring that the organization can not only withstand crises but also emerge stronger.

Decisiveness in crisis leadership involves the ability to make swift and informed decisions despite uncertainty. A decisive leader assesses the situation quickly, considers the available options, and takes action, understanding that in many crisis scenarios, the cost of inaction can exceed the risks associated with making an imperfect decision. To cultivate decisiveness, leaders can practice scenario planning and decision-making exercises, enhancing their ability to evaluate options under pressure and make choices with confidence.

Effective communication is another cornerstone of crisis leadership. It entails conveying clear, concise, and transparent messages to various stakeholders, including employees, customers, and the public. Communication during a crisis must not only inform but also reassure and guide those affected by the situation. Leaders can develop their communication skills by engaging in active listening, practicing empathy, and learning to tailor their messaging for different audiences and mediums. Regular training in public speaking and media handling can also prepare leaders to manage the communication demands of a crisis.

Resilience, the capacity to endure stress and bounce back from adversity, is vital for leaders facing crises. Resilient leaders maintain a positive outlook, adapt to changing circumstances, and view challenges as opportunities for growth. Building resilience can involve personal development techniques such as stress management, mindfulness, and maintaining a strong support network. Encouraging a culture of resilience within the team, through team-building activities and promoting work-life balance, can also enhance the collective ability to navigate crises.

In addition to these core skills, effective crisis leadership also involves empathy, the ability to understand and share the feelings of others. Empathy ensures that decisions consider the human impact and helps maintain morale and trust during challenging times. Leaders can foster empathy by regularly engaging in reflective practices that encourage perspective-taking and by actively seeking to understand the needs and concerns of their team members.

By identifying and cultivating these essential qualities and skills, leaders can prepare themselves and their teams to manage crises effectively. This preparation not only involves personal development but also creating an environment that values and encourages the growth of these competencies. Through deliberate practice, feedback, and ongoing learning, leaders can enhance their crisis leadership capabilities, positioning their organizations for resilience and success in the face of adversity.

Effective decision-making in crisis situations is a critical skill for leaders, demanding a delicate balance between the need for swift action and the necessity for accuracy. The high-pressure environment of a crisis amplifies the challenges associated with making decisions, making it essential for leaders to employ strategies that enhance their ability to respond effectively.

One key strategy is to establish a clear decision-making framework before a crisis occurs. This framework should outline who is responsible for making decisions, the processes for rapidly gathering and analyzing information, and the channels for communicating decisions. By having a structure in place, leaders can make quicker decisions without sacrificing the thoroughness needed for accuracy.

Emphasizing the importance of situational awareness is another crucial strategy. Leaders must ensure they have access to real-time, reliable information to make informed decisions. This involves setting up systems for monitoring and reporting critical data and establishing a network of trusted advisors who can provide insights and perspectives. Being well-informed enables leaders to assess the situation accurately and decide with confidence.

Prioritizing decisions is also vital during a crisis. Leaders should identify which decisions need immediate attention and which can wait. This prioritization helps focus efforts on critical issues that will have the most significant impact on the organization's ability to navigate the crisis.

Another strategy is to embrace adaptive decision-making. Crises are dynamic situations where new information can change the landscape rapidly. Leaders must be prepared to adjust their decisions as new data becomes available. This adaptive approach allows for flexibility and responsiveness, ensuring that decisions remain relevant as the situation evolves.

Encouraging input from diverse perspectives can enhance decision-making quality. Involving team members from different areas of the organization can provide a broader understanding of the crisis and its impacts. This inclusivity helps in identifying potential pitfalls and opportunities that might not be apparent from a single viewpoint.

To balance speed and accuracy, leaders can also use a "satisficing" approach, aiming for decisions that are good enough to meet the current needs rather than perfect. This pragmatic approach acknowledges the constraints of time and information during a crisis, focusing on practicality and effectiveness.

Leaders should cultivate a mindset of resilience and learning. Not every decision will lead to the desired outcome, especially in a crisis. Being open to learning from decisions, whether successful or not, is crucial for continuous improvement and preparedness for future crises.

Effective decision-making in crisis situations requires preparation, informed and adaptive approaches, prioritization, inclusivity, and a balance between speed and accuracy. By employing these strategies, leaders can navigate the complexities of crisis decision-making, leading their organizations through challenging times with confidence and agility.

Effective communication during crises is paramount for leaders, serving as a critical tool for managing the situation and mitigating its impact. The principles of effective crisis communication, both internally within the organization and externally with stakeholders, revolve around clarity, conciseness, and transparency. Crafting messaging that adheres to these principles can significantly influence the organization's ability to navigate through crises successfully.

Clarity is essential in crisis communication. Messages must be straightforward and easy to understand, avoiding any technical jargon that could confuse or mislead the audience. Leaders should articulate the situation's specifics, what is being done to address it, and what is expected from the audience, whether they are employees, customers, or the wider public. Clear communication helps to eliminate rumors and misinformation, which can proliferate rapidly during a crisis.

Conciseness is equally important. In a crisis, time is of the essence, and attention spans may be limited due to stress and anxiety. Messages should be brief and focused, conveying only the most critical information needed at the moment. This approach ensures that key points are communicated effectively without overwhelming the audience with too much detail.

Transparency builds trust. Being open about the nature of the crisis, its potential impacts, and the steps being taken to resolve it fosters trust among all stakeholders. While it may not always be possible to disclose all information, leaders should strive to be as transparent as circumstances allow. Acknowledging uncertainties and being honest about what is known and what is still being determined can go a long way in maintaining credibility and confidence.

In addition to these principles, effective crisis communication also involves:

- Timeliness: Communicating early and often is crucial. Even if all the details are not yet available, providing timely updates can prevent the spread of rumors and ensure that the organization is seen as the primary and reliable source of information.

- Empathy: Showing understanding and concern for those affected by the crisis demonstrates compassion and humanizes the organization. Messages should acknowledge the difficulties being faced and express genuine empathy and commitment to resolving the situation.

- Consistency: Ensuring that all communications are consistent across different channels and spokespersons is vital for avoiding confusion. This requires coordination and a unified communication strategy that all team members follow.

- Adaptability: As the situation evolves, so too should the communication strategy. Leaders must be prepared to adjust their messaging based on new information, changing circumstances, or the effectiveness of initial communications.

Effective crisis communication is a dynamic and strategic process that requires careful planning and execution. By adhering to the principles of clarity, conciseness, and transparency, and by incorporating timeliness, empathy, consistency, and adaptability into their communication strategies, leaders can guide their organizations through crises with confidence and integrity.

Managing teams and resources during crises is a crucial aspect of leadership that requires a nuanced approach, especially during high-stress periods. The ability to navigate these challenges effectively can significantly impact an organization's resilience and recovery. Leaders must adopt various techniques to ensure their teams remain productive, motivated, and cohesive when facing adversity.

Effective team management during crises begins with clear and transparent communication. Leaders should provide regular updates on the situation, the measures being taken, and any changes in roles or processes. This transparency helps to alleviate uncertainty and builds trust within the team.

Prioritizing the well-being of team members is also essential. High-stress periods can take a toll on individuals both emotionally and physically. Leaders should encourage their teams to take breaks, offer support through counseling services if available, and be flexible with work arrangements. Recognizing the signs of stress and burnout and addressing them proactively can help maintain team morale and prevent long-term productivity issues.

Adapting leadership styles to the needs of the situation and the team is another critical technique. Some circumstances may require a more directive approach to decision-making, while others may benefit from collaborative strategies that involve input from team members. The key is to balance decisiveness with empathy, ensuring that team members feel supported and valued even as they are guided through the crisis.

Maintaining focus on the organization's goals and values can provide a sense of purpose and direction amidst the chaos of a crisis. Leaders should remind their teams of the bigger picture and how their efforts contribute to the organization's resilience and recovery. This sense of purpose can be a powerful motivator during challenging times.

Delegating responsibilities effectively is also important. Leaders must assess their team's strengths and allocate tasks in a way that maximizes individual and collective capabilities. Empowering team members by entrusting them with meaningful responsibilities can boost confidence and foster a sense of ownership over the crisis response efforts.

Fostering a culture of flexibility and adaptability is crucial. Crises often lead to rapid changes in priorities and processes. Leaders should encourage their teams to be open to change and to approach new challenges with a problem-solving mindset. This adaptability is key to navigating the uncertainties of a crisis successfully.

Recognizing and celebrating small victories can have a significant positive impact on team morale. Acknowledging the hard work and achievements of team members, even during a crisis, can reinforce a positive team culture and motivate individuals to continue contributing their best efforts.

Managing teams and resources effectively during crises requires a blend of clear communication, empathy, adaptable leadership, focus on well-being, and recognition of team efforts. By employing these techniques, leaders can ensure their teams not only survive the crisis but emerge stronger and more cohesive.

Allocating and managing resources efficiently in a crisis is a critical task that demands strategic foresight and adaptability. Leaders must quickly assess the situation, identify the most pressing needs, and allocate resources in a way that supports immediate response efforts while also considering long-term recovery. This often involves reallocating budgets, personnel, and other resources from less critical areas to address the crisis effectively. Prioritizing actions that will have the most significant impact on mitigating the crisis is essential, as is maintaining flexibility to adapt resource allocation as the situation evolves.

Equally important is the process of learning from crises through post-crisis analysis and feedback. Once the immediate crisis has been managed, conducting a thorough review of the organization's response is crucial for identifying what worked well and what did not. This analysis should be comprehensive, involving input from all levels of the organization to gain a multifaceted understanding of the crisis management efforts. Key areas for review include decision-making processes, communication effectiveness, resource allocation, and team coordination.

From this analysis, leaders can identify valuable lessons learned and insights that can inform future crisis management planning and response strategies. This may involve revising existing crisis management plans, developing new training programs, or implementing new tools and technologies to enhance future responses. Engaging the entire organization in the learning process ensures that these insights translate into meaningful changes that improve resilience and preparedness.

Implementing changes based on feedback and insights gained from the crisis is an essential step in closing the loop of the crisis management process. It demonstrates an organization's commitment to continuous improvement and its ability to adapt based on experience. This not only prepares the organization for future crises but also builds confidence among stakeholders in the organization's leadership and resilience capabilities.

Efficiently allocating and managing resources during a crisis and engaging in a thorough post-crisis analysis and feedback process are vital components of effective crisis management. These practices ensure that organizations not only navigate crises effectively but also emerge stronger, more prepared, and with enhanced capabilities for managing future challenges.

Building organizational resilience and preparing for future crises are strategic imperatives that enable businesses to navigate uncertainties and rebound from setbacks stronger than before. This resilience is not inherent but can be developed through deliberate efforts and strategies aimed at enhancing the organization's capacity to withstand and adapt to crises.

One foundational strategy is to foster a culture of resilience. This involves nurturing an organizational mindset that values adaptability, continuous learning, and proactive problem-solving. Leaders play a crucial role in cultivating this culture by modeling resilience, encouraging innovation, and supporting team members in taking calculated risks and learning from failures.

Enhancing communication networks within the organization is another key strategy. Effective and efficient communication channels ensure that critical information flows freely and promptly, enabling faster responses to emerging threats. Regularly testing and updating these communication systems can prevent bottlenecks during crises.

Diversifying operations and resources also contribute significantly to resilience. By not relying on a single supplier, market, or operational method, organizations can reduce their vulnerability to specific crises. Diversification strategies might include developing alternative supply chains, exploring new markets, and investing in versatile technologies.

Investing in employee development and well-being is essential for building a resilient workforce. Employees who are well-trained, engaged, and supported are more likely to be committed and capable of navigating challenges. This includes providing opportunities for skill development, promoting work-life balance, and ensuring a supportive work environment.

Developing robust crisis management and business continuity plans is crucial. These plans should be comprehensive, covering various potential crises and outlining specific response strategies. Regularly reviewing and updating these plans based on new insights and changing environmental factors ensures they remain relevant and effective.

Conducting regular scenario planning exercises and drills can enhance preparedness. By simulating different crisis scenarios, organizations can identify potential gaps in their plans and responses, providing valuable insights into areas needing improvement.

Learning from past crises is vital for continuous improvement. This involves conducting thorough post-crisis analyses to extract lessons learned and applying these insights to refine crisis management plans. Engaging the entire organization in this learning process can foster a collective sense of responsibility and resilience.

Staying informed about emerging trends and potential threats allows organizations to anticipate and prepare for future crises. This proactive stance involves monitoring relevant environmental, technological, and geopolitical developments and assessing their potential impacts on the organization.

Building resilience and preparing for future crises require a multifaceted approach that encompasses fostering a resilient culture, enhancing communication, diversifying operations, investing in employees, developing and refining crisis management plans, conducting scenario planning, learning from past crises, and staying informed about emerging threats. Through these strategies, organizations can develop the resilience needed to face future challenges with confidence and agility.

Strategies for Skill Development

In the evolving landscape of leadership, the pursuit of excellence is an unending journey, underscored by the necessity for leaders to engage in continuous skill development. This journey, which forms the core of the upcoming chapter, "Strategies for Skill Development," is essential for leaders to remain adept and responsive to the multifaceted challenges that define the contemporary business world. The chapter aims to guide leaders through the myriad pathways available for enhancing their leadership capabilities, emphasizing the importance of a proactive approach to learning and growth.

As leaders navigate through the complexities of modern organizational environments, the need for a diverse set of skills becomes increasingly apparent. From strategic acumen and emotional intelligence to digital proficiency and the ability to foster innovation, the spectrum of skills relevant to today's leaders is broad and dynamic. This chapter explores the significance of identifying these critical skills and outlines methods for leaders to assess their current competencies and pinpoint areas ripe for development.

Understanding that growth often begins with self-reflection, the chapter checks into practical methods for self-assessment and the utilization of feedback mechanisms, such as performance reviews, to identify skill gaps. It highlights the value of embracing external perspectives in shaping a comprehensive view of a leader's developmental needs.

Exploring avenues for skill enhancement, the chapter navigates through the options for formal education, including leadership degrees and specialized courses, and discusses the impact these programs can have on a leader's strategic and operational insights.

It also weighs the benefits against the commitments these formal education pathways entail.

The narrative then shifts to the dynamic world of professional workshops and seminars, emphasizing their role in providing focused, practical learning experiences. The chapter offers guidance on selecting workshops that align with a leader's specific developmental goals, maximizing the benefits of these learning opportunities.

Online learning platforms and digital resources are presented as flexible and accessible means for leaders to expand their knowledge base and acquire new skills. The chapter provides strategies for evaluating the quality of online learning materials and integrating them effectively into a leader's development plan.

Personalized development strategies, such as mentorship and coaching, are explored for their profound impact on a leader's growth journey. The chapter discusses how to establish fruitful mentoring relationships and engage with coaches to receive tailored advice and feedback.

The importance of peer networks and learning communities is highlighted as a source of mutual support and shared wisdom. The chapter illustrates how engaging with fellow leaders can offer fresh perspectives, encouragement, and a sense of camaraderie on the path to leadership excellence.

In introducing "Strategies for Skill Development," this chapter sets the stage for leaders to embark on a deliberate and structured journey of continuous learning. By embracing the multitude of development avenues available and fostering a mindset of perpetual growth, leaders can ensure they remain effective and influential in an ever-changing business environment.

The imperative for continuous skill development in leadership cannot be overstated in an era marked by rapid technological advances, evolving global markets, and shifting societal expectations. This necessity stems from the understanding that the competencies which once propelled leaders to success are now merely the baseline. To navigate the complexities of the contemporary business landscape, leaders must commit to an ongoing process of learning and adaptation.

Continuous skill development ensures that leaders can not only respond to immediate challenges with agility and confidence but also anticipate future trends and prepare their organizations accordingly. It fosters innovation, enhances decision-making, and strengthens the ability to lead diverse and distributed teams. Moreover, leaders who prioritize their development set a powerful example for their organizations, cultivating a culture of learning that elevates the entire workforce.

Identifying the key skills relevant to contemporary leadership challenges is the first step in this journey of continuous development. These skills can broadly be categorized into several areas:

- Strategic Thinking and Visioning: The ability to anticipate future trends, articulate a clear vision, and develop strategies that align with long-term organizational goals is crucial. Leaders must navigate the balance between short-term performance and long-term growth, making decisions that propel the organization forward in an increasingly competitive landscape.

- Emotional Intelligence: The capacity to understand and manage one's emotions and to recognize and influence the emotions of others has never been more important. Emotional intelligence underpins effective communication, conflict resolution, and the ability to inspire and motivate teams.

- Adaptability and Resilience: In a world where change is the only constant, leaders must be able to pivot quickly and maintain their composure in the face of adversity. This includes being open to new ideas, embracing innovation, and leading teams through transitions with a steady hand.

- Digital Literacy: As technology continues to transform industries, leaders need to understand and leverage digital tools and platforms. This doesn't mean becoming technical experts but rather developing a solid understanding of the digital landscape and how it impacts their business.

- Cross-Cultural Competency: With global operations becoming the norm, leaders must navigate cultural differences and lead diverse teams. Understanding and respecting cultural nuances can enhance team cohesion and drive global strategies.

- Ethical Leadership and Social Responsibility: Today's leaders are expected to navigate complex ethical dilemmas and drive initiatives that contribute to societal well-being. This requires a strong moral compass and a commitment to principles that transcend profit.

Addressing these contemporary leadership challenges requires a multifaceted approach to skill development. Leaders must engage in self-assessment to identify gaps in their competencies, seek feedback from peers and subordinates, and pursue targeted learning opportunities. Whether through formal education, professional development programs, or self-directed learning, the goal is to cultivate a broad range of skills that enable effective leadership in today's dynamic world.

The importance of continuous skill development for leaders cannot be underestimated. By identifying and cultivating the key skills required to meet contemporary challenges, leaders can ensure their effectiveness, inspire their teams, and lead their organizations to sustained success.

Assessing leadership skills and identifying areas for development is a critical process that enables leaders to understand their strengths and pinpoint where they need to grow. This process of self-reflection and feedback is essential for continuous improvement and effective leadership.

Self-assessment is a foundational method where leaders take a reflective look at their own performance, behaviors, and outcomes. This might involve asking oneself key questions about leadership style, decision-making processes, and the impact of their actions on the team and organization. Various tools and frameworks, such as emotional intelligence assessments and leadership competency models, can provide structured approaches to self-assessment, helping leaders to systematically evaluate their skills and effectiveness.

In addition to self-reflection, utilizing feedback mechanisms is crucial for gaining external perspectives on leadership performance. Feedback can come from a variety of sources, including peers, supervisors, and direct reports. One effective approach is the 360-degree feedback process, which collects perceptions of a leader's performance from multiple stakeholders. This comprehensive feedback provides a well-rounded view of a leader's strengths and areas for development.

Performance reviews also serve as a valuable tool for identifying leadership skill gaps. These reviews, typically conducted on a regular basis, offer an opportunity for structured dialogue about performance, goals, and development needs. By comparing self-assessments with insights from performance reviews, leaders can gain a clearer understanding of their effectiveness and areas where they need to focus their development efforts.

To translate these assessments into actionable development plans, leaders should prioritize the areas identified as needing improvement and set specific, measurable goals for enhancing their skills. This might involve seeking out targeted training programs, finding a mentor or coach, or engaging in new projects that challenge them to develop and apply new skills.

The process of assessing leadership skills and identifying areas for development is not a one-time event but an ongoing journey. As leaders progress in their careers and face new challenges, their development needs will evolve. Continuously engaging in self-assessment, seeking feedback, and participating in performance reviews ensures that leaders remain aware of their strengths and development needs, allowing them to adapt and grow in their roles.

Effective leadership development relies on a combination of introspection, external feedback, and a commitment to ongoing learning. By actively engaging in these processes, leaders can enhance their skills, address gaps, and continue to lead their teams and organizations successfully.

Formal education and training programs offer structured pathways for leaders to enhance their skills and knowledge. Options such as leadership degrees, MBAs, and specialized courses provide comprehensive learning experiences designed to equip leaders with the tools needed for effective leadership. These programs cover a wide range of topics, including strategic management, organizational behavior, finance, and marketing, among others, providing a well-rounded education that can be directly applied to leadership roles.

Leadership degrees, often offered at both undergraduate and graduate levels, focus specifically on developing the skills necessary for effective leadership, such as communication, decision-making, and team management. MBA programs, on the other hand, provide a broader education in business management while also offering leadership training as a core component or specialization. Specialized courses, including executive education programs, workshops, and seminars, offer targeted learning opportunities on specific aspects of leadership and management.

The benefits of formal education in leadership development are significant. These programs not only provide theoretical knowledge but also offer practical applications through case studies, group projects, and sometimes internships or consultancy projects with real companies. Participants can gain insights from experienced faculty and industry practitioners, network with peers, and develop a deeper understanding of the challenges and opportunities in leadership. Formal education also signals a commitment to professional development, which can enhance a leader's credibility and career prospects.

Formal education comes with limitations. The time and financial investment required for degree programs or specialized courses can be substantial, making them inaccessible for some individuals. The theoretical focus of some programs may not fully address the practical realities and dynamic challenges faced by leaders in their specific contexts or industries. Additionally, the rapidly changing business landscape can outpace the curriculum offered in some formal education programs, potentially leaving gaps in contemporary skills and knowledge.

To maximize the benefits of formal education, leaders should carefully evaluate programs based on their relevance to current leadership challenges, the practical applicability of the curriculum, and the opportunities for networking and real-world experience. Seeking programs that offer flexibility, such as part-time or online options, can also help mitigate some of the limitations associated with time and financial commitments.

Formal education and training programs play a valuable role in leadership development, offering a structured approach to enhancing skills and knowledge. While evaluating the benefits and limitations of these options, leaders should consider their personal development goals, the specific needs of their leadership roles, and the practical applicability of the education offered to ensure that their investment in formal education yields meaningful returns in their professional growth and effectiveness as leaders.

Professional workshops, seminars, and short courses play a crucial role in the continuous development of leadership skills. These focused learning experiences are designed to offer intensive training on specific topics, allowing leaders to quickly acquire new skills or deepen existing ones. Unlike formal degree programs, workshops and seminars typically span a few days to several weeks, making them a practical option for busy professionals seeking to enhance their capabilities without a long-term commitment.

The role of these professional development opportunities is multifaceted. They provide a platform for leaders to stay abreast of the latest trends, theories, and practices in leadership and management. Workshops and seminars are often led by industry experts and thought leaders, offering participants insights into cutting-edge strategies and the chance to learn from the experiences of successful leaders. Furthermore, these settings facilitate networking, allowing leaders to connect with peers from various sectors, fostering a community of learning and exchange of ideas.

When selecting workshops, seminars, and short courses, it's essential to consider several factors to ensure the investment is both relevant and effective:

Identify Specific Learning Goals: Begin by clarifying what you aim to achieve through the program. Whether it's improving communication skills, learning new strategies for conflict resolution, or understanding the nuances of digital transformation, having clear objectives will guide your selection process.

1. Research the Program's Content and Structure: Look for programs that offer a balance between theoretical insights and practical applications. Programs should include interactive elements such as case studies, group discussions, and simulation exercises to facilitate hands-on learning.

2. Consider the Instructors' Expertise: The quality of a workshop or seminar often depends on the experience and knowledge of the instructors. Look for programs led by instructors with a strong track record in the field, including both academic credentials and real-world experience.

3. Evaluate the Program's Relevance to Your Industry: Ensure that the program content is applicable to your specific context. Programs that offer industry-specific insights or case studies can be particularly valuable.

4. Assess Networking Opportunities: Consider programs that attract participants from a variety of sectors and roles. Networking with other professionals can provide new perspectives and opportunities for collaboration.

5. Check for Flexibility and Accessibility: For busy leaders, finding programs that offer flexibility in terms of scheduling and location (including online options) can be crucial. This ensures that learning and development can be integrated into your professional life without significant disruptions.

6. Seek Feedback from Previous Participants: If possible, speak to colleagues or peers who have attended the programs you're considering. Their insights can help you gauge the effectiveness and impact of the program.

Professional workshops, seminars, and short courses offer a targeted and efficient way to enhance leadership skills. By carefully selecting programs that align with their learning goals, leaders can ensure they are investing in their professional development in a manner that is both impactful and practical.

In today's fast-paced and digitally connected world, online learning and digital platforms provide leaders with unprecedented access to flexible and accessible opportunities for skill development. These platforms offer a plethora of courses, webinars, and other educational materials that cater to a wide range of leadership topics, from the basics of effective management to specialized knowledge in areas like digital transformation and emotional intelligence. The advantage of online learning lies in its adaptability to the learner's schedule, allowing leaders to engage with content at their convenience and pace, making it a perfect fit for the demanding schedules of today's professionals.

Assessing the quality and applicability of online resources is a critical step to ensure that the investment in online learning translates into tangible benefits and skill enhancement. Evaluating the credentials of course providers and instructors is essential, as reputable sources are more likely to offer content that is both high-quality and relevant. Reading reviews and testimonials from past participants can provide valuable insights into the course's effectiveness and practical applicability.

The most impactful online courses typically feature interactive and engaging content, such as quizzes, simulations, and discussion forums, to foster active learning and retention. A thorough review of the course curriculum is also important to ensure that it aligns with personal learning goals and addresses the challenges contemporary leaders face. Additionally, courses that offer certification or accreditation can add value, especially when the credentials are recognized within the industry.

Many online learning platforms allow potential learners to preview course content or access introductory modules for free. Taking advantage of these previews can offer a glimpse into the teaching style, quality of material, and relevance to professional development needs, aiding in the decision-making process.

By carefully selecting online learning opportunities that meet these criteria, leaders can effectively leverage digital education to enhance their skills and leadership capabilities. The key to success with online learning is choosing resources that not only contribute to knowledge growth but also offer practical insights and strategies that can be applied in real-world leadership situations.

Mentorship and coaching are powerful tools in the arsenal of leadership development, offering personalized guidance and feedback that can significantly enhance a leader's capabilities. The impact of these relationships on leadership development is profound, as they provide a platform for learning from the experiences and insights of seasoned professionals. Mentorship, often a longer-term relationship, focuses on the holistic development of the mentee, offering advice, support, and encouragement. Coaching, which can be more structured and time-bound, typically concentrates on specific development areas, helping leaders to improve their performance and achieve specific goals.

Finding the right mentor or coach is a critical step in leveraging these relationships for leadership development. The ideal mentor or coach should not only possess the experience and skills that align with the leader's development needs but also share similar values and have a genuine interest in helping others grow. Compatibility is key to a productive mentorship or coaching relationship, as trust and respect form the foundation of effective learning.

Making the most of these relationships involves clear communication from the outset regarding goals, expectations, and the nature of the support needed. It's important for leaders to be open to feedback, willing to engage in self-reflection, and ready to take action based on the guidance received. Regular meetings or check-ins help maintain momentum and ensure that the relationship remains focused and productive.

Leaders should approach mentorship and coaching with a mindset of active engagement, viewing these relationships as a two-way street where both parties contribute to the dialogue. Being prepared with specific questions or topics for discussion can maximize the value of each interaction. Additionally, implementing the insights and strategies discussed, then reviewing the outcomes with the mentor or coach, can facilitate practical learning and growth.

Mentorship and coaching offer a unique blend of personal support, professional guidance, and accountability that can accelerate leadership development. By carefully selecting a mentor or coach and actively engaging in the relationship, leaders can unlock new levels of insight, performance, and personal growth, setting the stage for continued success in their leadership journey.

Engaging with peer networks and professional communities offers substantial benefits for leadership development, providing a platform for exchanging ideas, sharing challenges, and learning from the experiences of others in similar roles. These networks and communities facilitate a collaborative learning environment where leaders can gain new perspectives, stay informed about industry trends, and discover innovative solutions to common problems.

The benefits of participating in peer networks and learning communities extend beyond simple knowledge exchange. They offer a sense of camaraderie and support, reducing the isolation that leaders sometimes feel in their roles. Through these interactions, leaders can build valuable relationships that may lead to collaborative opportunities, mentorship, and even career advancement. Furthermore, exposure to diverse viewpoints and approaches to leadership can inspire creativity and encourage a more adaptive leadership style.

To actively participate and maximize learning from peer networks and professional communities, leaders should adopt several strategies. First, identifying networks that align with their professional interests and development goals is crucial. This might involve joining industry-specific associations, online forums, or local leadership groups. Once a suitable network is identified, leaders should engage regularly by attending meetings, contributing to discussions, and sharing their own experiences and insights.

Active participation also involves asking questions and seeking advice on specific challenges. This openness not only aids in personal development but also contributes to the collective knowledge of the community. Additionally, volunteering for leadership roles within these networks, such as organizing events or leading special interest groups, can provide valuable experience in leadership and project management.

Building meaningful relationships within these networks requires a commitment to genuine interaction and mutual support. Networking should not be approached merely as a means to an end but as an opportunity to contribute to the growth and success of the community as a whole. This might involve mentoring newer members, collaborating on projects, or facilitating connections between others.

Applying the insights and lessons learned from peer interactions to one's leadership practice is essential for tangible growth. Reflecting on these learnings, experimenting with new approaches, and sharing outcomes with the network can create a cycle of continuous improvement and learning.

Peer networks and professional communities offer a rich resource for leadership development, providing opportunities for learning, collaboration, and support. By actively engaging with these networks, adopting a mindset of contribution and openness, and applying learned insights, leaders can enhance their skills, expand their perspectives, and strengthen their leadership effectiveness.

Creating personal development plans with clear goals and milestones is a strategic approach to leadership growth, enabling leaders to chart a path for their professional and personal evolution. This process begins with a thorough self-assessment to identify strengths, areas for improvement, and specific skills or knowledge gaps that need to be addressed. Based on this assessment, leaders can set clear, achievable goals that are aligned with their career aspirations and the demands of their leadership roles.

Each goal within the personal development plan should be accompanied by specific milestones and a timeline, making the process measurable and time-bound. This structure not only facilitates tracking progress but also provides motivation as milestones are achieved. Incorporating both short-term and long-term goals allows for immediate wins while keeping the focus on broader career objectives.

To enhance the effectiveness of personal development plans, leaders should incorporate a variety of learning and development activities tailored to their goals. This might include formal education, attending workshops and seminars, participating in mentorship or coaching relationships, engaging with peer networks, and leveraging online learning opportunities. Diverse learning experiences enrich the development process, catering to different learning styles and providing a broader range of insights and skills.

Regular review and adjustment of development plans are crucial to ensure continuous progress and adaptation. Leaders should schedule periodic reviews of their plans, ideally on a quarterly basis, to assess their progress toward goals, reflect on what they have learned, and make adjustments as necessary. These reviews provide an opportunity to celebrate achievements, re-evaluate goals that may no longer be relevant, and identify new areas for development.

During these reviews, it's important to consider any changes in the leadership context, such as shifts in organizational priorities, industry trends, or personal career opportunities, that may impact the relevance and feasibility of the goals set. Flexibility in adapting the development plan ensures that it remains aligned with evolving career objectives and the dynamic nature of leadership challenges.

Seeking feedback from peers, mentors, and supervisors can enrich the review process, offering external perspectives on progress and areas where further development may be needed. This feedback can inform adjustments to the plan, ensuring it effectively addresses both strengths and weaknesses.

Personal development plans and goal setting are foundational elements of effective leadership development. By setting clear goals, regularly reviewing and adjusting plans, and incorporating diverse learning experiences, leaders can ensure they are continuously growing and evolving to meet the challenges of modern leadership. This proactive approach to development not only enhances individual leadership capabilities but also contributes to the overall strength and resilience of the organizations they lead.

The journey of leadership development is both complex and continuous, underscoring the importance of a multifaceted approach to skill enhancement. As explored throughout this discourse, effective leadership in the modern world demands more than a static set of skills; it requires an ongoing commitment to growth, adaptation, and learning. From formal education and targeted workshops to the invaluable insights gained through mentorship, coaching, and peer networks, each component plays a crucial role in shaping well-rounded leaders capable of navigating the complexities of contemporary organizational challenges.

This exploration has highlighted the need for leaders to engage in regular self-assessment, set clear development goals, and actively seek out diverse learning opportunities. Whether it's enhancing emotional intelligence, cultivating strategic thinking, or staying abreast of digital innovations, the areas for development are as varied as they are critical. The process of continuously updating and refining one's skill set not only benefits the individual leader but also has a profound impact on their teams and organizations, fostering cultures of resilience, innovation, and excellence.

Encouraging leaders to commit to lifelong learning and continuous improvement is more than an academic exercise; it's a call to action in a world where change is the only constant. The dedication to personal and professional growth ensures that leaders remain effective, relevant, and prepared to lead their organizations toward success, irrespective of the challenges that lie ahead.

The multifaceted approach to skill development in leadership is not merely a strategy for individual advancement but a cornerstone of effective, responsive, and visionary leadership. As leaders commit to this journey of lifelong learning, they not only enhance their own capabilities but also inspire those around them to pursue excellence, adaptability, and continuous growth. This commitment to development and improvement is what ultimately defines successful leadership in an ever-evolving global landscape.

The Importance of Continuous Learning

In the dynamic tapestry of personal and professional development, continuous learning emerges as a pivotal thread, weaving through the fabric of growth and adaptability. Defining continuous learning involves recognizing it as an ongoing process of acquiring new knowledge, skills, and insights, regardless of one's stage in life or career. It transcends traditional education, encompassing a broad spectrum of formal and informal learning opportunities. The significance of adopting a lifelong learning mindset in today's rapidly evolving world cannot be overstated; it is the cornerstone upon which individuals can build a resilient and fulfilling career, particularly in leadership roles.

We research the myriad benefits of continuous learning for leaders, highlighting how an unwavering commitment to personal growth contributes to leadership effectiveness, adaptability, and resilience. It explores the crucial link between lifelong learning and innovation, underscoring the role of continuous learning in driving organizational growth and navigating the complexities of the modern business landscape.

Identifying personal learning paths is essential for leaders aiming to align their development efforts with their career goals and leadership aspirations. The chapter offers insights into techniques for leaders to pinpoint their unique learning needs and interests, facilitating the creation of a tailored learning journey that propels them toward their objectives.

The discourse then navigates the distinction between formal education and informal learning, examining the roles and benefits of each. It advocates for a balanced approach that combines the structured rigor of formal educational programs with the flexibility and immediacy of informal learning opportunities, such as self-directed exploration and experiential learning.

Leveraging digital and online learning resources is presented as a strategy for navigating the vast landscape of available educational content. The chapter provides guidance on evaluating and selecting high-quality online learning resources that complement personal learning paths and enhance leadership skills.

Integrating learning into daily routines emerges as a practical strategy for embedding continuous learning into the fabric of everyday life. The chapter offers practical tips for developing habits and routines that foster an environment conducive to ongoing development, ensuring that learning becomes a natural and integral part of the leader's lifestyle.

Learning from experience, through reflection and application, is highlighted as a critical component of continuous learning. The chapter discusses the importance of reflecting on both successes and failures and applying new knowledge and skills in real-world scenarios to deepen understanding and facilitate true learning.

The role of networking and collaborative learning in enriching the continuous learning journey is also examined. Professional networks and learning communities provide invaluable opportunities for collaborative growth, knowledge sharing, and learning from the experiences of peers and mentors.

Addressing common obstacles to continuous learning, such as time constraints, lack of motivation, and resource limitations, the chapter outlines strategies to overcome these challenges and maintain momentum in the learning journey.

The chapter closes with a discussion on setting and reviewing learning goals, offering techniques for establishing realistic and meaningful objectives that evolve with personal and professional growth. It encourages leaders to embrace continuous learning not just as an academic pursuit but as a vital component of effective leadership and a fulfilling life.

Continuous learning in the context of personal and professional development represents an enduring commitment to acquiring new knowledge, skills, and understanding throughout one's life and career. It is the proactive pursuit of learning opportunities to enhance one's abilities, adapt to change, and navigate the complexities of the modern workplace and society at large. This concept transcends formal education, encompassing a wide array of learning experiences, from structured programs and courses to informal learning through experiences, reflections, and interactions.

The significance of a lifelong learning mindset in today's rapidly evolving world cannot be overstated. In an era characterized by technological advancements, shifting economic landscapes, and changing societal norms, the only constant is change itself. A lifelong learning mindset equips individuals with the agility to adapt to these changes, not just to survive but to thrive. It fosters a sense of curiosity and openness to new ideas, encouraging individuals to seek out challenges and learn from them.

For leaders, in particular, embracing continuous learning is essential for staying ahead of industry trends, understanding emerging technologies, and leading teams effectively in diverse and dynamic environments. It enables them to model growth and adaptability, inspiring their teams to embrace similar attitudes towards learning and development.

A lifelong learning mindset contributes to personal fulfillment and resilience. It encourages individuals to explore their interests and passions, leading to a more engaging and satisfying life. By continuously expanding their horizons, individuals can better cope with stress and navigate personal and professional setbacks, viewing them as opportunities for growth rather than insurmountable obstacles.

Defining continuous learning as an integral component of personal and professional development and recognizing the importance of a lifelong learning mindset are foundational steps in preparing for the challenges and opportunities of the 21st century. This mindset is not just beneficial but necessary for individuals aiming to lead meaningful, productive, and adaptable lives in an ever-changing world.

Continuous learning is a pivotal element in the realm of leadership, significantly enhancing leadership effectiveness, adaptability, and resilience. Its role in driving innovation and fostering organizational growth is equally profound, marking it as a cornerstone for dynamic and forward-thinking leadership.

Leaders who engage in continuous learning exhibit a higher degree of effectiveness. This ongoing educational journey equips them with a diverse skill set and a deep well of knowledge, enabling them to navigate complex challenges with insight and dexterity. By staying abreast of the latest trends, theories, and practices, these leaders can make informed decisions, craft strategic initiatives, and guide their teams with confidence. Their commitment to learning also sets a powerful example for their teams, cultivating a culture of curiosity and growth within the organization.

Adaptability and resilience, crucial attributes for today's leaders, are significantly bolstered by continuous learning. The rapid pace of change in the modern business environment demands leaders who can pivot quickly and effectively in response to new challenges. Continuous learning prepares leaders for this reality, fostering a mindset that is open to change and capable of thriving in uncertainty. This adaptability is underpinned by resilience, the ability to recover from setbacks and persist in the face of adversity. Lifelong learning nurtures resilience by providing leaders with the tools and perspectives needed to view challenges as opportunities for growth and learning.

The impact of continuous learning extends beyond individual leadership effectiveness, driving innovation and organizational growth. Leaders committed to learning are more likely to foster an environment that encourages innovation, where new ideas are welcomed and experimentation is valued. This environment is conducive to breakthroughs and can significantly contribute to the organization's competitive edge and growth. Continuous learning fuels this innovative spirit by exposing leaders to diverse ideas and approaches, which can spark creative solutions to problems and open up new avenues for business development.

Organizations led by lifelong learners are better positioned to adapt to market shifts, technological advancements, and evolving customer expectations. These leaders can steer their organizations through transformational changes, capitalizing on opportunities for expansion and improvement. The knowledge and skills gained through continuous learning enable leaders to foresee trends, adapt strategies accordingly, and lead their organizations to sustained success in an ever-changing landscape.

The benefits of continuous learning in leadership are manifold, enhancing leadership effectiveness, fostering adaptability and resilience, driving innovation, and contributing to organizational growth. Leaders who embrace a lifelong learning mindset are not only better equipped to face the challenges of today but are also prepared to seize the opportunities of tomorrow, leading their organizations to new heights of success.

Identifying personal learning paths is a critical step for leaders aiming to enhance their effectiveness and fulfill their leadership potential. This process involves a deliberate approach to understanding one's own unique learning needs, interests, and aligning these with overarching career goals and leadership aspirations. By tailoring a personal learning path, leaders can ensure that their development efforts are both meaningful and strategically focused.

The first technique in identifying personal learning needs is self-reflection. Leaders should take time to introspect on their current skill set, leadership style, and areas where they feel less confident. Reflecting on feedback received from peers, subordinates, and superiors can also provide valuable insights into areas requiring development. Questions regarding which skills would most significantly impact their leadership effectiveness or what knowledge gaps exist can guide this reflection process.

Another technique involves setting clear and specific career goals and leadership aspirations. Understanding where one wants to go is crucial in determining what skills and knowledge are necessary to get there. Leaders should consider both short-term objectives and long-term visions for their careers, including the types of roles they aspire to and the impact they wish to have within their organizations or industries.

Once leaders have a clear understanding of their learning needs and career aspirations, they can begin tailoring their personal learning path. This involves selecting learning opportunities that directly address identified needs and align with their goals. Options might include formal education programs, such as leadership courses or an MBA, for foundational knowledge and skills. For more specific competencies, targeted workshops, seminars, or online courses can provide focused learning in areas like digital transformation, emotional intelligence, or strategic decision-making.

Leaders should also consider experiential learning opportunities, such as taking on new projects, roles, or responsibilities that push them out of their comfort zones. These experiences can be particularly effective for developing practical skills and leadership capabilities. Networking with professionals in desired fields or roles can also offer insights into necessary skills and learning opportunities.

Incorporating feedback mechanisms throughout the learning process is essential. Regularly soliciting feedback from mentors, peers, and team members on progress can help leaders adjust their learning path as needed. This ensures that the development efforts remain relevant and aligned with evolving leadership roles and industry demands.

Leaders should adopt a flexible and adaptive approach to their personal learning paths. The landscape of leadership and business is constantly changing, and what may be a relevant skill today could evolve tomorrow. Leaders must be prepared to continually reassess their learning needs and adapt their development strategies accordingly.

Identifying personal learning paths requires a combination of self-reflection, goal setting, strategic selection of learning opportunities, experiential challenges, and ongoing feedback. By carefully tailoring their development efforts to align with their unique needs and aspirations, leaders can ensure they are continually growing and evolving to meet the demands of modern leadership.

In the landscape of leadership development, both formal education and informal learning play pivotal roles, each offering distinct benefits and catering to different aspects of a leader's growth. Understanding the interplay between structured learning and self-directed exploration is crucial for leaders seeking to maximize their development potential.

Formal education, encompassing degree programs, certifications, and structured courses, offers a comprehensive and systematic approach to learning. These programs provide a foundational knowledge base, critical thinking skills, and an understanding of theoretical frameworks that can be applied in leadership contexts. The benefits of formal education include access to expert faculty, a structured curriculum that covers a breadth of relevant topics, and the opportunity to earn credentials that can enhance professional credibility and career prospects. Formal programs also offer networking opportunities, connecting students with peers, alumni, and industry professionals.

On the other hand, informal learning opportunities, such as on-the-job experiences, mentoring relationships, self-study, and participation in professional communities, offer flexibility and immediacy that formal education often cannot. Informal learning allows leaders to tailor their development to specific needs and interests, applying new insights and skills directly to their work in real-time. This type of learning is often experiential, allowing leaders to learn from successes and failures in a practical context. The benefits of informal learning include its adaptability to individual learning styles, the ability to address immediate challenges and opportunities, and the potential for continuous, lifelong learning beyond the confines of structured programs.

Balancing formal education with informal learning involves recognizing the unique value each brings to leadership development and integrating them in a way that supports one's personal and professional goals. Leaders might pursue formal education to gain a broad understanding of leadership principles and management strategies while engaging in informal learning to develop specific skills or address immediate challenges. For example, a leader might complete an MBA to build a strong foundation in business and leadership theory while simultaneously seeking out a mentor for guidance on navigating organizational politics or leading change initiatives.

To effectively balance structured learning with self-directed exploration, leaders should:

- Identify their learning objectives and assess which areas might benefit most from formal education versus informal learning.

- Seek out formal educational programs that offer flexibility, such as part-time schedules or online options, to accommodate ongoing professional responsibilities.

- Actively engage in informal learning activities, setting personal goals for reading, networking, or experimenting with new approaches in their leadership practice.
- Reflect regularly on learning experiences, both formal and informal, to integrate new knowledge and skills into their leadership approach.

The synergy between formal education and informal learning can provide a holistic framework for leadership development. By thoughtfully balancing structured learning opportunities with self-directed exploration, leaders can create a personalized development path that fosters continuous growth, adaptability, and effectiveness in their leadership roles.

In today's digital age, the abundance of online courses, webinars, and digital platforms offers leaders a wealth of resources for continuous learning and development. Navigating this vast landscape effectively requires a strategic approach to identify, evaluate, and select the most relevant and high-quality online learning resources that align with one's leadership goals and needs.

The first step in leveraging these digital resources is to clearly define your learning objectives. Whether it's enhancing specific leadership skills, such as strategic thinking or emotional intelligence, or gaining knowledge in new areas like digital transformation, having clear goals will guide your search and selection of online learning opportunities.

Once objectives are set, the next step involves exploring the vast array of available resources. This exploration can include massive open online courses (MOOCs) offered by universities and specialized institutions, webinars hosted by industry experts, and digital platforms dedicated to professional development. Many reputable educational institutions and professional organizations offer courses specifically designed for leadership development, covering a wide range of topics relevant to today's leaders.

Evaluating the quality of online learning resources is critical. Look for courses and webinars offered by credible institutions and recognized experts in the field. Check the curriculum to ensure it covers the topics you're interested in and assesses the learning outcomes to see if they match your objectives. Reading reviews and testimonials from past participants can provide insights into the effectiveness of the course or webinar and the quality of the content.

Selecting the right online learning resources also involves considering the format and delivery of the content. Interactive courses that include discussions, case studies, and practical exercises can offer a more engaging and effective learning experience than those that rely solely on video lectures. Additionally, consider the time commitment required and ensure it fits into your schedule, especially if balancing professional responsibilities.

To make the most of digital and online learning resources, leaders should also be proactive in applying the knowledge and skills gained to their leadership practice. Reflecting on how new insights can be integrated into daily work, discussing key learnings with peers or mentors, and taking on projects or roles that allow for practical application can enhance the learning experience and solidify new skills.

Staying organized and committed is essential when engaging with digital learning. Setting aside dedicated time for online learning, tracking progress, and holding oneself accountable can help maintain momentum and ensure continuous development.

The digital and online landscape offers a treasure trove of learning opportunities for leaders willing to explore and invest in their development. By clearly defining learning goals, conducting thorough research, evaluating the quality and relevance of resources, and actively applying new knowledge, leaders can leverage digital and online learning to enhance their skills, adaptability, and effectiveness in an ever-evolving world.

Integrating learning into daily routines is a powerful strategy for leaders seeking to foster a culture of continuous improvement, both within themselves and their organizations. By making learning a regular part of everyday life, leaders can seamlessly acquire new knowledge and skills without the need for significant disruptions to their work or personal schedules. Here are practical tips for weaving learning into the fabric of daily routines and developing habits that promote continuous learning:

1. Start with Intentionality: Begin each day with a clear intention to learn something new. Setting this intention can help keep you open to learning opportunities throughout the day, whether it's from a conversation, a challenge, or a new task.

2. Leverage the Power of Microlearning: Break down learning into small, manageable segments that can be easily incorporated into your daily routine. For example, dedicate 15 minutes in the morning to reading an article or watching a video related to your leadership goals. Microlearning makes it easier to consistently engage with new material without feeling overwhelmed.

3. Utilize Technology and Tools: Take advantage of the plethora of digital tools and platforms available for learning. Podcasts, audiobooks, and mobile learning apps can be excellent resources for learning on the go, allowing you to make the most of downtime or multitask effectively during commutes or exercise.

4. Schedule Learning Breaks: Just as you might schedule meetings or tasks, block off time in your calendar specifically for learning activities. These dedicated slots ensure that learning becomes a non-negotiable part of your day, rather than something you only do when you find spare time.

5. Apply Learning Immediately: Look for immediate applications of what you learn in your work or personal life. Applying new concepts or skills as soon as possible helps reinforce the learning and demonstrates the practical value of your efforts.

6. Reflect Daily: End your day with a brief reflection on what you've learned and how you've applied it. This reflection can help solidify the knowledge and also provide insights into what you want to learn next.

7. Cultivate Curiosity: Foster a mindset of curiosity and openness to new ideas and experiences. Encouraging yourself and your team to ask questions and explore various subjects can create an environment where learning is naturally integrated into daily activities.

8. Share Your Learning: Discussing what you've learned with others not only reinforces your understanding but also promotes a learning culture within your team or organization. Sharing can take the form of informal discussions, formal presentations, or collaborative learning sessions.

9. Embrace Diverse Learning Sources: Diversify your learning sources to include not just professional development materials but also content from unrelated fields. This diversity can inspire creativity, foster innovation, and help you draw connections between seemingly disparate concepts.

10. Set and Review Learning Goals: Regularly set specific, achievable learning goals and review your progress towards them. This goal-setting and review process can help keep you accountable and ensure that your learning efforts are aligned with your broader personal and professional objectives.

By integrating learning into daily routines and developing habits that support continuous learning, leaders can ensure that they are constantly evolving and staying ahead in a rapidly changing world. These practices not only enhance personal growth and leadership effectiveness but also contribute to building a culture of lifelong learning within their organizations.

Learning from experience, which encompasses a spectrum of successes and failures, is a cornerstone of both personal and professional development. Central to extracting meaningful insights from these experiences is the practice of reflection. This introspective process allows individuals to dissect their actions and outcomes, understanding the why and how behind each event and contemplating future improvements. Coupled with the active application of new knowledge and skills in real-world scenarios, reflection deepens understanding and equips individuals with the ability to adeptly navigate complex challenges.

Reflection serves as a mirror to both successes and failures. Through careful consideration of successful outcomes, individuals can identify effective strategies and behaviors that can be replicated in future endeavors. Conversely, failures are transformed into rich learning opportunities, offering clarity on missteps and illuminating pathways for growth and improvement. This perspective shifts the perception of failures from setbacks to valuable lessons, fostering a culture of resilience and perpetual growth.

The true value of reflection is realized when new insights are applied to actual situations. This practical application tests the feasibility of learned lessons, allowing individuals to adjust their strategies based on real-time feedback and results. The transition from theoretical learning to practical application ensures that knowledge is not only retained but also becomes an integral part of one's decision-making process and leadership style.

To effectively harness the power of learning from experience, individuals can incorporate several practices into their routine. Maintaining a reflection journal offers a structured way to document daily experiences, lessons learned, and potential future applications. Seeking diverse perspectives through feedback from peers, mentors, or coaches can enrich the reflective process, providing additional layers of insight. Allocating specific times for reflection ensures this critical activity is recognized as a priority, while experimenting with new approaches in familiar situations encourages innovation and adaptability. Finally, analyzing the outcomes of these applications provides a feedback loop for continuous improvement, allowing for the refinement of strategies and approaches as necessary.

Engaging in this iterative cycle of reflection and application not only bolsters individual leadership capabilities but also has the potential to drive collective growth and success within teams and organizations. By committing to this process, leaders can cultivate an environment of continuous learning and development, enhancing their effectiveness, adaptability, and resilience in the face of an ever-evolving landscape.

The role of networking and collaborative learning in personal and professional development is profound, offering a dynamic avenue for growth beyond traditional educational frameworks. Professional networks and communities serve as fertile ground for collaborative learning, where individuals can share knowledge, gain insights from peers and mentors, and collectively navigate the complexities of their fields. This collaborative approach to learning harnesses the collective wisdom of the community, enabling individuals to tap into a diverse pool of experiences and perspectives.

Utilizing professional networks and communities for collaborative learning involves actively engaging with these groups, participating in discussions, and contributing one's own knowledge and experiences. Such engagement not only aids in one's development but also enriches the learning experience for the entire community. Networking events, professional associations, online forums, and social media platforms offer numerous opportunities for connecting with like-minded professionals who share similar interests and challenges.

Sharing knowledge within these networks is a two-way street; it involves not just seeking advice and insights but also offering one's expertise to others. This exchange fosters a culture of generosity and mutual support, where the focus shifts from competition to collaboration. Learning from peers and mentors through this shared knowledge can accelerate personal growth, offering practical advice and strategies that are directly applicable to real-world scenarios.

Mentors, in particular, play a crucial role in this learning ecosystem. They provide guidance, feedback, and support, drawing on their wealth of experience to help mentees navigate their career paths and development challenges. The mentor-mentee relationship, built on trust and respect, offers a personalized learning experience that can significantly impact an individual's growth.

Engaging in collaborative learning within professional networks also encourages the development of soft skills, such as communication, teamwork, and leadership. These skills are critical in today's collaborative work environments and can greatly enhance an individual's effectiveness and influence within their organization.

The role of networking and collaborative learning in development is invaluable, offering a platform for continuous growth, knowledge exchange, and the strengthening of professional relationships. By actively participating in professional networks and communities, individuals can enhance their learning experience, benefit from the collective wisdom of their peers, and contribute to the development of others. This collaborative approach not only accelerates personal and professional growth but also fosters a culture of learning and generosity that can have a lasting impact on entire industries and fields.

Overcoming obstacles to continuous learning is essential for sustaining personal and professional growth amidst the demands of daily life. Common challenges such as time constraints, fluctuating motivation, and limited resources can hinder one's ability to engage in ongoing learning. However, with strategic approaches, these barriers can be navigated successfully, ensuring that the journey of learning remains vibrant and productive.

Time constraints often emerge as a primary challenge, with busy schedules leaving little room for additional learning activities. One effective strategy to overcome this is to integrate learning into existing routines. This could involve listening to educational podcasts during commutes, dedicating a small segment of the lunch break to reading industry-related articles, or setting aside a brief period each day for focused learning. By making learning a part of daily habits, individuals can ensure consistent engagement without requiring significant time allocations.

Maintaining motivation can also be challenging, especially when the immediate benefits of learning are not apparent. Setting clear, achievable goals can help sustain motivation by providing a sense of direction and purpose. Celebrating milestones and reflecting on the progress made can reinforce the value of continuous learning and reinvigorate one's commitment. Additionally, choosing learning activities that are genuinely interesting and relevant to one's career aspirations or personal interests can make the learning process more enjoyable and engaging.

Resource limitations, including access to learning materials or financial constraints related to formal education programs, can further complicate the learning journey. Leveraging free or low-cost online resources, such as MOOCs (Massive Open Online Courses), webinars, and open-access journals, can provide high-quality learning opportunities without a significant financial investment. Joining professional associations or community groups can also offer access to exclusive learning materials, workshops, and networking events, often at a reduced cost for members.

To maintain momentum in learning journeys, it's important to adopt a flexible and adaptable mindset. Recognizing that learning paths may need to shift in response to new interests, career changes, or evolving industry trends can help individuals stay responsive and open to new learning opportunities. Building a support network of peers, mentors, and colleagues who value learning can provide encouragement, advice, and accountability, helping to sustain momentum even when challenges arise.

Overcoming obstacles to continuous learning requires a combination of strategic planning, goal setting, and leveraging available resources. By integrating learning into daily routines, maintaining motivation through goal achievement and interest alignment, and utilizing diverse and accessible resources, individuals can navigate common challenges and sustain their learning journeys. This commitment to continuous learning not only enriches personal and professional development but also ensures adaptability and resilience in an ever-changing world.

Setting and reviewing learning goals is a pivotal process in the continuous learning journey, ensuring that efforts are aligned with personal and professional aspirations and adapting to changing circumstances. Here's a structured approach to establishing realistic and meaningful goals and maintaining their relevance over time.

Setting Learning Goals

1. Reflect on Needs and Aspirations: Begin by assessing your current skill set, professional responsibilities, and long-term career aspirations. Identify areas where there is a gap between your current abilities and where you need or want to be. This reflection helps in pinpointing specific learning objectives that are both meaningful and aligned with your broader goals.

2. Make Goals SMART: Adopt the SMART criteria—Specific, Measurable, Achievable, Relevant, and Time-bound—to frame your learning goals. For instance, rather than setting a vague objective like "improve leadership skills," a SMART goal would be "complete a leadership development course and implement learned strategies in team management over the next quarter."

3. Prioritize Your Goals: Given that time and resources are limited, prioritize your learning goals based on their potential impact on your personal and professional growth. Focus on areas that offer the most significant benefits, considering both immediate needs and long-term value.

Reviewing and Updating Learning Goals

1. Schedule Regular Reviews: Set periodic reviews (e.g., quarterly or bi-annually) to assess your progress towards your learning goals. This regular check-in allows you to reflect on what you've learned, evaluate its application in real-world scenarios, and identify any adjustments needed.

2. Adapt to Changes: Personal interests, career paths, and industry landscapes are dynamic. As such, be prepared to update your learning objectives in response to new opportunities, challenges, or shifts in your professional environment. This flexibility ensures that your learning efforts remain relevant and targeted.

3. Seek Feedback: Incorporate feedback from peers, mentors, and supervisors in your review process. External perspectives can provide valuable insights into your progress, highlight areas for improvement, and suggest new directions for learning.

4. Celebrate Achievements and Set New Goals: Recognizing and celebrating milestones not only boosts motivation but also marks the completion of learning cycles. Use these moments to set new goals, leveraging the confidence and insights gained from your achievements to tackle more challenging or diverse learning objectives.

Techniques for Sustained Engagement

- Integrate Learning with Action: Enhance the relevance of your learning goals by immediately applying new knowledge and skills to practical tasks or projects. This integration fosters deeper understanding and retention.

- Leverage Varied Learning Resources: Diversify your learning approaches by combining formal education, online courses, mentoring, and experiential learning to keep the process engaging and comprehensive.

- Maintain a Learning Log: Documenting your learning experiences, reflections, and applications can provide a tangible record of your growth, serving as both a motivational tool and a resource for future planning.

By thoughtfully setting and regularly reviewing learning goals, individuals can ensure that their continuous learning efforts are purposeful, responsive to their evolving needs, and effectively integrated into their personal and professional development journey.

The journey of personal and professional development is inexorably linked to the commitment to lifelong learning. This commitment is not merely an academic endeavor but a fundamental ethos that distinguishes transformative leaders from the rest. The importance of adopting a lifelong learning mindset cannot be overstated; it is the bedrock upon which sustained growth, adaptability, and innovation are built. In a world characterized by rapid technological advancements, evolving market dynamics, and shifting societal expectations, the ability to continuously acquire and apply new knowledge and skills is paramount.

For leaders, the embrace of continuous learning transcends personal benefit, extending its impact to the teams they lead and the organizations they serve. Effective leadership in the 21st century demands more than a static skill set; it requires a proactive and persistent pursuit of growth and development. Leaders who embody a lifelong learning mindset inspire those around them, fostering cultures of curiosity, resilience, and agility. These are the organizations that not only survive but thrive amidst change and uncertainty.

Continuous learning is the catalyst for innovation and creativity. It challenges conventional wisdom, encourages the exploration of new ideas, and facilitates the discovery of novel solutions to complex problems. Leaders who are committed to their own development are better equipped to navigate the complexities of the modern business landscape, drive organizational growth, and make meaningful contributions to their industries and communities.

The path of continuous learning is as diverse as it is rewarding, encompassing formal education, informal learning experiences, digital and online resources, and the rich insights gained from networking and collaborative endeavors. By setting clear learning goals, regularly reviewing and adapting these objectives, and integrating learning into daily routines, leaders can ensure that their development journey is both strategic and fulfilling.

As we look to the future, the call to action for leaders is clear: Embrace continuous learning as a fundamental component of effective leadership. This commitment not only enhances individual capability and adaptability but also sets the foundation for building resilient, innovative, and successful organizations. In the end, the pursuit of lifelong learning is not just about acquiring knowledge; it is about fostering a mindset that embraces change, seeks out challenges, and continually strives for excellence.

Section 2: Adapting Leadership Styles to a Changing World

In Section 2 of "Navigating the New Normal: Leadership Strategies for a Post-Pandemic World," we explore the critical theme of adapting leadership styles to the rapidly evolving business landscape shaped by the COVID-19 pandemic and its aftermath. The way leaders guide, motivate, and inspire their teams has fundamentally shifted. This section discusses the nuances of these changes and offers insights into how effective leadership can not only adapt to these changes but also thrive within them.

The onset of the pandemic brought about an era of unprecedented change, propelling organizations into a future where the traditional boundaries of workspaces and workstyles were redefined. Leaders faced the challenge of managing remote or hybrid teams, fostering collaboration in virtual settings, and ensuring productivity amidst uncertainty. Such challenges have necessitated a reevaluation and adjustment of leadership approaches.

This section begins by examining the necessity for flexible and adaptive leadership styles in the post-pandemic world. It discusses the shift from conventional, hierarchical leadership models to more agile, empathetic, and collaborative approaches. We dig into how leaders can effectively manage remote and hybrid teams, a skill that has become crucial in today's work environment. This includes navigating the challenges of communication, engagement, and team cohesion in a virtual or semi-virtual context.

We also present case studies of leaders who have successfully adapted their leadership styles during the pandemic. These real-life examples offer valuable insights into practical strategies and approaches that have proven effective in navigating these complex times. Moreover, this section addresses the critical aspect of fostering resilience and innovation in teams. In a world where change is the only constant, leaders must not only adapt themselves but also cultivate an environment where their teams can be resilient, agile, and innovative.

As you journey through Section 2, you will gain a deeper understanding of the dynamic nature of leadership in the modern era. The insights and strategies presented here aim to equip you with the tools to effectively adapt your leadership style, ensuring that you are well-prepared to lead your teams confidently and effectively in a world that continues to evolve unpredictably.

The Need for Flexible Leadership Styles

In the wake of the global pandemic, the landscape of leadership has undergone a significant transformation, necessitating a shift towards more flexible leadership styles. This evolution reflects the urgent need for adaptability in navigating the complexities of the new normal—a world marked by unprecedented changes and challenges. Flexible leadership, characterized by the ability to adjust strategies, leadership approaches, and management practices in real-time, has emerged as a critical competency for leaders aiming to steer their organizations through post-pandemic recovery and beyond.

The importance of adaptability in leadership cannot be overstated. The pandemic has not only disrupted traditional business models but also prompted a reevaluation of what effective leadership looks like in an increasingly volatile, uncertain, complex, and ambiguous (VUCA) environment. Leaders are now required to pivot quickly in response to changing circumstances, balancing the need for decisive action with the flexibility to adapt to new information and evolving situations.

This introduction to flexible leadership styles examines the paradigm shift from rigid, hierarchical leadership models to more dynamic, agile approaches. It explores how the pandemic has accelerated the transition to leadership that values adaptability, resilience, and open communication. The characteristics of flexible leadership, such as the ability to embrace change, foster innovation, and maintain resilience in the face of adversity, are examined in detail.

In the chapters that follow, we will explore strategies for leading effectively in remote and hybrid work environments, the role of flexible leadership in crisis management and rapid decision-making, and how such leaders can empower teams, promote autonomy, and build a culture of trust and inclusivity. Additionally, the necessity of cultural sensitivity, the imperative of continuous learning, and practical steps for implementing flexible leadership in practice will be discussed.

As we conclude this introduction, it becomes clear that the post-pandemic world demands a new breed of leaders—ones who are not only adept at navigating the current challenges but are also prepared to evolve with the changing landscape. The following chapters will provide insights, strategies, and case studies to guide leaders in developing and applying flexible leadership styles, ultimately encouraging them to embrace adaptability as a core component of their leadership practice.

Flexible leadership, in the context of post-pandemic challenges, embodies the capacity of leaders to dynamically adjust their styles, strategies, and approaches in response to the rapidly changing circumstances of the business landscape. This adaptability is paramount in navigating the aftermath of the global pandemic, which has introduced a series of unprecedented shifts in how organizations operate, how teams are managed, and how business goals are pursued. Flexible leadership transcends traditional, rigid management paradigms, advocating for a more fluid, responsive approach to leadership that is sensitive to the nuances of the current environment.

The essence of flexible leadership lies in its focus on adaptability—a quality that has become indispensable in the post-pandemic world. The abrupt shift to remote work, the necessity of maintaining productivity amidst global uncertainty, and the ongoing adjustments to new ways of working have all underscored the need for leadership that is not only proactive but also highly adaptable. Leaders today must be capable of pivoting strategies quickly, embracing technological advancements, and fostering a culture of resilience and innovation within their teams.

The importance of adaptability in leadership approaches to effectively navigate the new normal cannot be overstated.

Adaptability allows leaders to respond to unforeseen challenges with agility, to make informed decisions amidst uncertainty, and to maintain organizational cohesion in a landscape marked by constant change. It involves a willingness to learn and evolve, to question existing assumptions, and to explore new opportunities for growth. In doing so, adaptable leaders are better positioned to guide their organizations through recovery and toward sustainable success in a post-pandemic world.

In sum, flexible leadership is not merely a preference but a necessity in the face of the post-pandemic challenges. It requires a departure from conventional leadership models towards more dynamic, agile approaches that prioritize adaptability, resilience, and continuous learning. As organizations navigate the complexities of the new normal, the ability of leaders to adapt and evolve will be critical in shaping their future trajectory.

The pandemic has fundamentally altered the landscape of leadership, necessitating a significant shift in traditional leadership models. This transformation is characterized by a move away from rigid, hierarchical styles of leadership towards more dynamic, agile approaches. The changes brought about by the global health crisis have not only disrupted how businesses operate but have also reshaped the expectations and needs of employees, highlighting the limitations of conventional leadership in navigating through such unprecedented times.

Historically, leadership models often emphasized top-down decision-making, with leaders at the top of the hierarchy setting direction and employees following established protocols to execute tasks. This approach, while providing clear structure and authority lines, often lacked the flexibility and responsiveness needed to adapt to rapid changes in the business environment. The pandemic, with its sudden onset and far-reaching impacts, exposed these limitations, demonstrating the need for leadership that is more adaptable, collaborative, and responsive to the evolving needs of both the organization and its people.

The transition to more dynamic, agile leadership approaches is marked by several key shifts:

- From Command and Control to Empowerment and Collaboration: Leaders are increasingly recognizing the value of empowering employees and encouraging collaboration. This shift fosters a more inclusive environment where diverse perspectives are welcomed, and innovation is nurtured, enabling organizations to respond more effectively to changing circumstances.

- Emphasis on Flexibility and Adaptability: The pandemic underscored the importance of being able to pivot quickly in response to new information or changing conditions. Agile leadership approaches prioritize flexibility, allowing leaders and their teams to adapt strategies and operations as needed, often in real-time.

- Increased Focus on Emotional Intelligence and Empathy: The challenges of the pandemic, including the shift to remote work and the stresses associated with health concerns and economic uncertainty, highlighted the need for leaders to demonstrate empathy and emotional intelligence. Understanding and addressing the emotional well-being of team members became as important as managing productivity and performance.

- Leveraging Technology for Leadership and Communication: The widespread adoption of remote work necessitated the use of digital tools not only for operational purposes but also for leadership and communication. Leaders have had to become adept at using technology to maintain team cohesion, foster collaboration, and ensure effective communication across distributed teams.

- Resilience and Crisis Management as Core Competencies: The pandemic has made it clear that resilience and effective crisis management are critical competencies for leaders. The ability to navigate through crises, maintain focus on long-term goals, and lead teams through uncertainty has become essential for organizational survival and success.

This shift in leadership paradigms, from hierarchical and fixed to dynamic and agile, reflects a broader transformation in the business world—one that values adaptability, inclusivity, and resilience. As organizations continue to navigate the post-pandemic landscape, the leaders who embrace these agile approaches are the ones most likely to thrive, driving their organizations forward in an era defined by constant change.

Flexible leadership is characterized by a set of key traits and behaviors that allow leaders to navigate the complexities of the modern business environment effectively. At the core of flexible leadership lie adaptability, openness, and resilience—qualities that enable leaders to respond to changing scenarios with agility and insight. These leaders possess the ability to adjust their strategies, approaches, and management styles in real-time, ensuring their teams and organizations can pivot in response to new challenges and opportunities.

Adaptability is perhaps the most defining trait of a flexible leader. It involves the willingness and capacity to change course when circumstances demand it, whether due to shifts in market dynamics, technological advancements, or unforeseen crises. This trait is complemented by openness, which reflects a leader's readiness to consider new ideas, embrace innovation, and listen to diverse perspectives. Openness fosters a culture of continuous learning and experimentation, crucial for sustaining growth and competitiveness.

Resilience stands as another pillar of flexible leadership, embodying the strength and perseverance leaders need to withstand setbacks and navigate through periods of uncertainty. Resilient leaders maintain a positive outlook, focusing on long-term objectives while addressing immediate challenges. Their resilience not only helps sustain their own motivation but also serves to inspire and bolster the morale of their teams.

Balancing firm decision-making with adaptability is a nuanced aspect of flexible leadership. Effective leaders recognize when to stand firm on decisions that align with core values and strategic objectives and when flexibility is required to adapt to new information or evolving circumstances. This balance is critical for maintaining direction and integrity while being responsive to the needs of the moment.

Flexible leadership also entails a commitment to communication and collaboration. By fostering open lines of communication and encouraging collaborative problem-solving, leaders can harness the collective expertise and creativity of their teams. This collaborative approach enhances decision-making quality and ensures that diverse viewpoints are considered in the formulation of strategies and solutions.

Flexible leadership is defined by a dynamic interplay of adaptability, openness, resilience, and a balanced approach to decision-making. Leaders who embody these characteristics are better equipped to lead their organizations through the complexities and uncertainties of today's business landscape, driving success in an ever-evolving world.

Adapting to remote and hybrid work environments presents a unique set of challenges and opportunities for leaders accustomed to traditional office settings. The transition necessitates a reevaluation of leadership strategies to maintain effectiveness, team cohesion, and productivity across dispersed teams. In navigating the nuances of distance leadership, several key strategies emerge as essential for success.

Clear and consistent communication is paramount in remote and hybrid settings. Leaders must cultivate an environment where open dialogue is encouraged, ensuring that team members feel connected despite physical distances. This involves not only regular updates and check-ins via video conferencing but also an openness to feedback and concerns from the team. The use of varied communication tools, tailored to different needs and preferences, helps maintain a seamless flow of information and keeps everyone on the same page.

Building trust and autonomy within the team becomes increasingly important as traditional oversight mechanisms become less feasible. Demonstrating confidence in the team's abilities by delegating responsibilities and empowering individuals to make decisions fosters a culture of accountability and ownership. This shift towards outcome-based management, rather than focusing on hours worked, underscores the value of trust in achieving results.

Maintaining team cohesion in a remote or hybrid environment requires intentional efforts to sustain social connections and a sense of belonging among team members. Initiatives such as virtual team-building exercises, informal catch-ups, and celebrating successes together can help bridge the gap created by physical separation. These activities reinforce the team's shared goals and values, contributing to a unified and motivated group.

The effective use of technology is a critical component of successful remote and hybrid leadership. Beyond selecting appropriate tools for collaboration and project management, leaders must ensure that the team is proficient with these technologies. Providing training and ongoing support minimizes technical difficulties and enhances overall efficiency.

Flexibility and empathy are crucial as team members navigate the personal and professional challenges of remote work. Leaders should recognize and accommodate the diverse circumstances faced by their team, offering support and adjustments as needed. This empathetic approach not only alleviates stress but also reinforces a supportive and inclusive culture.

Ensuring inclusivity is vital to prevent feelings of isolation among remote team members. Leaders should strive for equitable participation in meetings, discussions, and decision-making processes, ensuring that all voices are heard and valued regardless of their physical location.

Embracing continuous learning and adaptation is fundamental in the evolving landscape of remote and hybrid work. Leaders should remain open to refining their approaches based on feedback and the changing needs of the team and organization. This commitment to improvement ensures that leadership practices remain effective and responsive to the challenges and opportunities of remote and hybrid work environments.

Leading effectively in remote and hybrid settings involves a multifaceted approach that emphasizes communication, trust, technology use, empathy, and inclusivity. By embracing these strategies, leaders can overcome the challenges of distance leadership and cultivate thriving, cohesive teams that are well-equipped to navigate the complexities of the modern work landscape.

In the realm of crisis management and rapid decision-making, flexible leadership plays a pivotal role in navigating organizations through turbulent times. The ability to make swift decisions while maintaining a balance between speed and thoroughness is a hallmark of effective leadership during periods of uncertainty. Flexible leaders are adept at assessing situations quickly, gathering essential information, and making informed choices that safeguard the interests of their organizations and stakeholders.

The essence of flexible leadership in crisis management lies in the capacity to adapt leadership style and decision-making processes to the demands of the situation. Crises often require leaders to depart from conventional planning and deliberation routines, demanding immediate action to mitigate risks and capitalize on time-sensitive opportunities. However, the urgency to act swiftly does not negate the need for thoughtful consideration. Flexible leaders excel at walking this tightrope, ensuring that decisions are made quickly but not hastily, and are based on the best available information.

Balancing speed and thoroughness in decision-making involves a nuanced understanding of the crisis at hand. It requires leaders to prioritize effectively, focusing on decisions that have the most significant impact on the immediate well-being of the organization and its people. This often means identifying the most critical issues, allocating resources efficiently, and delegating tasks to trusted team members to expedite action.

To achieve this balance, flexible leaders rely on a robust communication network that allows for rapid information flow and feedback. They create an environment where team members feel empowered to share insights and updates in real-time, which in turn, facilitates quicker, more informed decision-making. Moreover, these leaders are prepared to adjust their strategies as new information emerges, demonstrating resilience and a willingness to pivot when necessary.

Incorporating a level of thoroughness in rapid decision-making also involves drawing on past experiences and lessons learned. Flexible leaders use their knowledge of previous crises to inform their actions, applying proven strategies while remaining open to innovative solutions. They also understand the importance of reflecting on decisions post-crisis, analyzing outcomes, and integrating new learnings into future crisis management plans.

The role of flexible leadership in crisis management and rapid decision-making is critical in guiding organizations through challenges with agility and foresight. By mastering the balance between speed and thoroughness, flexible leaders ensure that their organizations can respond effectively to crises, minimizing negative impacts while positioning themselves for recovery and growth in the aftermath. This balanced approach not only enhances the resilience of the organization but also builds trust and confidence among stakeholders, reinforcing the leader's ability to navigate through uncertainty.

Flexible leaders play a pivotal role in fostering environments where autonomy and empowerment flourish. By promoting these values, they enable teams to harness their full potential, driving innovation and adaptability within the organization. The essence of empowering teams and delegating authority lies in the leader's ability to trust their team members, providing them with the freedom to make decisions and take action based on their expertise and insights.

Empowering teams begins with a clear communication of goals and expectations. Flexible leaders articulate the organization's vision and how each team member's contributions align with achieving these objectives. This clarity not only motivates but also provides a framework within which team members can exercise autonomy, making strategic decisions that propel the organization forward.

Delegation is a critical technique for empowering teams, and it requires more than merely assigning tasks. It involves entrusting team members with responsibilities that challenge them, encouraging growth and development. Effective delegation is underpinned by a deep understanding of each team member's skills, strengths, and areas for improvement. Flexible leaders match tasks with the team members best equipped to handle them, ensuring a higher likelihood of success and satisfaction.

Trust-building is essential for effective delegation and empowerment. It is cultivated over time through consistent, transparent interactions and by demonstrating faith in team members' abilities. Trust is reinforced when leaders support their teams' decisions and provide constructive feedback, even when outcomes fall short of expectations. This support fosters a safe environment for experimentation and learning, crucial components of a dynamic and innovative workplace.

Flexible leaders also recognize the importance of providing teams with the resources and tools they need to succeed. This might include access to training, mentorship opportunities, and the necessary technological tools. Equipping teams with these resources demonstrates a commitment to their success and empowers them to take initiative and ownership of their projects.

Creating opportunities for team members to contribute to decision-making processes further empowers individuals and reinforces their value to the organization. This inclusive approach not only leverages diverse perspectives for better decision-making but also enhances team cohesion and morale.

In dynamic environments, flexibility and adaptability are key. Leaders must be prepared to adjust their delegation and empowerment strategies as circumstances change, maintaining open lines of communication and being receptive to feedback from their teams. This adaptability ensures that empowerment and delegation practices remain effective, even as the organization evolves.

Flexible leaders who prioritize empowering their teams and delegating authority foster a culture of trust, innovation, and accountability. By effectively leveraging these techniques, they enable their teams to operate with a high degree of autonomy, driving organizational success in an ever-changing business landscape.

In today's globalized and interconnected world, the need for cultural sensitivity and inclusivity in leadership has never been more pronounced. Leaders are increasingly required to navigate a diverse landscape of cultural norms, values, and expectations, both within their teams and in the broader organizational context. This reality calls for leadership styles that are not only adaptive to diverse teams but also actively promote an environment of inclusivity and respect.

Cultural sensitivity in leadership involves an awareness and understanding of the diverse cultural backgrounds and perspectives that team members bring to the table. It requires leaders to recognize and honor differences, whether they pertain to national cultures, ethnic backgrounds, religious beliefs, or personal values. By fostering an atmosphere where diversity is viewed as a strength, leaders can enhance team cohesion, creativity, and problem-solving capabilities.

Adapting leadership approaches to accommodate this diversity involves several key practices. It starts with active listening and open dialogue, where team members feel valued and heard.

Leaders should encourage sharing of diverse viewpoints and experiences, facilitating learning and mutual understanding among team members. This practice not only enriches the team's collective knowledge but also builds trust and respect.

Inclusivity goes beyond mere tolerance of differences; it involves creating opportunities for all team members to contribute fully to the team's objectives. Leaders must be vigilant in identifying and dismantling any barriers to full participation, whether they stem from unconscious biases, organizational structures, or communication practices. This might involve implementing flexible working arrangements, providing training on unconscious bias, or ensuring that team activities and celebrations are accessible and respectful of all members' cultural norms.

Adapting leadership approaches to diverse teams and global challenges requires ongoing education and self-reflection. Leaders should commit to continuously expanding their understanding of different cultures and perspectives, seeking out resources, training, and experiences that broaden their worldview. This commitment to personal growth not only enhances a leader's cultural sensitivity but also models the importance of lifelong learning to their teams.

In navigating global challenges, leaders with culturally sensitive and inclusive approaches are better equipped to forge strong relationships with international partners, customers, and colleagues. They can effectively bridge cultural divides, fostering collaboration and innovation across geographic and cultural boundaries.

Cultural sensitivity and inclusivity are not optional extras but essential components of effective leadership in the 21st century. By embracing and integrating these principles into their leadership styles, leaders can build teams that are not only more cohesive and productive but also reflective of the diverse world in which we live. This approach not only benefits the organization but also contributes to a more inclusive and understanding global community.

In the ever-evolving landscape of modern business, the importance of continuous learning and self-improvement for leaders cannot be overstated. As the pace of change accelerates, driven by technological advancements, shifting market dynamics, and global challenges, leaders must remain lifelong learners to effectively navigate and shape the future of their organizations. This commitment to personal and professional growth ensures that leaders can adapt their strategies, innovate, and lead with confidence in an uncertain world.

Continuous learning enables leaders to stay informed about emerging trends and challenges, equipping them with the knowledge and skills necessary to respond proactively. It involves a proactive approach to education, seeking out new information, perspectives, and experiences that can enhance leadership effectiveness. Leaders who prioritize learning demonstrate a curiosity and openness to change, qualities that are infectious and can inspire a culture of learning throughout the organization.

Strategies for staying informed and responsive include leveraging a variety of learning resources, such as industry publications, academic research, and professional networks. Engaging with thought leaders through conferences, webinars, and social media can provide insights into future trends and innovative practices. Additionally, leaders can benefit from cross-disciplinary learning, exploring subjects outside their immediate area of expertise to gain a broader perspective on complex problems.

Another key strategy is to foster a feedback-rich environment within the organization, where insights from employees, customers, and partners are valued and used to inform decision-making. This openness to feedback not only aids in personal growth but also ensures that the organization remains agile and responsive to the needs of its stakeholders.

Implementing structured reflection practices is also vital. By regularly reflecting on successes, failures, and the lessons learned, leaders can deepen their understanding of their own leadership styles, the impact of their decisions, and areas for future improvement. This reflective practice can be enhanced through coaching or mentoring relationships, which provide a space for guided self-exploration and development.

Embracing experimentation and risk-taking as part of the learning process encourages innovation and adaptability. Leaders who are willing to try new approaches, and learn from both successes and failures, model the resilience and flexibility needed to thrive in times of change.

Learning and evolving with change is a fundamental aspect of effective leadership. By embracing continuous learning and self-improvement, leaders not only enhance their own capabilities but also contribute to the creation of adaptable, forward-thinking organizations. The strategies for staying informed, engaging with diverse perspectives, and fostering an environment of feedback and reflection are essential for navigating the complexities of the modern business environment and leading with vision and integrity.

Implementing flexible leadership in practice involves a deliberate shift towards adaptability, openness, and resilience in one's leadership approach. This transition requires leaders to develop and refine a set of skills and behaviors that enable them to navigate the complexities of the modern business environment effectively. Practical steps and action plans can guide leaders in this journey, fostering a leadership style that is responsive to change and capable of harnessing the full potential of their teams.

One foundational step is to cultivate a mindset of continuous learning and curiosity. Leaders should actively seek out new knowledge, perspectives, and experiences, embracing opportunities to grow both personally and professionally. This might involve participating in leadership development programs, attending industry conferences, or engaging in cross-functional projects within the organization. By modeling a commitment to learning, leaders inspire their teams to embrace a similar mindset, creating a culture of continuous improvement.

Developing emotional intelligence is another critical aspect of flexible leadership. Leaders must be attuned to their own emotions and those of their team members, demonstrating empathy and understanding in their interactions. This emotional awareness facilitates effective communication, conflict resolution, and team cohesion, especially in times of change or uncertainty. Techniques such as active listening, reflective practice, and seeking feedback can enhance a leader's emotional intelligence over time.

Building strong relationships based on trust is essential for flexible leadership. Trust enables leaders to delegate effectively, empowering team members with autonomy and authority to make decisions. To build trust, leaders should demonstrate consistency, reliability, and transparency in their actions and decisions. They should also provide support and resources to help team members succeed, showing confidence in their abilities and contributing to a positive and empowering work environment.

Adapting communication strategies to fit the needs of diverse teams and situations is another practical step. Leaders should utilize various communication channels and styles to ensure clarity and inclusiveness, tailoring their approach to reach and engage all team members effectively. This might involve combining traditional meetings with digital communication tools, providing regular updates to keep everyone informed, and creating opportunities for open dialogue and feedback.

Embracing a flexible approach to problem-solving and decision-making allows leaders to respond swiftly and effectively to emerging challenges. This involves being open to new ideas, willing to experiment with different solutions, and ready to pivot strategies based on evolving circumstances. Encouraging a similar flexibility and creativity among team members can lead to innovative solutions and a more agile organization.

Case studies of successful flexible leadership often highlight leaders who have navigated their organizations through periods of significant change or crisis. For example, leaders who swiftly transitioned their teams to remote work during the pandemic while maintaining productivity and morale demonstrated flexible leadership in action. These leaders adjusted their communication and management strategies to support their teams, leveraged technology to facilitate collaboration, and prioritized the well-being of their employees, ensuring business continuity and resilience in the face of unprecedented challenges.

Implementing flexible leadership in practice requires a multifaceted approach that emphasizes continuous learning, emotional intelligence, trust-building, adaptive communication, and innovative problem-solving. By developing and applying these flexible leadership styles, leaders can navigate the complexities of the modern business landscape, driving success and sustainability for their organizations in an ever-changing world.

The necessity of flexible leadership styles in the post-pandemic world has been underscored by the unprecedented challenges and rapid changes organizations have faced. The global crisis has highlighted the limitations of traditional, rigid leadership approaches and illuminated the path toward more dynamic, responsive ways of leading. Flexible leadership, characterized by adaptability, resilience, and a commitment to continuous learning, has emerged as essential for navigating the complexities and uncertainties of today's business environment.

Leaders are encouraged to embrace adaptability as a core component of their leadership practice. This adaptability is not merely about reacting to changes as they occur but proactively anticipating shifts, fostering a culture of innovation, and empowering teams to thrive in the face of adversity. It involves a willingness to question the status quo, experiment with new strategies, and pivot directions when necessary, all while maintaining a clear vision and purpose.

The transition to flexible leadership requires a conscious effort to develop the skills and mindset needed to lead with agility. Leaders must cultivate an environment where learning is continuous, communication is open and inclusive, and diversity of thought is valued. By doing so, they can create resilient organizations capable of withstanding challenges and seizing opportunities in the post-pandemic landscape.

The journey toward flexible leadership is both a personal and organizational imperative in the post-pandemic era. Leaders who embrace adaptability, foster a culture of learning and innovation, and build resilient teams will not only navigate the challenges of today but also shape the future of their organizations. The call to action for leaders is clear: to embrace flexibility and adaptability as foundational elements of their leadership approach, ensuring their organizations can thrive in an ever-evolving world.

Leading Remote and Hybrid Teams

The emergence of remote and hybrid work models marks a significant shift in the landscape of work in the post-pandemic era. This transformation, accelerated by the global health crisis, has not only redefined where work happens but also how it is led and managed. Leading remote and hybrid teams presents a unique set of challenges and opportunities for leaders accustomed to traditional office environments. This next chapter delves into the intricacies of managing dispersed teams, exploring strategies for effective communication, trust-building, goal-setting, and leveraging technology for collaboration.

The rise of remote and hybrid work models necessitates a reevaluation of leadership practices to address the challenges of distance management. These challenges include maintaining clear and consistent communication across different locations and time zones, fostering trust and strong relationships without regular face-to-face interactions, and ensuring team members remain engaged and motivated. However, these models also offer opportunities for greater flexibility, access to a wider talent pool, and potential improvements in work-life balance for team members.

Establishing effective communication is foundational to the success of remote and hybrid teams. This section will outline strategies for ensuring that all team members are aligned, informed, and connected, regardless of their physical location. It will also highlight the tools and technologies that can facilitate seamless communication and collaboration.

Building trust and relationships from a distance requires intentional effort and techniques tailored to virtual environments. This part of the chapter will provide insights into overcoming the limitations imposed by limited in-person interactions and fostering a culture of trust and mutual respect.

Setting clear expectations and goals is crucial for remote and hybrid teams to thrive. Leaders must articulate measurable objectives that align with broader organizational goals, ensuring team members understand their roles and responsibilities. This segment will offer best practices for goal-setting and alignment in dispersed teams.

Leveraging technology for collaboration has become indispensable in remote and hybrid work settings. An overview of collaboration tools and software, along with tips for integrating technology into team workflows, will be provided to enhance productivity and teamwork.

Maintaining team engagement and morale in a remote or hybrid context poses unique challenges, such as combating feelings of isolation and disconnection. Strategies for keeping teams motivated and connected will be explored, addressing the nuances of remote team dynamics.

Balancing flexibility with productivity is a key concern in remote and hybrid models. This section will discuss techniques for effective time management, promoting flexibility while avoiding burnout, and ensuring team members remain productive and focused.

Adapting performance management strategies for dispersed teams involves providing constructive feedback and recognizing achievements in a virtual setting. Approaches to performance management and feedback that are suited to remote and hybrid environments will be examined.

Cultivating an inclusive team culture is essential for ensuring that all team members feel valued and included, regardless of their work location. Strategies for creating a cohesive and inclusive culture will be discussed, emphasizing the importance of equity and belonging in remote and hybrid teams.

Navigating challenges and resolving conflicts in remote and hybrid teams require proactive management and clear conflict resolution strategies. This section will identify common challenges and offer techniques for maintaining team harmony and addressing disputes effectively.

Encouraging continuous learning and development within remote and hybrid teams is vital for sustaining growth and adaptation. Resources and approaches for ongoing professional development will be highlighted, ensuring teams remain competitive and innovative.

Leading remote and hybrid teams effectively requires a multifaceted approach, blending traditional leadership skills with new strategies tailored to the realities of remote and hybrid work. Leaders who embrace these strategies, continuously adapting and refining their approaches, will be well-positioned to navigate the challenges and capitalize on the opportunities presented by dispersed team management.

The rise of remote and hybrid work models in the post-pandemic era represents one of the most significant shifts in the workplace landscape in recent history. Triggered by the global health crisis, organizations worldwide were compelled to rapidly adopt remote work practices to ensure business continuity amidst lockdowns and social distancing measures. This emergency response has evolved into a more permanent transformation, with many organizations recognizing the benefits and potential of remote and hybrid work arrangements even as the immediate threat of the pandemic recedes.

This transition has not been without its challenges. Managing dispersed teams across different locations and time zones introduces complexities in communication, collaboration, and company culture. Leaders must navigate the nuances of ensuring team cohesion, maintaining productivity, and supporting the well-being of team members who may feel isolated or disconnected from the broader organizational community. Additionally, the blurred boundaries between work and home life present challenges in managing work-life balance and preventing burnout.

Despite these challenges, the shift to remote and hybrid work models also presents significant opportunities. Organizations can tap into a broader talent pool, no longer limited by geographical constraints, which can lead to more diverse and skilled teams. The flexibility offered by remote and hybrid work can also enhance employee satisfaction and retention, as team members appreciate the ability to structure their work around their personal lives. Furthermore, the adoption of digital tools and platforms for collaboration and communication can lead to efficiencies and innovations in how work is conducted, potentially accelerating digital transformation initiatives.

The rise of remote and hybrid work models thus marks a pivotal moment in redefining the future of work. Leaders are tasked with steering their teams through the challenges while seizing the opportunities presented by this new normal. Success in this endeavor requires adaptability, empathy, and a commitment to continuous learning and innovation, ensuring that organizations can thrive in the post-pandemic world.

Establishing effective communication is crucial in remote and hybrid work environments, where the physical cues and immediate feedback of traditional office settings are absent. Clear and consistent communication bridges the gap created by physical distance, ensuring that team members remain aligned, informed, and connected. Implementing strategies and leveraging tools and technologies are key steps in fostering a communication-rich environment.

The foundation of effective communication in dispersed teams is setting clear expectations around communication norms and channels. Leaders should define which mediums are to be used for different types of communication, such as email for non-urgent matters and instant messaging for quick queries. Establishing regular check-ins, such as daily stand-ups or weekly team meetings via video conferencing, ensures ongoing alignment and provides opportunities for team members to raise concerns, share updates, and stay connected with the wider team.

Creating an environment that encourages open dialogue is another critical strategy. This involves promoting a culture where questions are welcomed, feedback is encouraged, and all team members feel valued and heard. Encouraging informal virtual interactions, such as virtual coffee breaks or social hours, can also help maintain the social fabric of the team, fostering relationships and trust that are essential for effective collaboration.

The use of technology plays a significant role in facilitating effective communication within remote and hybrid teams. Video conferencing tools, such as Zoom or Microsoft Teams, enable face-to-face interactions, helping to build rapport and clarify communication through visual cues. Collaboration platforms, like Slack or Microsoft Teams, offer spaces for real-time messaging, project discussions, and document sharing, keeping everyone on the same page. Additionally, project management tools like Asana or Trello can help track tasks and progress, providing transparency and accountability.

To enhance the effectiveness of these tools, leaders should ensure that team members are equipped with the necessary skills and training to use them effectively. This might involve providing access to tutorials, conducting training sessions, or offering one-on-one support for less tech-savvy team members. It's also important to regularly assess the effectiveness of communication tools and strategies, soliciting feedback from the team and being prepared to adapt and evolve practices in response to their needs and preferences.

Establishing effective communication within remote and hybrid teams requires a deliberate approach that combines clear expectations, a culture of openness, and the strategic use of technology. By implementing these strategies, leaders can ensure that their teams remain cohesive, engaged, and productive, regardless of their physical locations.

Building trust and relationships from a distance in a virtual environment requires deliberate effort and strategies tailored to overcome the inherent challenges of limited face-to-face interaction. Trust is the foundation of effective teamwork and is particularly crucial in remote and hybrid settings, where the physical distance can amplify misunderstandings and hinder the spontaneous interactions that often build camaraderie in traditional office environments.

One effective technique for fostering trust is to prioritize transparent and open communication. Leaders should regularly share updates about the organization, projects, and any changes in policies or strategies. Transparency about challenges and uncertainties also plays a crucial role, as it demonstrates honesty and vulnerability, encouraging team members to reciprocate.

Creating opportunities for team members to interact informally is another key strategy. Virtual coffee breaks, online team-building activities, or casual catch-ups can replicate the water-cooler conversations of office settings. These interactions allow team members to connect on a personal level, sharing stories, interests, and experiences outside of work tasks, which can strengthen bonds and build trust.

Consistent and fair recognition of contributions and achievements is vital in a virtual environment. Acknowledging individual and team successes in team meetings or communication platforms not only boosts morale but also reinforces the value of each team member's work. Recognition fosters a sense of belonging and appreciation, crucial components of a trusting relationship.

Setting clear expectations and providing regular feedback are also important. When team members understand what is expected of them and receive constructive feedback on their performance, it reduces uncertainties and builds confidence in the leadership. Moreover, inviting feedback from team members demonstrates respect for their opinions and insights, further enhancing trust.

Another technique involves investing in one-on-one time with team members. Personal check-ins allow leaders to understand individual challenges, aspirations, and circumstances, tailoring support to each team member's needs. This individual attention strengthens relationships, making team members feel valued and supported.

Leaders can also encourage collaboration and peer support among team members. Facilitating project collaborations or peer mentoring opportunities can help build inter-team trust and foster a supportive team dynamic. When team members rely on each other and work closely together, it naturally enhances trust and cohesion.

Adapting leadership styles to be more empathetic and understanding can significantly impact trust-building in remote settings. Leaders who show genuine care for their team members' well-being, especially considering the unique challenges of remote work, such as isolation or work-life balance issues, cultivate an environment where trust thrives.

In conclusion, building trust and strong working relationships from a distance requires a multifaceted approach focused on transparent communication, recognition, personal connections, and empathy. By employing these techniques, leaders can overcome the challenges of limited face-to-face interaction, fostering a culture of trust and collaboration that underpins successful remote and hybrid teams.

In the landscape of remote and hybrid work, setting clear and measurable goals for teams is more critical than ever. The absence of a physical office environment can lead to uncertainties about priorities and expectations unless goals are explicitly defined. Clear goals provide direction, foster accountability, and ensure that team efforts are aligned with the broader objectives of the organization.

The importance of setting clear, measurable goals lies in their ability to guide team members towards desired outcomes, facilitating focus and efficiency. Goals act as a roadmap, helping teams navigate their tasks and responsibilities, especially when direct oversight is minimized. Measurable goals also allow for tracking progress and evaluating performance, enabling leaders and teams to adjust strategies as needed to stay on course.

Best practices for aligning team objectives with organizational goals begin with understanding the strategic vision and priorities of the organization. Leaders should translate these overarching objectives into specific, actionable goals for their teams, ensuring relevance and contribution to the broader mission. This alignment ensures that every team member's work directly supports the organization's success, creating a sense of purpose and motivation.

Engaging team members in the goal-setting process is another best practice that promotes buy-in and commitment. By involving team members in discussions about objectives, leaders can harness their insights, encourage ownership of goals, and tailor expectations to the team's capabilities and resources. This collaborative approach also helps identify potential challenges and opportunities, enriching the goal-setting process.

SMART (Specific, Measurable, Achievable, Relevant, Time-bound) criteria are invaluable in setting clear and measurable goals. Applying these criteria ensures that goals are well-defined, quantifiable, realistic, aligned with team and organizational objectives, and bound by a specific timeframe. SMART goals provide clarity and focus, making it easier for teams to understand what is expected and how success will be measured.

Regularly reviewing and adjusting goals is crucial, especially in the dynamic context of remote and hybrid work. Changes in market conditions, organizational priorities, or team capabilities may necessitate revisions to goals. Periodic check-ins allow leaders and teams to assess progress, celebrate achievements, address obstacles, and recalibrate goals as necessary to remain aligned with organizational objectives.

Communication plays a pivotal role in the goal-setting process. Clearly articulating goals, expectations, and the rationale behind them ensures that team members are informed and aligned. Utilizing digital tools and platforms can facilitate the sharing of goals, progress updates, and feedback, keeping everyone engaged and focused, regardless of their physical location.

Setting clear and measurable goals is foundational to the success of remote and hybrid teams. By aligning team objectives with organizational goals, engaging team members in the goal-setting process, applying SMART criteria, regularly reviewing progress, and communicating effectively, leaders can foster a focused, accountable, and motivated team environment that drives organizational success in the post-pandemic world.

Leveraging technology for collaboration is a cornerstone of success for remote and hybrid teams, enabling seamless communication, project management, and team cohesion regardless of physical locations. The array of collaboration tools and software available today offers diverse functionalities to support various aspects of virtual teamwork. Integrating these technologies into team workflows effectively can significantly enhance productivity, engagement, and overall team dynamics.

Collaboration tools and software suitable for remote and hybrid teams span several categories, each addressing different needs. Communication platforms like Slack and Microsoft Teams facilitate real-time messaging and team discussions, offering features such as chat rooms, direct messaging, and integration with other tools. Video conferencing tools such as Zoom, Google Meet, and Microsoft Teams enable face-to-face meetings and presentations, crucial for maintaining personal connections and ensuring clarity in communication.

Project management software, including Trello, Asana, and Monday.com, provides teams with the ability to plan, track, and manage projects and tasks in a centralized location. These platforms often feature task assignments, deadlines, progress tracking, and collaboration spaces, helping keep everyone aligned and accountable. File sharing and collaboration platforms like Google Drive, Dropbox, and OneDrive allow team members to store, share, and work on documents simultaneously, ensuring easy access to information and facilitating real-time collaboration.

To effectively integrate technology into team workflows, leaders should first assess the specific needs of their team and the functionalities required to support their work processes. Selecting tools that integrate well with each other can streamline workflows and reduce the cognitive load associated with switching between platforms. Providing training and resources to ensure all team members are proficient in using the selected tools is also essential, as this ensures that technology serves as an enabler rather than a barrier to collaboration.

Establishing clear guidelines and best practices for using collaboration tools can further enhance their effectiveness. This might include norms around response times, appropriate use of different communication channels, and document management practices. Encouraging and modeling the use of collaboration tools for both work-related and informal interactions can help build a culture of openness and connectivity, fostering a sense of community within the team.

Regularly reviewing the effectiveness of the technology tools in use is crucial. Soliciting feedback from team members on the tools' impact on their work, any challenges encountered, and suggestions for improvement can provide valuable insights for refining the technology strategy. Being open to exploring new tools and technologies as they emerge can also help teams stay at the forefront of collaboration best practices.

Leveraging technology for collaboration is pivotal in supporting the productivity and cohesion of remote and hybrid teams. By carefully selecting tools that meet the team's needs, providing necessary training and support, establishing clear usage guidelines, and remaining adaptable to changes and feedback, leaders can ensure that technology acts as a powerful enabler of effective, efficient, and enjoyable teamwork.

Maintaining team engagement and morale in remote and hybrid environments is crucial for sustaining productivity and fostering a positive workplace culture, despite the physical distances. This challenge requires thoughtful strategies to ensure team members feel connected, valued, and motivated. Addressing the issues of isolation and disconnection is paramount in these settings, where the lack of face-to-face interactions can impact team dynamics and individual well-being.

One effective strategy is fostering a strong sense of community among team members. This can be achieved through regular virtual meetings that not only focus on work-related topics but also allow time for personal check-ins and casual conversations. Creating virtual spaces for team members to share personal news, hobbies, or interests can help replicate the social interactions that occur naturally in office environments, reducing feelings of isolation.

Recognizing and celebrating achievements is another key strategy for boosting morale. Public acknowledgment of individual and team successes during virtual meetings, through company-wide communications, or on digital recognition platforms can provide a sense of accomplishment and appreciation. Celebrating milestones, anniversaries, and professional achievements fosters a positive atmosphere and reinforces the value of each team member's contributions.

Ensuring clear communication of goals, roles, and expectations also plays a significant role in maintaining engagement. When team members understand how their work contributes to the larger organizational objectives, they are more likely to feel motivated and aligned with the team's mission. Regular updates on company performance, future plans, and changes in strategy can help team members feel informed and involved.

Providing opportunities for professional development and growth is crucial for keeping team members engaged. Offering access to online courses, webinars, and workshops allows individuals to acquire new skills and knowledge, enhancing their career prospects and contributing to their sense of progress and achievement. Encouraging participation in cross-functional projects or committees can also provide valuable learning experiences and broaden team members' networks within the organization.

Addressing the challenges of isolation requires a proactive approach to mental health and well-being. Implementing initiatives such as virtual wellness sessions, access to counseling services, or regular check-ins can support team members' emotional health. Encouraging a healthy work-life balance, with flexible work hours when possible, can also help mitigate the stress and burnout that can accompany remote work.

Building a culture of open feedback and communication is essential for identifying and addressing issues of disconnection and morale. Creating an environment where team members feel comfortable voicing their concerns, challenges, and suggestions for improvement enables leaders to take timely action to address potential problems. Regular surveys or feedback sessions can provide insights into team sentiment and engagement levels.

Maintaining team engagement and morale in remote and hybrid settings involves a multifaceted approach that emphasizes community, recognition, clear communication, professional development, well-being, and open feedback. By implementing these strategies, leaders can create a supportive and motivating environment that counteracts the challenges of isolation and disconnection, ensuring that team members remain engaged, productive, and connected.

Balancing flexibility with productivity in remote and hybrid work settings is a nuanced challenge that demands careful consideration. The autonomy offered by remote work can enhance work-life balance and personal autonomy but also requires disciplined time management to maintain productivity. Avoiding burnout, a common risk in environments where work and personal spaces overlap, is crucial for sustaining long-term effectiveness and well-being.

To navigate these challenges, leaders and teams can adopt several techniques for effective time management and maintaining a healthy balance:

- Structured Scheduling: While remote work offers flexibility, establishing a structured schedule can help delineate work hours from personal time, ensuring dedicated blocks for focused work while preserving time for rest and personal activities. Encouraging team members to set and share their work hours can also facilitate collaboration by making it clear when everyone is available.

- Prioritization and Goal Setting: Identifying and focusing on high-priority tasks ensures that efforts are concentrated on activities with the highest impact. Techniques like the Eisenhower Box or the Pareto Principle (80/20 rule) can help in categorizing tasks by urgency and importance, guiding daily and weekly planning.

- Use of Productivity Tools: Digital tools like time tracking software, task managers, and calendar applications can aid in organizing tasks, setting reminders, and visualizing how time is spent. These tools can be instrumental in identifying time sinks and optimizing work patterns for better efficiency.

- Regular Breaks and Downtime: Incorporating regular breaks into the workday, such as the Pomodoro Technique, can prevent fatigue and maintain high levels of concentration. Encouraging team members to take time off and disconnect outside work hours is vital for preventing burnout and promoting well-being.

- Clear Communication of Availability: In remote and hybrid settings, it's essential to communicate availability clearly to colleagues and leaders. Setting boundaries, such as "do not disturb" times, and respecting others' boundaries can help manage expectations and reduce the pressure to be always on.

- Empowering Team Autonomy: Leaders can foster a culture of trust by empowering team members to manage their schedules and workloads, provided they meet their objectives and maintain productivity. This autonomy can boost morale and motivation, as team members feel trusted and valued.

- Mindful Meetings: Evaluating the necessity and frequency of meetings can free up significant time for focused work. Adopting practices like agenda setting, limiting meeting durations, and considering asynchronous communication alternatives can minimize disruptions and enhance productivity.

- Personalized Work Strategies: Recognizing that everyone has unique rhythms and preferences for when and how they work best can allow individuals to tailor their work strategies. Encouraging team members to discover and leverage their peak productivity periods can lead to more efficient work practices.

Balancing flexibility with productivity requires a conscious effort to create structures and practices that support focused work, while also allowing for the personal flexibility that makes remote and hybrid work appealing. By adopting these techniques, teams can navigate the challenges of remote work environments, maintaining productivity and safeguarding against burnout.

Adapting performance management strategies for remote and hybrid teams requires a nuanced approach that considers the unique dynamics of dispersed work environments. Traditional methods of evaluating performance, often reliant on physical presence and observable behaviors, must evolve to accommodate the realities of remote and hybrid work. This evolution involves establishing clear, measurable objectives, leveraging technology for ongoing feedback, and finding innovative ways to recognize and celebrate achievements.

In the context of remote and hybrid teams, performance management hinges on setting clear expectations and goals that are aligned with organizational objectives. Leaders must articulate what success looks like for each role, ensuring that team members understand their responsibilities and how their contributions impact the broader mission. This clarity is foundational for accountability and helps guide individuals in prioritizing their efforts.

Providing constructive feedback in a virtual setting challenges leaders to maintain open lines of communication and foster a culture of trust. Regular virtual check-ins offer a platform for discussing progress, addressing challenges, and offering support. These conversations should be framed positively, focusing on development and growth rather than solely on critique. Emphasizing strengths and achievements can motivate team members, while targeted feedback on areas for improvement should be accompanied by concrete suggestions and opportunities for skill development.

Recognizing achievements becomes particularly important in remote and hybrid settings, where team members may feel their efforts go unnoticed. Leaders should seize opportunities to celebrate successes, both big and small, in virtual team meetings, company-wide communications, or through digital recognition platforms. Public acknowledgment not only validates the individual's contributions but also reinforces the behaviors and outcomes that the organization values.

Leveraging technology plays a crucial role in modern performance management. Digital tools can facilitate continuous feedback, allowing team members to receive timely insights into their performance. These platforms can also support peer feedback mechanisms, promoting a culture of recognition and collective growth. Additionally, project management and productivity tools provide objective data on task completion and time management, offering another layer of insight into performance.

Adapting performance management for remote and hybrid teams also involves recognizing the personal challenges team members may face in these environments. Leaders should adopt a flexible and empathetic approach, considering factors such as work-life balance, mental health, and the home working environment in their assessments. This holistic view ensures that performance management is fair, supportive, and conducive to long-term engagement and productivity.

Effective performance management and feedback in remote and hybrid teams demand clear communication, measurable goals, regular and constructive feedback, and meaningful recognition of achievements. By adapting these strategies to the virtual context, leaders can support their teams' development, motivation, and alignment with organizational goals, ensuring success in the dispersed work environment.

Cultivating an inclusive team culture in remote and hybrid work environments is essential for fostering a sense of belonging and equity among team members, regardless of their physical location. The challenges of remote work, such as potential feelings of isolation or disconnection, make it imperative for leaders to intentionally build and maintain an environment where every team member feels valued, heard, and included.

Ensuring inclusivity and equity involves recognizing and addressing the unique challenges and barriers that remote and hybrid work settings may pose to different team members. This could include differences in access to technology, varying home working conditions, or the diverse personal responsibilities that team members juggle alongside their work commitments. Leaders need to adopt flexible and empathetic approaches, offering support and accommodations where necessary to ensure all team members can participate fully and equitably in team activities and work processes.

Creating a cohesive and inclusive team culture starts with open and transparent communication. Leaders should encourage regular sharing of ideas, feedback, and concerns, creating channels where team members can express themselves without fear of judgment. This open dialogue fosters mutual understanding and respect, laying the foundation for a supportive team environment.

Another effective strategy is to celebrate diversity and encourage team members to share their backgrounds, experiences, and perspectives. This could be facilitated through virtual team-building activities, cultural exchange sessions, or dedicated discussion forums. Such initiatives not only enrich the team's collective knowledge but also highlight the value of diverse viewpoints in driving creativity and innovation.

Building inclusivity also means ensuring that all team members have equal access to opportunities for professional development, advancement, and participation in decision-making processes. Leaders should be mindful of potential biases in these areas, actively seeking to identify and remove any barriers that might prevent full participation by all team members.

Promoting an inclusive team culture requires continuous effort and reflection. Leaders should regularly assess the effectiveness of their inclusivity strategies, seeking feedback from the team and being willing to make adjustments as needed. This ongoing commitment to inclusivity not only enhances team cohesion and morale but also contributes to the overall performance and success of the organization.

Fostering an inclusive team culture in remote and hybrid environments is a multifaceted challenge that demands intentional actions and policies. By ensuring equity, celebrating diversity, facilitating open communication, and providing equal opportunities for all team members, leaders can create a supportive and inclusive work environment that empowers every individual to thrive.

Navigating challenges and resolving conflicts in remote and hybrid team management requires a proactive and nuanced approach, given the unique dynamics of dispersed work settings.

Common challenges include communication breakdowns, feelings of isolation among team members, and difficulties in maintaining a shared team culture. Additionally, the lack of face-to-face interaction can exacerbate misunderstandings and conflicts, making it essential for leaders to cultivate strong communication skills and conflict resolution strategies.

Identifying and addressing these challenges begins with fostering an environment of open communication. Leaders should encourage team members to voice their concerns and feedback early, creating a culture where issues are addressed promptly before they escalate. Regular check-ins and team meetings can provide forums for discussing challenges, while anonymous feedback tools can help surface issues that team members may feel uncomfortable raising openly.

When conflicts arise, adopting a structured approach to resolution is crucial. This involves first acknowledging the conflict and the parties involved, followed by a thorough understanding of the differing perspectives. Leaders should facilitate a dialogue that allows each party to express their views in a respectful and constructive manner, focusing on identifying the root causes of the conflict rather than assigning blame.

Techniques for effective conflict resolution include active listening, where leaders give full attention to the concerns being expressed and acknowledge the emotions involved. This empathy can help de-escalate tensions and demonstrate a commitment to finding a resolution. Employing problem-solving strategies that focus on finding mutually beneficial solutions can also guide the parties toward reconciliation. This might involve compromise, collaboration, or adapting processes and communication styles to prevent similar conflicts in the future.

Maintaining team harmony in remote and hybrid settings also involves building a strong sense of community and shared purpose among team members. Leaders can foster this by celebrating collective achievements, facilitating team-building activities that transcend work-related tasks, and reinforcing the team's shared goals and values. These initiatives can help mitigate feelings of isolation and promote a sense of belonging and cohesion.

In addition to these strategies, training in conflict resolution and communication skills can equip both leaders and team members with the tools needed to navigate disagreements effectively. Encouraging a mindset of continuous improvement, where the team learns from each conflict and adapts its practices accordingly, can also help minimize future disputes.

Navigating challenges and resolving conflicts in remote and hybrid teams require a deliberate focus on communication, empathy, and proactive problem-solving. By creating an environment where issues are addressed openly and constructively, leaders can maintain team harmony, ensuring that the team remains cohesive and productive in the face of the unique challenges presented by dispersed work environments.

Encouraging continuous professional development within remote and hybrid teams is essential for ensuring that individuals and the team as a whole remain competitive and adaptive in a rapidly changing work environment. This commitment to learning and development not only enhances the skills and capabilities of the team but also contributes to job satisfaction and career progression for individual members. Leaders play a pivotal role in fostering a culture of continuous learning, utilizing a range of resources and approaches to support ongoing skill and team development.

Creating a culture that values learning begins with leadership example. Leaders who actively engage in their own professional development and share their learning experiences demonstrate the value of continuous growth, inspiring their team members to pursue similar paths. This can be further supported by integrating learning and development goals into the team's broader objectives, ensuring that professional growth is recognized as a priority alongside project and performance targets.

To facilitate continuous learning, leaders can leverage a variety of resources and platforms. Online courses, webinars, and virtual workshops offer flexible, accessible options for skill development, covering a wide range of topics relevant to the team's needs and individual career aspirations. Encouraging team members to obtain certifications or participate in industry conferences can also provide valuable learning opportunities and networking experiences.

Mentoring and coaching are powerful tools for personal and professional development, particularly in remote and hybrid settings where one-on-one interactions may be less frequent. Pairing team members with mentors either within or outside the organization can facilitate knowledge sharing, offer guidance, and support career development. Similarly, providing access to professional coaches can help individuals work on specific areas of growth, such as leadership skills, communication, or time management.

Peer learning groups within the team can foster a collaborative learning environment where team members share insights, challenges, and best practices with each other. These groups can focus on specific skills, technologies, or project management methodologies, creating a forum for collective problem-solving and innovation.

To support continuous learning and development effectively, it's important for leaders to provide the necessary time and resources. This might involve allocating dedicated learning hours during the workweek, providing budgets for course fees and materials, or offering incentives for completing professional development activities.

Regularly reviewing and updating individual and team development plans ensures that learning goals remain aligned with changing team objectives, project requirements, and individual career paths. This process, coupled with feedback and recognition for achievements in learning and development, reinforces the importance of continuous growth.

Fostering continuous professional development within remote and hybrid teams requires a multifaceted approach that combines leadership support, access to diverse learning resources, and the creation of a culture that values and rewards growth. By prioritizing continuous learning and development, leaders can ensure their teams remain agile, motivated, and equipped to meet the challenges and opportunities of the modern workplace.

The effective leadership of remote and hybrid teams in the evolving landscape of work necessitates a dynamic and thoughtful approach, blending traditional leadership virtues with strategies tailored to the nuances of dispersed team management. This entails fostering clear and open communication, building trust and relationships despite the physical distances, setting clear and measurable goals, leveraging technology for collaboration, and maintaining team engagement and morale. Additionally, balancing flexibility with productivity, managing performance and providing constructive feedback, cultivating an inclusive team culture, navigating challenges and resolving conflicts, and encouraging continuous learning and development are all crucial components of successful remote and hybrid team leadership.

The key to navigating these multifaceted responsibilities lies in the leader's ability to adapt and evolve. The post-pandemic era has underscored the importance of flexibility, empathy, and resilience in leadership. Leaders are called upon to continuously assess and refine their approaches, staying attuned to the needs of their team members and the demands of the external environment. This adaptive leadership is not a fixed destination but a journey of ongoing growth and development, requiring a commitment to learning, openness to feedback, and a willingness to embrace change.

Leaders are encouraged to view the management of remote and hybrid teams not just as a challenge to be overcome but as an opportunity to innovate and reimagine the possibilities of teamwork and organizational culture. By embracing the strategies outlined, leaders can harness the potential of their dispersed teams, driving productivity, fostering a sense of belonging, and achieving organizational goals.

The effective leadership of remote and hybrid teams demands a comprehensive and adaptable approach. By prioritizing communication, trust, inclusivity, and continuous improvement, leaders can navigate the complexities of dispersed team management successfully. The future of work is undoubtedly more flexible and distributed, and leaders who are prepared to continuously adapt and refine their approaches will be well-positioned to lead their teams to success in this new landscape.

Case Studies of Adaptation

The onset of the pandemic brought about unprecedented changes, testing the resilience and adaptability of leaders across various sectors. The rapid shift in market dynamics, the transition to remote work, supply chain disruptions, and the pressing need for rapid decision-making under uncertainty have all underscored the critical importance of leadership adaptation. This next chapter enquires about how leaders across industries navigated the complexities introduced by the pandemic, providing valuable insights into the strategies and qualities that underpin successful adaptation.

The purpose of examining these case studies is to illuminate the diverse challenges faced by leaders and the innovative approaches they employed to steer their organizations through turbulent times. From technology companies making a swift transition to remote work to retail giants navigating supply chain disruptions, each case study offers a unique perspective on leadership in action. Through these narratives, we aim to explore the effective communication practices, team engagement techniques, and productivity maintenance strategies that have proven successful in various contexts.

In the healthcare sector, the pandemic posed unparalleled challenges, putting immense pressure on leadership to manage resources, support staff, and ensure patient care. The case studies will highlight how healthcare executives rose to the occasion, implementing effective crisis management strategies and adapting to the rapidly evolving situation.

The educational sphere also faced a significant upheaval as leaders were tasked with transitioning to online learning. These case studies will shed light on how educational leaders maintained the quality of education and supported their staff and students through this transition, ensuring continuity and access to learning.

The hospitality industry, hit hard by travel restrictions, required leaders to rethink and reinvent their business models to survive. By examining how leaders in this sector adapted, we can gain insights into the resilience and creativity required to preserve customer relationships and navigate through periods of low demand.

In the banking and finance sector, economic uncertainty prompted leaders to focus on risk management and maintaining customer trust. The strategies deployed by leaders in this context reveal the importance of clear communication and strategic decision-making in sustaining operations and customer confidence.

Small businesses, with their limited resources, had to demonstrate exceptional agility and innovation to adapt to changing market conditions. Through a focus on community engagement and rapid innovation, small business leaders found ways to thrive, offering lessons in resilience and adaptability.

Non-profit organizations faced the dual challenge of sustaining operations and continuing to make an impact. The leadership strategies employed in this sector to navigate fundraising challenges, volunteer engagement, and program delivery provide valuable lessons in sustaining mission-driven work under difficult circumstances.

Leaders of global corporations had to navigate the added complexity of leading across borders, dealing with varying regulations, cultures, and market dynamics. These case studies will explore how global leaders managed international teams and adapted strategies to ensure cohesive operations worldwide.

The lessons learned from these case studies of adaptation during the pandemic highlight the essential qualities and strategies that contribute to successful leadership. By summarizing key takeaways and insights, this chapter aims to equip leaders with the knowledge and inspiration needed to navigate future challenges, emphasizing the enduring importance of adaptability, resilience, and innovation in leadership.

The pandemic ushered in a period of unprecedented changes, challenging the foundational norms of how societies operate, businesses function, and leaders lead. Across the globe, organizations faced abrupt shifts to remote work, significant disruptions in supply chains, and a pressing need for rapid adaptation to safeguard the health and well-being of employees while ensuring business continuity. This period of crisis highlighted the critical importance of leadership flexibility, innovation, and resilience.

The purpose of examining real-world examples of leadership adaptation during the pandemic is twofold. Firstly, it provides concrete insights into the strategies and approaches that leaders across various sectors employed to navigate through the crisis. These case studies serve as a testament to human ingenuity and resilience, offering valuable lessons on managing teams, pivoting business models, and maintaining operations under extreme uncertainty. Secondly, analyzing these examples fosters a deeper understanding of the qualities that define effective leadership in times of crisis. By reflecting on these adaptations, leaders can glean insights into fostering agility, fostering a culture of innovation, and building resilient organizations capable of withstanding future challenges.

In essence, the exploration of how leaders adapted to the challenges brought about by the pandemic is not merely an academic exercise. It is a crucial endeavor for distilling practical wisdom and actionable strategies that can inform leadership practices in navigating any form of adversity. This examination underscores the adaptability, creativity, and steadfastness required to lead successfully through uncharted territories, providing a roadmap for future leaders to follow in the face of uncertainty.

One notable example of a technology company successfully transitioning to remote work is Twitter. In the early stages of the pandemic, Twitter was among the first major tech companies to announce that it would allow employees to work from home "forever" if they chose to, signaling a significant shift towards embracing remote work as a permanent option. This decision highlighted the company's adaptability and its commitment to employee safety and well-being.

- Strategies Used for Effective Communication: Twitter implemented several strategies to ensure clear and effective communication among its remote workforce. The company leveraged digital tools and platforms, such as Slack for instant messaging and Zoom for video conferencing, to facilitate seamless communication. To replace the spontaneous conversations that occur in an office setting, Twitter encouraged the use of virtual "water cooler" channels where employees could engage in informal chats and social interactions.

- Team Engagement: To keep teams engaged, Twitter focused on maintaining a strong sense of community and connection among its dispersed employees. The company organized virtual events, including team-building activities, wellness sessions, and all-hands meetings, to foster a sense of belonging and to keep the company culture alive. Twitter also made efforts to ensure that remote work policies were inclusive, taking into account the diverse needs and challenges faced by employees in different locations and circumstances.

- Maintaining Productivity: Recognizing the potential challenges of remote work in terms of productivity, Twitter took proactive steps to support its employees. This included providing resources for setting up home offices, offering flexibility in work hours to accommodate different time zones and personal responsibilities, and setting clear expectations around work outputs. The company also adopted agile methodologies and tools for project management, ensuring that teams could collaborate effectively and maintain productivity from a distance.

Twitter's transition to remote work demonstrates how technology companies can successfully adapt to new ways of working, leveraging digital tools to maintain communication, engagement, and productivity. The company's experience underscores the importance of flexibility, support, and a strong company culture in navigating the shift to remote work, offering valuable insights for other organizations facing similar transitions.

A prime example of navigating supply chain disruptions is Walmart's response during the pandemic. As one of the world's largest retailers, Walmart faced unprecedented challenges in keeping its shelves stocked and fulfilling online orders as consumer demand surged and global supply chains were strained. The company's strategic response showcased adaptive leadership and innovative solutions that kept its operations running smoothly despite the challenges.

- Adapting Supply Chain Strategies: Walmart rapidly adjusted its supply chain strategies to respond to the fluctuating demand and supply constraints. The company increased its focus on local suppliers and diversified its vendor base to mitigate the risk of disruptions. This shift not only helped maintain inventory levels but also supported local economies during a critical time.

- Leveraging Technology and Data Analytics: Walmart utilized advanced data analytics and forecasting tools to better predict demand patterns and adjust its inventory management practices accordingly. This technology-enabled approach allowed the company to be more agile in its response, reallocating resources efficiently to where they were needed most.

- Expanding E-Commerce and Delivery Services: Recognizing the shift in consumer behavior towards online shopping, Walmart accelerated the expansion of its e-commerce platform and delivery services. The company introduced new options like curbside pickup and contactless delivery to meet customer needs safely and efficiently. These initiatives helped Walmart continue serving customers despite lockdowns and social distancing measures.

- Leadership and Employee Support: Walmart's leadership played a critical role in navigating the crisis, with clear communication and decisive actions that prioritized the safety and well-being of employees and customers. The company implemented health and safety measures across its stores and distribution centers and provided additional financial support to employees, acknowledging their crucial role in the company's operations during the pandemic.

- Strengthening Customer Relationships: Throughout the crisis, Walmart maintained a strong focus on customer service, adapting its operations to ensure customers could access essential goods. The company's efforts to keep prices stable and shelves stocked, despite supply chain challenges, reinforced customer trust and loyalty.

Walmart's response to the supply chain disruptions during the pandemic demonstrates the effectiveness of adaptive leadership, strategic innovation, and a commitment to employees and customers. By swiftly adjusting its strategies, leveraging technology, and prioritizing safety and service, Walmart was able to navigate the challenges and continue fulfilling its role as a critical retailer during a time of need.

During the pandemic, healthcare leaders faced unprecedented challenges, including overwhelming patient loads, resource shortages, and the physical and emotional toll on healthcare workers. One notable example of effective healthcare leadership during this crisis is the Mayo Clinic, a globally recognized healthcare organization based in the United States.

- Leadership Challenges: Healthcare executives at the Mayo Clinic and similar institutions confronted critical issues such as rapidly increasing COVID-19 cases, shortages of personal protective equipment (PPE), ventilators, and other essential medical supplies, and the need to quickly expand hospital capacity to treat COVID-19 patients while continuing to provide care for other conditions. Additionally, ensuring the safety and well-being of frontline healthcare workers was a paramount concern.

- Effective Strategies in Crisis Management: The Mayo Clinic's response to the pandemic was multifaceted. Early in the crisis, the organization formed a COVID-19 Response Team to coordinate its strategy across its network of hospitals. This team focused on developing protocols for patient care, testing, and safety measures to protect both patients and staff.

- Resource Allocation: To address the issue of resource shortages, the Mayo Clinic implemented innovative solutions, including the in-house development of COVID-19 testing capabilities to reduce reliance on external suppliers. The organization also optimized the use of PPE through conservation strategies and explored new supply chains to procure necessary equipment. Moreover, the clinic reconfigured hospital spaces and expanded ICU capacity to accommodate the influx of COVID-19 patients.

- Staff Support: Recognizing the immense pressure on healthcare workers, the Mayo Clinic prioritized staff support. This included implementing mental health resources and support programs to address the emotional and psychological strain on employees. The clinic also ensured transparent and frequent communication with its workforce, providing updates on the evolving situation, changes in protocols, and resources available to staff.

- Innovation and Adaptation: The Mayo Clinic embraced telemedicine to reduce the risk of virus transmission, expanding virtual care options for patients. This not only helped in managing patient load but also ensured that individuals with other medical needs continued to receive care.

- Community Engagement and Public Health Leadership: Beyond its internal response, the Mayo Clinic took a leading role in public health advocacy, emphasizing the importance of preventive measures such as social distancing, mask-wearing, and vaccination. The clinic's experts frequently engaged with the media and public forums to provide evidence-based information and guidance.

The Mayo Clinic's response to the pandemic highlights the critical role of healthcare leadership in navigating crises. Through effective crisis management, strategic resource allocation, staff support, and community engagement, healthcare leaders can guide their organizations through unprecedented challenges, ensuring patient care and staff well-being. These strategies underscore the importance of adaptability, innovation, and resilience in healthcare leadership.

A compelling example of educational leadership during the pandemic is the approach taken by Arizona State University (ASU). Under the leadership of President Michael Crow, ASU demonstrated remarkable agility in transitioning to online learning, ensuring continuity in education while prioritizing the well-being of both staff and students.

- Managing the Shift to Online Teaching: ASU was already at the forefront of digital education before the pandemic, which positioned it advantageously to expand its online offerings rapidly. The university's leadership accelerated the deployment of its existing online infrastructure to transition thousands of courses to virtual formats. Faculty members received support and training in online pedagogy, emphasizing interactive and engaging digital instruction.

- Techniques for Ensuring Quality Education: To maintain the quality of education in the virtual environment, ASU utilized its robust online learning platform, which features adaptive learning technologies to personalize the educational experience. The university also invested in high-quality production of online course materials and leveraged tools like virtual labs, simulations, and augmented reality to enrich the learning experience. Regular assessments and feedback mechanisms were put in place to monitor student engagement and comprehension, allowing for timely interventions when necessary.

- Supporting Staff: Recognizing the challenges faced by faculty in transitioning to online teaching, ASU provided comprehensive resources, including technical support, professional development workshops, and peer mentoring programs. This support helped faculty adapt to new teaching modalities, explore innovative instructional techniques, and effectively engage students in a remote setting.

- Supporting Students: To support students in the transition, ASU offered a wide range of services, from tech support and access to digital resources to counseling and wellness programs. The university made concerted efforts to ensure students had the necessary technology for online learning, including loaner laptops and Wi-Fi hotspots for those in need. Virtual advising and tutoring services were expanded to provide additional academic support.

- Community Engagement and Communication: Effective communication was central to ASU's strategy. The university maintained transparent and frequent communication with students, faculty, and the broader community about its response to the pandemic, changes to academic policies, and available resources. This open dialogue helped alleviate concerns and build trust within the university community.

Arizona State University's response to the pandemic underscores the importance of proactive leadership, technological preparedness, and a comprehensive support system in successfully managing the shift to online learning. By leveraging technology, prioritizing quality education, and providing robust support for both staff and students, educational leaders can navigate the challenges of remote teaching and learning, ensuring that education continues to thrive even in the face of unprecedented challenges.

A standout example of leadership adaptation in the hospitality industry amidst travel restrictions is the approach taken by Airbnb. As the pandemic severely impacted travel and tourism, Airbnb faced significant challenges, including a drastic drop in bookings and revenue. Under the leadership of CEO Brian Chesky, Airbnb swiftly pivoted its business model and implemented strategies to navigate the crisis, ultimately preserving customer relationships and setting the stage for recovery.

- Pivoting Business Models: Recognizing the shift in consumer behavior due to travel restrictions, Airbnb quickly adapted its offerings to focus on local and domestic travel experiences, catering to the rising interest in staycations and nearby getaways. The platform highlighted properties that offered unique, safe, and private accommodations, appealing to those looking for a change of scenery without venturing far from home.

- Introducing New Safety Standards: To address health and safety concerns, Airbnb introduced enhanced cleaning protocols for hosts, dubbed the "Enhanced Clean" program. This initiative, developed in partnership with medical experts, provided hosts with comprehensive guidelines for cleaning and sanitizing their spaces between guest stays. By prioritizing safety, Airbnb aimed to rebuild trust with travelers and encourage bookings even during the pandemic.

- Leveraging Technology for Virtual Experiences: Airbnb innovated its experiences offering by launching "Online Experiences," a collection of virtual activities hosted by locals around the world. These experiences ranged from cooking classes and art workshops to virtual tours, allowing hosts to continue earning income and providing guests with unique travel experiences from the safety of their homes. This move not only preserved customer relationships but also expanded Airbnb's market by making experiences accessible to a global audience.

- Supporting Hosts and Communities: Understanding the financial impact on its host community, Airbnb established a relief fund to provide financial assistance to hosts affected by cancellations. The company also facilitated hosts in offering accommodations to frontline workers and healthcare professionals, reinforcing Airbnb's commitment to community support during challenging times.

- Communicating with Transparency and Empathy: Throughout the crisis, Brian Chesky's leadership was characterized by transparent and empathetic communication. Chesky openly discussed the company's challenges and decisions, including the painful but necessary steps to reduce Airbnb's workforce. This transparency, combined with a clear focus on the company's long-term vision and values, helped maintain trust and loyalty among employees, hosts, and customers.

Airbnb's response to the pandemic showcases how adaptive leadership and innovative thinking can help navigate through crises. By pivoting its business model, prioritizing safety, leveraging technology for new offerings, supporting its community, and maintaining open communication, Airbnb was able to weather the storm and emerge as a leader in the recovery of the hospitality industry.

During the pandemic, the banking and finance sector faced significant economic uncertainty, with fluctuating markets, increased loan defaults, and a surge in demand for digital banking services. A notable example of leadership in this sector is Jamie Dimon, CEO of JPMorgan Chase, who navigated the bank through these turbulent times by implementing strategic risk management measures and focusing on maintaining customer trust.

- Navigating Economic Challenges: Under Dimon's leadership, JPMorgan Chase took proactive steps to assess and mitigate the financial risks posed by the pandemic. Recognizing the potential for a severe economic downturn, the bank increased its loan loss provisions, setting aside billions of dollars to cover potential loan defaults and protect its financial stability. This cautious approach was aimed at ensuring the bank could withstand the economic impact of the pandemic and continue supporting its customers and the broader economy.

- Maintaining Customer Trust: JPMorgan Chase prioritized maintaining customer trust through transparent communication and support for customers facing financial hardship. The bank offered forbearance and loan modification programs for clients affected by the pandemic, including deferring payments and waiving certain fees. By providing these relief measures, JPMorgan Chase demonstrated empathy and commitment to its customers, reinforcing trust and loyalty.

- Expanding Digital Banking Services: With the pandemic accelerating the shift towards digital banking, JPMorgan Chase invested in enhancing its online and mobile banking platforms to meet the increased demand for remote banking services. The bank introduced new digital tools and features to make online banking more accessible and user-friendly, ensuring customers could manage their finances safely from home. This focus on digital innovation not only addressed the immediate needs of customers but also positioned the bank as a leader in digital banking for the future.

- Supporting Businesses and the Economy: Recognizing the significant challenges faced by small businesses, JPMorgan Chase played a key role in administering the U.S. government's Paycheck Protection Program (PPP) loans, facilitating critical financial support to help businesses keep their workforce employed during the pandemic. The bank's efforts to streamline the application process and provide guidance to businesses on navigating the program underscored its commitment to economic recovery and support for the business community.

- Leadership and Communication: Throughout the crisis, Jamie Dimon's leadership was characterized by clear and consistent communication with stakeholders, including employees, customers, and regulators. By openly discussing the bank's strategies, challenges, and outlook, Dimon fostered a culture of transparency and resilience. His optimistic yet realistic outlook on the economy and the bank's role in supporting recovery efforts provided reassurance and confidence in the face of uncertainty.

JPMorgan Chase's response to the pandemic, guided by strategic risk management, customer support, digital innovation, and strong leadership, highlights the importance of adaptability and proactive planning in navigating economic challenges. The bank's actions during this period reinforced its commitment to its customers and the broader economy, showcasing effective leadership in the banking and finance sector amidst global economic uncertainty.

One compelling example of small business leadership demonstrating agility and innovation during the pandemic is that of Zingerman's Community of Businesses, a collection of food-related companies based in Ann Arbor, Michigan. Known for its deli, bakery, and other food services, Zingerman's faced significant challenges when the pandemic hit, including the temporary closure of dine-in services and a sudden drop in sales. The leadership's response highlighted the importance of agility, innovation, and community engagement in navigating the crisis.

- Agility in Business Operations: As the pandemic restrictions came into effect, Zingerman's quickly pivoted its business model to focus on mail order, delivery, and curbside pickup services. This shift required rapid changes in operations, from adjusting the workforce to adopting new health and safety protocols. The company's agile response allowed it to continue serving customers despite the dine-in closures, maintaining revenue streams in a challenging economic environment.

- Innovation in Product and Service Offerings: Recognizing the changing needs of its customers, Zingerman's innovated its product and service offerings. The company launched online cooking classes, tapping into the increased interest in home cooking during the lockdowns. It also created "food boxes" for delivery, offering curated selections of gourmet products and ingredients. These initiatives not only provided new revenue sources but also kept the brand relevant and connected with its customer base.

- Community Engagement and Support: Throughout the crisis, Zingerman's remained deeply committed to its community. The company launched a "pay-it-forward" program where customers could purchase meals for frontline workers and individuals in need. This initiative not only provided much-needed support to the community but also strengthened the bond between Zingerman's and its customers, reinforcing the company's reputation as a community-oriented business.

- Communication and Transparency: Effective communication with customers, employees, and the broader community was a key aspect of Zingerman's strategy. The leadership team was transparent about the challenges the business was facing, the measures being taken to ensure safety, and how the community could support the business and each other. This openness fostered trust and loyalty, crucial for sustaining the business through uncertain times.

- Employee Support and Engagement: Understanding the toll the pandemic was taking on its employees, Zingerman's focused on supporting its workforce, ensuring job security wherever possible, and offering flexibility to accommodate personal circumstances. The company's commitment to its employees fostered a positive work environment and motivated staff, critical for maintaining high-quality service during the crisis.

Zingerman's story exemplifies how small businesses can navigate challenging market conditions through agility, innovation, and a strong commitment to community engagement. By swiftly adapting its operations, exploring new avenues for revenue, and maintaining close connections with customers and the community, Zingerman's not only survived the pandemic but also reinforced its position as a beloved local business. This case underscores the potential of small businesses to thrive in adversity by staying flexible, creative, and community-focused.

During the pandemic, non-profit organizations faced significant challenges, including disruptions to fundraising activities, volunteer participation, and program delivery. A notable example of resilience and innovation in the non-profit sector is the approach taken by Feeding America, the United States' largest hunger-relief organization. Under the leadership of Claire Babineaux-Fontenot, Feeding America adapted its operations to meet the surge in demand for food assistance while navigating the pandemic's challenges.

- Adapting Fundraising Strategies: With traditional in-person fundraising events canceled due to social distancing measures, Feeding America shifted its focus to digital fundraising campaigns. The organization leveraged social media platforms, email marketing, and its website to reach donors, sharing compelling stories of the impact of their work during the pandemic. Feeding America also formed strategic partnerships with corporations and celebrities to amplify its fundraising efforts, securing essential funds to continue its operations.

- Volunteer Engagement: Recognizing the challenges of engaging volunteers safely, Feeding America implemented strict health and safety protocols across its network of food banks, allowing volunteer activities to continue where possible. The organization also introduced virtual volunteering opportunities, such as digital advocacy and remote support for administrative tasks, enabling supporters to contribute to the mission from their homes.

- Innovative Program Delivery: To address the increased demand for food assistance, Feeding America optimized its supply chain and distribution network, collaborating with local food banks to ensure the efficient delivery of food to communities in need. The organization utilized creative distribution methods, such as drive-through food pantries and partnerships with school districts to distribute meals to students learning remotely. These adaptations ensured that Feeding America could maintain its impact, reaching millions of individuals facing hunger.

- Communication and Transparency: Throughout the pandemic, Feeding America maintained transparent and frequent communication with its stakeholders, including donors, volunteers, and the communities it serves. By openly discussing the challenges faced and the strategies implemented to overcome them, the organization fostered trust and reinforced the importance of its mission.

- Supporting Staff and Building Resilience: Understanding the pressures faced by its staff, Feeding America focused on supporting its employees, providing resources for remote work, mental health support, and flexibility to manage personal and professional responsibilities. This focus on staff well-being was crucial for maintaining operational resilience and ensuring the organization could continue its vital work.

Feeding America's response to the pandemic exemplifies effective non-profit leadership in times of crisis. Through adaptive fundraising strategies, innovative program delivery, volunteer engagement, transparent communication, and a commitment to staff support, the organization not only sustained its operations but also expanded its impact in response to growing needs. This case study highlights the potential for non-profits to navigate challenges through resilience, innovation, and a deep commitment to their mission.

A notable example of leadership across borders during a crisis can be observed in the actions of Unilever, a global corporation with products sold in over 190 countries. Under the leadership of CEO Alan Jope, Unilever navigated the complexities of the pandemic by leveraging its global presence while adapting to local market conditions and regulations. This approach underscored the challenges and strategies inherent in leading a diversified international team through unprecedented times.

- Challenges Faced: One of the primary challenges for Unilever was the variation in pandemic impact and government response across the countries it operates in. This meant navigating a patchwork of regulations, from lockdowns to supply chain restrictions, all while ensuring the safety of employees and meeting consumer demand. Additionally, cultural differences influenced employee expectations regarding work arrangements and safety measures, requiring a nuanced approach to internal policies.

- Adapting to Local Regulations and Market Conditions: Unilever's leadership demonstrated agility by decentralizing decision-making, empowering local managers to make swift decisions based on their understanding of regional regulations and market dynamics. This local autonomy ensured that Unilever could quickly adapt its operations, from manufacturing to distribution, in line with local guidelines, minimizing disruptions.

- Leveraging Technology for Global Coordination: To maintain cohesion and ensure effective communication across its international teams, Unilever increased its reliance on digital tools and platforms. The company utilized virtual meeting software to facilitate cross-border collaboration, ensuring that teams remained aligned on global strategies while executing local adaptations. This technology-enabled approach was crucial for sharing best practices and insights across regions, fostering a sense of unity and purpose.

- Supporting Employees and Promoting Inclusivity: Recognizing the varied impacts of the pandemic on its global workforce, Unilever implemented flexible work arrangements and provided support for mental and physical health. The company's leadership emphasized inclusivity and understanding, acknowledging the different challenges faced by employees in various countries and adapting policies to support their well-being.

- Engaging with Local Communities: Beyond internal management, Unilever strengthened its commitment to the communities it serves, recognizing that the pandemic's impacts extended beyond its operations. The company launched several initiatives to support public health and economic resilience, from donating products to healthcare facilities to providing financial support to small businesses within its supply chain. These efforts not only helped address immediate needs but also reinforced Unilever's reputation as a responsible and caring corporate citizen.

- Continuous Learning and Flexibility: Unilever's approach to navigating the pandemic was characterized by a commitment to continuous learning and flexibility. The company regularly reviewed its strategies in light of new information and changing conditions, ready to pivot as necessary. This adaptability was key to Unilever's successful navigation of the pandemic's challenges.

Unilever's response to the pandemic illustrates the complexities of leading a global corporation through a crisis. By prioritizing local autonomy, leveraging technology for global coordination, supporting employees, engaging with communities, and maintaining flexibility, Unilever managed to navigate the challenges of different regulations, cultures, and market dynamics, showcasing the effectiveness of adaptive and empathetic leadership on a global scale.

The pandemic presented an array of unprecedented challenges across various sectors, from technology to healthcare, and education to global corporations, each facing unique hurdles. Through these challenges, leadership adaptation emerged as a pivotal theme, with agility, innovation, empathy, and resilience standing out as essential qualities for navigating through turbulent times. The case studies from different industries provide a wealth of lessons on effective crisis management, emphasizing the importance of being quick to adapt, embracing creativity in problem-solving, and maintaining a human-centric approach.

Agility and flexibility were undoubtedly at the forefront of successful adaptation. Leaders who swiftly responded to the evolving situation, whether through pivoting business models or adopting new operational strategies, managed to steer their organizations through the storm. This adaptability often hinged on empowering others to make decisions, enabling organizations to react promptly to immediate challenges.

Innovation also played a crucial role, with leaders who leveraged creative solutions not just surviving but in many cases finding new avenues for growth. This ranged from introducing new products and services to rethinking customer engagement and operational processes. Embracing technology for remote collaboration and customer service became a lifeline for many, illustrating the power of innovative thinking in overcoming obstacles.

The human aspect of leadership was magnified during the pandemic. Leaders who showed genuine empathy and provided robust support for their teams were able to preserve morale and foster resilience. Practices such as transparent communication, offering mental health support, and ensuring flexible work arrangements underscored the importance of considering the well-being of employees as integral to sustaining productivity and loyalty.

Effective communication and active community engagement were also key in maintaining trust and cohesion. By being clear, consistent, and genuine in their communications, leaders built a sense of solidarity and confidence among their teams and customers. Moreover, many leaders stepped up to support not just their organizations but also the wider community, enhancing their reputations and strengthening their social license to operate.

Looking beyond the immediate crisis, leaders who kept an eye on the long-term vision and strategic objectives of their organizations positioned themselves for recovery and future growth. This strategic foresight involved planning for the aftermath of the pandemic and anticipating future opportunities and challenges, highlighting the importance of balancing immediate crisis responses with long-term planning.

Resilience and a learning orientation became hallmarks of effective leadership during the pandemic. Leaders who cultivated these qualities within their organizations encouraged a culture where challenges were seen as opportunities for learning and growth. This approach not only helped organizations navigate the crisis but also prepared them for future uncertainties, proving that resilience and adaptability are key to enduring success.

The pandemic tested the mettle of leaders across the globe, offering profound lessons in leadership adaptability. The experiences of organizations across different industries underscore timeless leadership principles while providing fresh insights into managing in an ever-changing world. These lessons offer a guide for current and future leaders aiming to build organizations that are not only resilient and agile but also deeply humane and strategically forward-looking.

Promoting Resilience and Innovation

In the fast-evolving landscape of the modern workplace, the concepts of resilience and innovation have emerged as critical pillars for team success. Understanding how these qualities manifest within a team context, and the importance of actively cultivating them, sets the stage for navigating the complexities of today's dynamic work environment. This chapter probes the strategies and practices that foster resilience and innovation, illustrating how teams can not only withstand challenges but also thrive by embracing change and creativity.

Building a resilient team involves more than just preparing for specific challenges; it requires developing a mindset that views setbacks as opportunities for growth and learning. Strategies to foster this mindset include promoting psychological safety, where team members feel comfortable expressing vulnerabilities and uncertainties, and implementing training that enhances adaptability and problem-solving skills. Techniques such as scenario planning and resilience workshops can equip teams with the tools to bounce back from setbacks with greater strength and wisdom.

Creating an environment that fosters innovation demands a departure from traditional, hierarchical approaches to management. It involves cultivating a culture that values curiosity, encourages experimentation, and rewards creative thinking. Overcoming barriers to innovation means dismantling the fear of failure and encouraging a trial-and-error approach to problem-solving. Establishing practices such as idea-sharing forums, innovation labs, or hackathons can stimulate creative thinking and collaborative innovation.

Leadership plays a crucial role in promoting both resilience and innovation. Leaders who model resilient behaviors and demonstrate an openness to new ideas pave the way for their teams to do the same. Balancing support with appropriately challenging tasks can stimulate team members to stretch their capabilities and explore new possibilities. Furthermore, leaders can foster a culture of innovation by setting clear expectations for creative contributions while providing the necessary resources and autonomy to explore new ideas.

Effective communication is the backbone of a team's resilience and innovative capacity. Practices that reinforce a positive outlook, celebrate incremental successes, and provide constructive feedback on efforts to innovate are essential. Feedback mechanisms that are specific, timely, and focused on growth can inspire team members to pursue improvement and novel solutions with vigor.

Encouraging risk-taking and learning from failures are also vital components. Creating a safe space where taking calculated risks is encouraged—and where failures are viewed as learning opportunities—can significantly enhance a team's innovative output. Strategies that analyze setbacks in a structured, non-judgmental manner help in extracting valuable lessons and turning potential discouragements into stepping stones for future success.

Empowering teams for autonomous innovation involves granting team members the freedom to initiate and pursue projects, with leaders providing guidance to ensure alignment with broader organizational goals. This balance between autonomy and direction fosters a sense of ownership among team members, driving motivation and commitment to innovative endeavors.

Leveraging diversity for innovative problem-solving recognizes that diverse perspectives and backgrounds bring a wealth of ideas and approaches to the table. Inclusive leadership that actively seeks out and values these diverse viewpoints can significantly enhance a team's problem-solving capabilities and creative output.

Implementing practices for sustained innovation requires embedding innovation into the fabric of the team's regular activities and goals. Continuous improvement processes, open innovation platforms, and regular innovation audits can ensure that the pursuit of novel solutions becomes a routine aspect of team dynamics.

Through real-world case studies, this chapter will showcase teams that have successfully navigated the twin challenges of cultivating resilience and fostering innovation. These examples will provide practical insights and lessons that can be applied across various contexts, illustrating the transformative power of resilience and innovation in achieving team success.

Integrating resilience and innovation into team dynamics is not a one-time initiative but a continuous effort. This chapter aims to equip leaders with the knowledge and tools to continually nurture these essential qualities, ensuring their teams are poised to meet the challenges of the modern workplace with agility, creativity, and strength.

Understanding resilience and innovation within a team context is crucial for navigating the complexities of today's dynamic work environment. Resilience, in this sense, refers to a team's ability to withstand pressures, adapt to change, and recover quickly from difficulties, turning challenges into opportunities for growth. Innovation, on the other hand, is about a team's capacity to generate new ideas, embrace creative solutions, and implement changes that drive progress and competitive advantage.

Cultivating these qualities is essential in the modern workplace for several reasons. First, the rapid pace of technological advancements and the constant shift in market demands require teams to be resilient, adaptable, and continuously evolving. Teams that can bounce back from setbacks and view failures as learning opportunities are better positioned to maintain momentum and stay ahead of the curve.

Second, the global nature of business and the increasing complexity of problems demand innovative thinking. Teams that foster a culture of creativity and experimentation are more likely to develop breakthrough solutions and improve processes, products, and services. Innovation becomes not just a strategy for success but a means of survival in an increasingly competitive landscape.

Cultivating resilience and innovation contributes to a more engaged and motivated workforce. Teams that are empowered to tackle challenges and encouraged to explore new ideas feel more valued and invested in their work. This not only enhances job satisfaction and retention but also attracts top talent looking for dynamic and forward-thinking environments.

Resilience and innovation are interlinked qualities that feed into each other; resilience provides the stability and strength to navigate uncertainty, while innovation drives change and growth. Together, they form a powerful combination that enables teams to thrive in today's fast-paced and ever-changing work environment, making the cultivation of these qualities a strategic imperative for leaders and organizations.

Building a foundation of resilience within teams is a multifaceted endeavor that hinges on the development of a mindset geared toward adaptability, learning, and growth in the face of challenges. This process begins by creating an atmosphere of openness and psychological safety, where team members feel comfortable sharing ideas, concerns, and mistakes without fear of retribution. Such an environment encourages dialogue about obstacles and failures, shifting the focus from blame to learning and collective problem-solving. Leaders play a crucial role in this by demonstrating empathy, actively listening, and acknowledging their own vulnerabilities.

Equally important is the establishment of clear expectations and shared goals that align with the organization's broader mission. This alignment not only fosters team cohesion but also imbues team members with a sense of purpose, motivating them to persevere through difficulties. Goals should be both realistic and flexible, allowing the team to adapt as needed while maintaining a clear direction.

Promoting a growth mindset within the team encourages members to view challenges as opportunities for personal and professional development. This can be achieved by celebrating efforts, rewarding curiosity, and emphasizing the value of continuous learning. Providing opportunities for training and development reinforces the belief that skills and abilities can be enhanced through hard work and persistence.

Effective communication and collaboration are vital to ensuring that team members feel supported and are working in concert toward common objectives. Regular check-ins and open feedback mechanisms can help identify and address potential issues early, while collaboration among diverse team members can lead to creative solutions to challenges, boosting the team's overall adaptability.

Emotional resilience is key to managing stress and maintaining well-being. Leaders can support their team's emotional health by advocating for work-life balance, offering mental health resources, and setting an example in managing their own stress. Strengthening team bonds through various team-building activities can also enhance morale and a sense of unity, which are essential during tough times.

Resilient teams are those that are prepared for setbacks, viewing them as part of the learning journey. Practices such as scenario planning and risk assessments can prepare teams for potential challenges, while debriefs and after-action reviews following setbacks offer valuable lessons. Celebrating the overcoming of obstacles and the insights gained from failures reinforces the team's ability to recover and grow from experiences.

Empowering team members by granting them autonomy and encouraging them to take initiative builds a sense of ownership and responsibility. When leaders trust their teams to make decisions and tackle problems, it boosts confidence and fosters a proactive stance towards change and uncertainty.

Cultivating resilience within teams is an ongoing process that requires leaders to foster a supportive and adaptable culture. Through strategic actions and a commitment to growth and development, leaders can equip their teams to navigate adversity successfully and emerge stronger, ready to face the dynamics of the modern work environment.

Creating an environment that fosters innovation involves cultivating a workplace culture where creativity and innovative thinking are not just encouraged but are integral to the organization's DNA. This requires deliberate efforts from leaders to nurture an atmosphere where new ideas are welcomed, risk-taking is supported, and diverse perspectives are valued. Such an environment empowers individuals to think outside the box and pursue novel solutions to complex problems.

To establish this culture, leaders must first demonstrate their commitment to innovation through their actions and decisions. This includes allocating resources to support innovative projects, celebrating creative achievements, and setting strategic priorities that emphasize the importance of innovation. By visibly valuing creativity and innovation, leaders set a tone that encourages team members to contribute their ideas and solutions.

One of the critical steps in fostering an innovative environment is removing barriers to creativity. This often means addressing organizational silos that hinder collaboration and information sharing, streamlining bureaucratic processes that slow down experimentation, and challenging the "we've always done it this way" mindset that stifles new thinking. Leaders can encourage cross-functional teams, simplify approval processes for testing new ideas, and create forums for sharing innovative practices across the organization.

Cultivating an open-minded approach to problem-solving is essential for innovation. This involves encouraging curiosity and a willingness to question assumptions and explore multiple solutions. Leaders can facilitate this by promoting a culture of learning where failure is seen as a valuable part of the innovation process. Recognizing and analyzing failures not as setbacks but as learning opportunities fosters a resilient and innovative mindset among team members.

Diversity and inclusivity also play a crucial role in fostering innovation. By bringing together individuals with different backgrounds, experiences, and perspectives, organizations can tap into a broader range of ideas and solutions. Leaders should strive to create inclusive teams and ensure that all voices are heard and considered in the innovation process, leveraging the collective intelligence of the workforce.

Creating a safe space for experimentation is another key factor. This means providing team members with the freedom to explore new ideas without fear of negative consequences for taking risks. Establishing innovation labs, hackathons, or dedicated time for pursuing passion projects can encourage experimentation and creativity.

Communication and transparency about the organization's innovation goals and processes help maintain alignment and build trust. Leaders should communicate the strategic importance of innovation, how it contributes to the organization's success, and how individuals can participate in and contribute to innovative efforts.

Creating an environment that fosters innovation requires leaders to actively cultivate a culture that embraces creativity, supports risk-taking, values diversity, and promotes an open-minded approach to problem-solving. By overcoming barriers to innovation and empowering team members to experiment and learn from failures, organizations can unleash the creative potential of their workforce and drive sustainable innovation.

Leaders play a pivotal role in promoting resilience and innovation within their teams, serving both as models of these qualities and as catalysts for fostering an environment where they can flourish. The way leaders navigate challenges, encourage experimentation, and balance support with challenge significantly impacts the team's ability to adapt, innovate, and thrive even in uncertain conditions.

Modeling resilience is fundamental. Leaders demonstrate this quality by how they respond to setbacks, uncertainties, and pressures. By maintaining a positive outlook, focusing on solutions rather than problems, and showing a willingness to adapt strategies in response to changing circumstances, leaders can inspire their teams to embrace a similar resilience. This involves openly sharing experiences of overcoming difficulties, which can normalize challenges as part of the growth process and show team members that persistence and flexibility can lead to success.

Encouraging innovative thinking requires leaders to create a culture of curiosity and openness where new ideas are welcomed and valued. Leaders can foster this environment by asking open-ended questions that stimulate creative thinking, encouraging team members to explore and present new ideas, and by showing genuine interest and enthusiasm for innovative solutions. Providing resources and opportunities for learning and exploration also signals a commitment to innovation.

Balancing support and challenge is crucial in stimulating growth and creativity. Leaders support their teams by providing the necessary resources, guidance, and encouragement to pursue new ideas. This support also includes offering constructive feedback that helps refine ideas and push them towards realization. However, equally important is presenting team members with challenges that stretch their capabilities and prompt them to think creatively to find solutions. This delicate balance ensures team members feel both empowered and motivated to tackle complex problems and pursue innovative projects.

Leaders also play a key role in removing barriers to resilience and innovation. This may involve cutting through bureaucratic red tape that stifles creativity, advocating for the team's ideas with higher management, or reallocating resources to support innovative initiatives. By actively working to eliminate obstacles, leaders can ensure their teams have the freedom and support needed to innovate effectively.

Creating a safe space for risk-taking and failure is another critical aspect of a leader's role in promoting innovation. Leaders should emphasize that failure is often a stepping stone to success, not a reason for punishment. Celebrating both successes and valuable lessons from failures reinforces a culture where risk-taking is seen as an essential part of the innovation process.

In promoting resilience and innovation, effective leaders strike a balance between providing direction and allowing autonomy. They set clear visions and goals that inspire innovative thinking while giving team members the freedom to explore how best to achieve these objectives. This approach encourages ownership and engagement, as team members feel their contributions are meaningful and valued.

The leader's role in promoting resilience and innovation is multifaceted, requiring them to model these qualities, balance support with challenge, and create an environment that nurtures creativity and adaptability. By doing so, leaders can cultivate teams that are not only equipped to navigate the complexities of today's work environment but are also poised to drive forward with innovative solutions and resilience.

Effective communication is pivotal in supporting resilience and facilitating innovative ideas within teams. It acts as the backbone of a resilient organization, ensuring that team members feel connected, understood, and supported through challenges and changes. By adopting specific communication strategies, leaders can reinforce resilience, encourage open dialogue, and inspire improvement and innovation.

One key strategy is to maintain transparency in communication. Leaders who openly share information about organizational changes, challenges, and strategies foster an atmosphere of trust.

This transparency helps team members understand the context of their work, the challenges ahead, and how they can contribute to overcoming them. When team members are well-informed, they are more likely to feel secure and confident in their ability to adapt to changes, thereby enhancing resilience.

Creating regular check-ins and open forums for discussion is another effective communication practice. These sessions allow team members to express concerns, share experiences, and brainstorm solutions collaboratively. Leaders should encourage participation from all team members and actively listen to their inputs. Such interactions not only help in identifying potential issues early but also promote a culture where everyone feels their voice is heard and valued, contributing to a collective sense of resilience.

Positive reinforcement plays a crucial role in building resilience. Recognizing and celebrating achievements, no matter how small, can significantly boost morale. Leaders should make it a point to acknowledge the hard work and successes of their teams, linking these achievements to the team's resilience and capacity to innovate. This recognition can be a powerful motivator, encouraging team members to continue pushing boundaries and developing innovative solutions.

When it comes to feedback, employing a constructive approach that focuses on growth and development is crucial. Feedback should be specific, actionable, and framed positively, highlighting areas of strength while also pointing out opportunities for improvement. Leaders can inspire innovation by suggesting alternative approaches or asking probing questions that encourage team members to think differently about problems and solutions. This kind of feedback not only facilitates improvement but also signals to team members that experimentation and learning from mistakes are valued.

Encouraging storytelling is another technique that can reinforce resilience and spur innovation. Sharing stories of past challenges, how they were overcome, and the lessons learned along the way can be incredibly inspiring. These narratives can serve as powerful examples of resilience in action, demonstrating the tangible results of persistence, adaptability, and creative problem-solving.

Fostering a forward-looking perspective is essential for resilience. Leaders should communicate a clear vision of the future that emphasizes growth and opportunity, even in the face of adversity. By framing challenges as stepping stones to future successes, leaders can help team members adopt a more resilient mindset that views obstacles as opportunities for learning and innovation.

Effective communication strategies are integral to supporting resilience and encouraging innovative thinking within teams. By maintaining transparency, facilitating open dialogue, employing positive reinforcement, providing constructive feedback, encouraging storytelling, and fostering a forward-looking perspective, leaders can create an environment where resilience is nurtured, and innovative ideas flourish. These practices not only enhance team cohesion and morale but also empower individuals to contribute their best work in the face of challenges.

Encouraging risk-taking and learning from failures is crucial for fostering an environment where innovation can thrive. This approach requires creating a safe space where team members feel supported in exploring new ideas and approaches, even when there's a possibility of failure. By valuing calculated risk-taking and viewing setbacks as essential learning opportunities, leaders can cultivate a culture of resilience and continuous improvement.

Creating such a safe space starts with leadership attitudes towards risk and failure. Leaders should openly discuss their own experiences with risk-taking, sharing both successes and lessons learned from failures. This transparency helps demystify failure, showing it as a natural part of the innovation process. Celebrating attempts at innovation, regardless of the outcome, reinforces the idea that taking calculated risks is valued and encouraged.

Strategies for learning from failures involve a structured approach to debriefing and analysis. When a project or initiative doesn't yield the desired results, conducting a thorough review to understand what happened, why it happened, and how it can be improved is essential. This process should be constructive, focusing on extracting actionable insights rather than assigning blame. Encouraging team members to participate in these reviews fosters a collective sense of ownership and learning.

Another effective strategy is to set clear expectations around risk-taking and failure. This involves defining what constitutes a 'calculated risk' and establishing boundaries within which team members can experiment. Providing guidelines on risk assessment and management empowers team members to make informed decisions about when and how to take risks.

Leaders can also encourage risk-taking and learning from failures by allocating resources specifically for experimentation. This might include setting aside time and budget for pilot projects, innovation labs, or hackathons. These resources provide a tangible means for team members to explore new ideas without the pressure of immediate success, fostering a more innovative and resilient team culture.

Fostering a growth mindset within the team is another crucial element. A growth mindset believes that abilities and intelligence can be developed through dedication and hard work. Leaders can nurture this mindset by emphasizing effort and progress over perfection, encouraging team members to view challenges as opportunities to expand their skills and knowledge.

Leveraging diversity and encouraging collaboration can enhance the team's capacity for risk-taking and learning from failures. Diverse teams bring a range of perspectives, experiences, and ideas to the table, enriching the brainstorming process and offering multiple angles for problem-solving. Collaborative efforts in risk-taking and innovation can lead to more robust solutions and a shared sense of accomplishment and learning.

Encouraging risk-taking and learning from failures requires creating an environment where experimentation is supported, setbacks are viewed as learning opportunities, and continuous improvement is prioritized. By adopting these strategies, leaders can build teams that are not only more innovative and resilient but also more engaged and motivated, driving the organization forward in an ever-changing landscape.

Empowering teams for autonomous innovation involves cultivating an environment where team members feel confident and supported in taking the initiative to explore new ideas and develop innovative solutions. This empowerment is crucial for fostering a culture of creativity and continuous improvement, where innovation can flourish organically. Achieving this requires a nuanced approach that balances granting autonomy with providing the necessary guidance to ensure efforts remain aligned with the broader organizational goals.

Leaders play a pivotal role in this process by setting clear expectations and providing a framework within which innovation can occur. This starts with communicating the organization's vision and strategic objectives, ensuring team members understand how their work contributes to the bigger picture. By doing so, leaders provide a sense of direction that guides innovative efforts, ensuring they are meaningful and aligned with the company's mission.

At the same time, granting autonomy is essential for sparking creativity. This means giving team members the freedom to pursue projects and ideas that interest them, even if these fall outside their regular duties or immediate team objectives. Such freedom signals trust in their capabilities and judgment, which can be incredibly motivating and lead to higher engagement and job satisfaction.

Autonomy does not mean a lack of support. Leaders should ensure that teams have access to the resources they need to bring their innovative ideas to life. This includes not only physical resources, such as budget and materials, but also access to knowledge, skills development opportunities, and mentorship. Leaders should foster an environment where asking for help and collaborating with others is encouraged, facilitating knowledge sharing and collective problem-solving.

To maintain alignment with organizational goals, leaders should implement regular check-ins and feedback mechanisms. These interactions allow leaders to stay informed about the progress of innovative projects and offer an opportunity to provide constructive feedback, helping to steer efforts in the right direction when necessary. Such guidance is crucial for ensuring that autonomy does not lead to misalignment with the company's strategic objectives.

Recognizing and celebrating successes, as well as learning from failures, reinforces the value of autonomous innovation. Public acknowledgment of innovative efforts, regardless of the outcome, emphasizes that taking initiative and pushing boundaries is appreciated and rewarded. This recognition can further inspire team members to pursue their innovative ideas.

Empowering teams for autonomous innovation requires a careful balance between granting freedom and providing direction. By setting clear expectations, offering support and resources, and maintaining open lines of communication, leaders can foster an environment where team members feel empowered to take initiative and develop innovative solutions. This not only enhances creativity and job satisfaction but also ensures that innovation efforts contribute to the organization's overall success.

Leveraging diversity for innovative problem-solving recognizes that the most creative and effective solutions often emerge from teams that bring a wide range of perspectives, experiences, and backgrounds to the table. The richness of diverse viewpoints can challenge conventional thinking, spark new ideas, and lead to breakthrough innovations that might not be possible in more homogenous groups. This approach to innovation is deeply rooted in the understanding that diversity goes beyond demographic differences to include diverse ways of thinking, problem-solving, and approaching challenges.

Inclusive leadership plays a critical role in harnessing this diversity for innovation. Leaders who value and utilize diverse viewpoints create an environment where all team members feel respected, valued, and empowered to contribute their unique insights. This starts with actively seeking and welcoming different perspectives, encouraging team members to share their ideas and experiences, and listening with an open mind. Inclusive leaders recognize that everyone, regardless of their role or background, has something valuable to contribute to the innovation process.

One effective strategy for leveraging diversity in problem-solving is to create diverse working groups or teams specifically for brainstorming and tackling complex projects. By intentionally assembling teams with members from different departments, disciplines, and cultural backgrounds, organizations can ensure a broad range of ideas and approaches are considered. This cross-pollination of perspectives can lead to more creative and comprehensive solutions.

Another important aspect of inclusive leadership is creating a culture of psychological safety where team members feel comfortable expressing their ideas and taking risks. This involves not only encouraging diverse viewpoints but also addressing any biases or barriers that might prevent certain voices from being heard. Leaders must be vigilant in identifying and dismantling these barriers, whether they are structural, cultural, or interpersonal, to ensure a genuinely inclusive environment.

Training and development opportunities focused on diversity and inclusion can also enhance a team's capacity for innovative problem-solving. By educating team members about the value of diversity and equipping them with the skills to collaborate effectively across differences, organizations can foster a deeper understanding and appreciation of diverse perspectives.

Recognizing and celebrating the successes that arise from diverse collaboration further reinforces the importance of leveraging diversity for innovation. Highlighting examples where diverse teams have developed successful solutions can serve as powerful motivation, demonstrating the tangible benefits of inclusive problem-solving.

Leveraging diversity for innovative problem-solving requires inclusive leadership committed to valuing and utilizing diverse viewpoints. By creating diverse teams, fostering a culture of psychological safety, addressing biases, providing relevant training, and celebrating successes, leaders can unlock the creative potential of their workforce. This approach not only leads to more innovative solutions but also contributes to a more dynamic, resilient, and inclusive organizational culture.

Implementing practices for sustained innovation involves creating systems and structures that embed innovation into the fabric of an organization's daily operations and long-term strategic goals. This commitment to continuous innovation requires more than just ad-hoc initiatives or sporadic brainstorming sessions; it necessitates a comprehensive approach that encourages creativity, experimentation, and iterative learning as ongoing processes.

To develop systems that support ongoing innovation, organizations must first establish clear frameworks that define what innovation means within their context, setting specific innovation objectives aligned with their overall strategic goals. This clarity helps in creating focused innovation efforts and ensures that creative endeavors contribute meaningfully to the organization's mission and vision.

Integrating innovation into the team's regular activities can be achieved by embedding innovation metrics into performance evaluations, encouraging team members to allocate time to innovation projects, and setting aside resources specifically for exploration and experimentation. By formally recognizing innovation efforts as part of job responsibilities, organizations signal their commitment to nurturing an innovative culture.

Creating cross-functional teams is another effective practice for fostering sustained innovation. These teams bring together diverse skills and perspectives, breaking down silos and encouraging collaborative problem-solving. Regularly rotating team members across different projects can also refresh the pool of ideas and prevent stagnation, ensuring a dynamic exchange of knowledge and insights.

Encouraging rapid prototyping and iterative development allows teams to experiment with new ideas in a low-risk environment. This approach emphasizes learning by doing, where feedback is continuously sought and used to refine concepts before full-scale implementation. Such a process not only accelerates innovation but also reduces the cost and risk associated with bringing new ideas to market.

Providing formal and informal learning opportunities is crucial for sustaining innovation. Workshops, seminars, and access to online learning resources enable team members to stay abreast of the latest trends, technologies, and methodologies in their field. Encouraging attendance at conferences and industry events can also inspire fresh thinking and provide insights into emerging challenges and opportunities.

To cultivate a culture where innovation is continuously nurtured, leaders must also create an environment that celebrates both successes and constructive failures. Recognizing and learning from failures as much as from successes reinforces the notion that innovation involves risk, and not every attempt will result in success. This mindset encourages team members to take calculated risks without fear of reprisal, knowing that their efforts are valued regardless of the outcome.

Maintaining open channels of communication about innovation efforts is vital. Sharing stories of innovation within the organization, whether through internal newsletters, meetings, or digital platforms, can inspire others and spread the innovative spirit. Highlighting ongoing projects, successes, and lessons learned fosters a sense of community around innovation efforts and invites wider participation.

Implementing practices for sustained innovation requires a strategic and systemic approach that integrates innovation into every aspect of the organization's operations and culture. By setting clear objectives, encouraging cross-functional collaboration, fostering an environment of continuous learning and experimentation, and celebrating both successes and failures, organizations can ensure that innovation remains a continuous and dynamic force driving their growth and evolution.

Exploring real-world examples of teams that have successfully cultivated resilience and innovation provides valuable insights into the practical application of these concepts. These case studies demonstrate how organizations across various industries have navigated challenges, leveraged diversity, and fostered environments that encourage creative problem-solving and adaptability.

One notable example is the global technology company, IBM, which has long emphasized a culture of continuous innovation and adaptability. Facing the dual challenges of rapidly evolving technology landscapes and shifting market demands, IBM embarked on a significant transformation, pivoting from hardware to cloud computing and AI technologies. This shift required not only technological innovation but also a cultural one, where employees were encouraged to embrace change, learn new skills, and think creatively. IBM's commitment to fostering an inclusive culture where diverse perspectives are valued has been key to its ongoing ability to innovate. The lesson here is the importance of aligning organizational culture with innovation goals, ensuring that employees are equipped and motivated to contribute to transformation efforts.

Another example comes from the healthcare sector, where the Mayo Clinic's response to the COVID-19 pandemic showcased remarkable resilience and innovation. Faced with the sudden need to treat a high volume of COVID-19 patients, the Mayo Clinic rapidly adapted its operations, expanding telehealth services to ensure continued patient care while minimizing virus exposure. The clinic also developed new testing methods and streamlined patient flow to manage the crisis effectively. This response was underpinned by a strong foundation of teamwork and a commitment to leveraging scientific research for innovative healthcare solutions. The Mayo Clinic's experience underscores the value of preparedness, adaptability, and a collaborative approach to innovation in responding to crises.

In the retail sector, Nike's response to the pandemic highlighted how consumer brands could innovate to maintain engagement and drive growth even as traditional retail channels were disrupted. Nike increased its investment in digital platforms, enhancing its e-commerce capabilities and launching innovative online marketing campaigns. This digital pivot not only helped Nike navigate the challenges posed by store closures but also strengthened its connection with customers through engaging online experiences. Nike's ability to quickly adapt and innovate in its marketing and sales strategies illustrates how resilience and innovation can drive success in changing market conditions.

These case studies reveal several key lessons that can be applied across different contexts. First, the importance of fostering a culture that supports continuous learning and adaptability, ensuring that teams are prepared to navigate change. Second, the value of leveraging technology and digital platforms for innovation, particularly in times of crisis. Third, the critical role of leadership in guiding organizations through transformation, by setting a clear vision, encouraging collaboration, and maintaining open communication. Finally, the examples highlight how organizations that embrace diversity and inclusivity are better positioned to generate creative solutions and adapt to new challenges.

The successful cultivation of resilience and innovation requires a multifaceted approach that encompasses leadership, culture, technology, and an unwavering focus on adaptation and growth. The lessons learned from these real-world examples offer valuable guidance for organizations looking to navigate their own challenges and seize opportunities for innovation.

Integrating resilience and innovation into team dynamics is essential for navigating the complexities of today's rapidly changing work environment. The exploration of strategies for promoting these qualities reveals the multifaceted approach required to cultivate an organizational culture that values adaptability, creative problem-solving, and continuous learning. As teams face unprecedented challenges and opportunities, the ability to bounce back from setbacks and to innovate becomes crucial for sustained success and growth.

The key strategies for fostering resilience and innovation encompass establishing a supportive and inclusive culture, setting clear goals aligned with organizational objectives, and encouraging open communication and collaboration. Leaders play a pivotal role in this process by modeling resilience and innovation themselves, demonstrating a commitment to these values in their decision-making and problem-solving approaches. By actively promoting a growth mindset, leaders can inspire their teams to view challenges as opportunities for learning and development.

Creating a safe space for experimentation and risk-taking is another critical aspect of fostering innovation. Leaders should encourage their teams to explore new ideas and approaches, providing the necessary resources and support to turn these ideas into actionable projects. Recognizing and celebrating both successes and constructive failures reinforces the value of experimentation and learning, encouraging a culture of continuous improvement.

Empowering team members to take initiative and contribute their unique perspectives enhances both resilience and innovation. Diversity of thought and experience enriches the problem-solving process, leading to more creative and effective solutions. Leaders can harness this diversity by facilitating inclusive discussions, valuing all contributions, and leveraging the strengths of each team member.

Balancing autonomy with guidance ensures that innovative efforts remain aligned with the team's goals and the broader organizational mission. Regular check-ins and feedback sessions provide opportunities for leaders to offer direction and support, helping to steer innovative projects toward successful outcomes while maintaining a focus on growth and development.

Integrating resilience and innovation into team dynamics requires deliberate efforts from leaders to cultivate an environment where these qualities are valued and nurtured. By adopting the strategies outlined, leaders can build teams that are not only equipped to navigate the uncertainties of the modern workplace but are also poised to drive innovation and growth. Encouraging leaders to continually foster resilience and innovation is vital for creating dynamic, adaptable, and forward-thinking organizations capable of thriving in an ever-changing landscape.

Section 3: Building a Resilient Leadership Pipeline

In Section 3 of "Navigating the New Normal: Leadership Strategies for a Post-Pandemic World," we shift our focus to a vital aspect of organizational sustainability and success: building a resilient leadership pipeline. The unprecedented challenges posed by the COVID-19 pandemic have underscored the need for leaders who are not only adept at handling immediate crises but are also capable of steering organizations through periods of uncertainty and change. This section is dedicated to exploring strategies and practices that can help organizations cultivate a cadre of leaders equipped for the future.

Resilience in leadership is more than just the ability to withstand adversity; it's about emerging from challenges stronger and more capable. As we navigate a business landscape marked by continuous change and uncertainty, the need for leaders who can adapt, learn, and lead with foresight has never been more critical.

We begin by discussing strategies for identifying potential leaders within the organization, looking beyond traditional indicators of leadership potential to include traits like adaptability, emotional intelligence, and innovative thinking. We then explore how organizations can invest in the development of these individuals through targeted training programs, mentorship, and opportunities for growth and challenge.

Mentoring and coaching emerge as key themes in this section, as we examine how experienced leaders can pass on their wisdom and insights to the next generation of leaders. This transfer of knowledge is critical in cultivating a resilient leadership pipeline, ensuring that emerging leaders are not only skilled and knowledgeable but also aligned with the organization's values and vision.

This section addresses the importance of preparing leaders for unexpected challenges and disruptions. The pandemic has taught us that the unexpected can happen at any time, and leaders must be equipped to navigate these situations with competence and composure.

As we conclude this section, we look towards the future of leadership development. We consider the ongoing evolution of leadership needs and how organizations can continuously adapt their strategies to build a pipeline of leaders who are not just fit for today's challenges but are also prepared for the unknowns of tomorrow.

Join us in this exploration of building a resilient leadership pipeline, a journey that is not just about developing individual leaders, but about fostering a culture of leadership that permeates every level of the organization and secures its future in an ever-changing world.

Developing Resilient Leaders

In the next chapter, "Developing Resilient Leaders," we explore the crucial role of resilience in leadership and the strategies for cultivating this vital attribute among leaders within an organization. Resilience, particularly in the context of leadership, involves the capacity to withstand adversity, adapt to change, and emerge from challenges stronger and more capable. This quality is increasingly recognized as indispensable for leaders who must navigate the complexities of today's rapidly evolving organizational landscapes, marked by frequent disruptions, uncertainty, and change.

The process of developing resilient leaders begins with identifying individuals within the organization who exhibit potential for resilience. This involves looking beyond traditional leadership criteria to recognize traits such as adaptability, emotional intelligence, and a positive approach to challenges. Utilizing various tools and assessments can help in pinpointing these resilience traits, setting the stage for targeted development efforts.

Cultivating a resilient mindset is central to this development. Strategies aimed at nurturing resilience include fostering adaptability, enhancing emotional intelligence, and teaching effective stress management techniques. These efforts contribute to building a foundation of resilience that enables leaders to manage personal and organizational pressures effectively.

Training and development programs play a critical role in equipping emerging leaders with the skills and knowledge necessary for resilience. Designing these programs to include experiential learning opportunities, simulations, and scenario planning can provide leaders with realistic challenges that foster resilience through hands-on experience.

Mentorship and coaching also emerge as powerful tools for developing resilience. Experienced leaders can offer invaluable guidance, support, and insights, helping to strengthen the resilience of emerging leaders. Establishing mentoring relationships and coaching programs focused on resilience can accelerate the development of this critical leadership quality.

Creating a supportive organizational culture is essential for reinforcing resilience. Organizational leaders must model resilience themselves and create an environment that encourages and values this quality. Strategies to achieve this include promoting open communication, recognizing and learning from failures, and providing support during challenges. Empowering leaders to face challenges head-on and learn from these experiences is crucial for resilience building. Encouraging risk-taking and viewing setbacks as learning opportunities can help leaders develop the confidence and skills needed to navigate future challenges.

Feedback and continuous improvement mechanisms are vital for refining resilience. Implementing systems that provide leaders with constructive feedback on their resilience capabilities and areas for improvement supports ongoing development and growth. Monitoring and evaluating the progress of resilience development is important for assessing the effectiveness of initiatives and making necessary adjustments. This ensures that efforts to build resilience are aligned with organizational goals and are producing the desired outcomes.

Incorporating resilience into leadership succession planning ensures that the organization maintains a pipeline of leaders equipped to handle future challenges. This forward-looking approach guarantees the sustainability and success of resilience-building efforts.

Developing resilient leaders is a comprehensive and ongoing process that requires commitment from both the organization and its leaders. By prioritizing resilience and implementing targeted strategies for its development, organizations can ensure they are prepared to meet the demands of an ever-changing world, fostering a leadership cadre that is not only resilient but also capable of leading with vision and strength.

In the context of leadership, resilience is defined as the capacity of leaders to withstand adversity, bounce back from setbacks, and lead their organizations through periods of uncertainty and change with strength and foresight. It encompasses the ability to manage stress effectively, maintain focus on organizational goals despite challenges, and adapt strategies in response to evolving circumstances. Resilient leaders possess a unique blend of emotional intelligence, problem-solving skills, and a positive outlook that enables them to turn obstacles into opportunities for growth and development.

The importance of resilient leaders in navigating organizational challenges and change cannot be overstated. In today's fast-paced and often unpredictable business environment, organizations frequently encounter disruptions that can range from technological advancements and market shifts to global crises like the COVID-19 pandemic. Resilient leaders play a crucial role in steering their organizations through such challenges, minimizing negative impacts while seizing opportunities for innovation and improvement.

Resilient leaders also foster a culture of resilience within their teams and the broader organization. By modeling adaptability, perseverance, and a constructive approach to facing difficulties, they inspire their teams to embrace change positively and proactively. This collective resilience is vital for maintaining morale, productivity, and engagement, even in the face of adversity. They are adept at managing their own emotions and those of their team members, providing support and encouragement when needed. Their emotional intelligence enables them to recognize signs of stress and burnout in their teams and to take action to address these issues, ensuring the well-being of their employees.

Resilient leaders are indispensable assets to any organization. Their ability to navigate challenges, inspire their teams, and adapt to change not only ensures the organization's survival during tough times but also positions it for future success and growth. Cultivating resilience in leadership is therefore a strategic imperative for organizations aiming to thrive in an ever-changing world.

Identifying potential resilient leaders within an organization involves looking beyond conventional leadership criteria to pinpoint individuals who exhibit specific traits and behaviors indicative of resilience. This process is essential for cultivating a leadership pipeline that can navigate and thrive amidst challenges and change.

The criteria for identifying potential resilient leaders include adaptability, emotional intelligence, a positive attitude towards challenges, and a track record of overcoming adversity. Adaptability refers to the ability to adjust strategies and approaches in response to new information or changing circumstances. Emotional intelligence encompasses self-awareness, self-regulation, empathy, and social skills, enabling leaders to manage their emotions and those of others effectively. A positive attitude towards challenges involves viewing difficulties as opportunities for growth and learning, rather than insurmountable obstacles. Lastly, a history of overcoming adversity demonstrates a candidate's proven capacity for resilience, showing that they have faced challenges head-on and emerged stronger.

In addition to these criteria, organizations can employ various tools and assessments to recognize resilience traits in potential leaders. Psychological assessments, such as the Resilience Scale for Adults (RSA) or the Connor-Davidson Resilience Scale (CD-RISC), can provide insights into an individual's resilience levels by measuring factors like personal competence, tolerance of negative affect, and positive acceptance of change. Behavioral interviews that explore candidates' past experiences with adversity, their responses to challenging situations, and their process of bouncing back can also reveal resilience traits.

360-degree feedback tools offer another avenue for identifying potential resilient leaders. By gathering feedback from a wide range of colleagues, including supervisors, peers, and direct reports, organizations can gain a comprehensive view of an individual's resilience as demonstrated through their interactions and performance in various situations.

Development centers and simulation exercises designed to mimic challenging scenarios can also be effective in assessing resilience. These exercises allow individuals to demonstrate their problem-solving skills, adaptability, and emotional intelligence in real-time, providing observers with valuable insights into their potential for resilient leadership.

Identifying potential resilient leaders requires a multifaceted approach that combines subjective assessments with objective measurements. By leveraging a combination of criteria, tools, and assessments, organizations can effectively pinpoint individuals who possess the resilience traits necessary to lead successfully through uncertainty and change.

Cultivating a resilient mindset among emerging leaders is crucial for preparing them to navigate the complexities of modern organizational life, where change is constant and challenges are inevitable. Developing this mindset involves a combination of fostering adaptability, enhancing emotional intelligence, and teaching effective stress management techniques. These elements work together to equip leaders with the capacity to endure setbacks, learn from experiences, and lead their teams with confidence and clarity.

Adaptability is foundational to resilience. It enables leaders to pivot in response to changing circumstances and to view disruptions not merely as obstacles but as opportunities for growth and innovation. Strategies for nurturing adaptability include encouraging continuous learning, promoting a culture of flexibility within the team, and providing opportunities for leaders to take on diverse roles and challenges. By pushing emerging leaders out of their comfort zones in a supportive environment, organizations can help them develop the agility needed to thrive in unpredictable conditions.

Emotional intelligence is another critical component of a resilient mindset. It encompasses self-awareness, self-regulation, empathy, and social skills, allowing leaders to manage their emotions and those of others effectively. Enhancing emotional intelligence can be achieved through targeted training programs, coaching, and feedback mechanisms that provide insights into emotional responses and interpersonal dynamics. Leaders with high emotional intelligence are better equipped to maintain composure under pressure, build strong relationships, and foster a positive team environment, all of which contribute to resilience.

Effective stress management is also integral to building resilience. Leaders must be able to recognize signs of stress in themselves and their teams and implement strategies to manage it constructively. This might involve teaching techniques such as mindfulness, deep breathing, or time management, as well as promoting a healthy work-life balance. Stress management training can empower leaders to maintain their well-being and performance even in high-pressure situations.

Incorporating experiential learning opportunities, such as simulations, role-playing exercises, and real-world projects, can further reinforce these aspects of resilience. Such experiences allow emerging leaders to practice adaptability, emotional intelligence, and stress management in contexts that mimic the challenges they will face in their leadership roles.

To nurture a resilient mindset effectively, organizations must create an environment that supports and values these qualities. This includes providing regular feedback that acknowledges efforts to adapt and overcome challenges, celebrating successes, and learning from failures. Leaders themselves should model resilience, demonstrating through their actions and attitudes that embracing change, managing emotions, and prioritizing well-being are key to sustaining performance and achieving organizational goals.

Cultivating a resilient mindset among emerging leaders is a multifaceted process that requires intentional development of adaptability, emotional intelligence, and stress management skills. By prioritizing these areas and embedding them into the leadership development journey, organizations can prepare their leaders to navigate the challenges of today's dynamic work environment with resilience and poise.

Designing effective training programs focused on developing resilience is essential for equipping leaders with the skills and mindset needed to navigate the complexities and uncertainties inherent in today's organizational environments. These programs should aim not only to impart knowledge but also to foster the practical application of resilience strategies through experiential learning, simulations, and scenario planning. Such an approach ensures that emerging leaders are not only cognizant of the principles of resilience but are also adept at applying them in real-world contexts.

Experiential learning is a cornerstone of effective resilience training. By engaging leaders in hands-on activities that mimic the challenges they are likely to face, training programs can provide a safe space for experimentation and learning. This might include team-building exercises that require collaborative problem-solving under pressure, or individual projects that stretch their capabilities and require them to adapt and persevere. The key is to create experiences that mirror the ambiguity and complexity of real-life situations, enabling leaders to practice resilience in a controlled, reflective environment.

Simulations offer another powerful tool for resilience training. These can range from computer-based simulations that model specific scenarios, such as crisis management exercises, to role-playing games that allow leaders to navigate interpersonal dynamics and conflict resolution. Simulations provide the opportunity for leaders to make decisions, see the consequences of their actions, and adjust their strategies in real-time. This iterative process of action, feedback, and adjustment is instrumental in building resilience, as it mirrors the cycle of learning and adaptation required in actual leadership roles.

Scenario planning is also an effective element of resilience training programs. By considering various future scenarios, including potential crises and disruptions, leaders can develop the foresight and flexibility needed to navigate uncertainty. Scenario planning exercises encourage leaders to think critically and creatively about how they would respond to different challenges, fostering a mindset that is proactive rather than reactive. These exercises can also highlight the importance of contingency planning and the need to remain adaptable in the face of changing circumstances.

Incorporating these elements into training programs requires careful planning and a commitment to creating learning experiences that are both challenging and supportive. Facilitators should be skilled in guiding reflection and discussion, helping leaders to extract lessons from their experiences and to understand how they can apply resilience strategies in their day-to-day roles. Providing ongoing support and resources, such as follow-up coaching or access to a community of practice, can further enhance the effectiveness of resilience training.

Training and development programs for resilience should aim to instill a deep understanding of the principles of resilience, coupled with the practical skills needed to apply these principles effectively. By incorporating experiential learning, simulations, and scenario planning, organizations can ensure that their leaders are not only prepared to face challenges but are also capable of leading with confidence and adaptability in an ever-changing world.

The role of mentorship and coaching in the development of resilience cannot be overstated, as they provide personalized support and guidance that can significantly accelerate a leader's ability to navigate adversity and change. These relationships offer a unique platform for emerging leaders to learn from the experiences and insights of seasoned professionals, helping them to build the skills, confidence, and mindset necessary for resilient leadership.

Mentorship and coaching impact resilience development in several key ways. Firstly, they provide a safe space for emerging leaders to explore their vulnerabilities, discuss challenges, and receive constructive feedback without the fear of judgment. This environment encourages open dialogue about failures and setbacks, transforming them into learning opportunities and building blocks for resilience.

Secondly, mentors and coaches can offer tailored advice and strategies for managing stress, overcoming obstacles, and adapting to change, drawing on their own experiences and professional knowledge. This personalized guidance is invaluable for helping emerging leaders develop practical resilience skills that are applicable to their specific contexts and challenges.

Mentorship and coaching relationships help reinforce the importance of emotional intelligence in resilient leadership. Through regular interactions, mentors and coaches can model effective emotional regulation, empathy, and social skills, demonstrating how these competencies contribute to resilience and success in leadership roles.

To establish mentoring programs that effectively foster resilience, organizations should consider the following best practices:

- Carefully Match Mentors and Mentees: Effective mentorship relationships are often based on mutual interests, complementary skills, and personalities. Careful matching can ensure that both parties benefit from the relationship, fostering a positive and productive dynamic.

- Provide Training for Mentors and Coaches: Equipping mentors and coaches with the skills to support resilience development is crucial. This might include training in active listening, providing constructive feedback, and guiding reflective practice.

- Set Clear Goals and Expectations: Both mentors and mentees should have a clear understanding of the goals of the mentorship, as well as the expectations for their roles within the relationship. This clarity can help focus the mentorship on specific areas of development, including resilience.

- Encourage Regular, Structured Meetings: Consistency and structure can enhance the effectiveness of mentorship and coaching. Regular meetings provide ongoing support for emerging leaders and ensure that resilience development is continuously addressed.

- Foster a Culture of Mentorship within the Organization: Creating an organizational culture that values and supports mentorship can encourage more experienced leaders to share their knowledge and insights. This culture can be fostered through recognition of mentoring contributions, sharing success stories, and providing resources for mentorship activities.

- Evaluate and Adapt the Program: Regular evaluation of the mentoring program can provide insights into its effectiveness and areas for improvement. Soliciting feedback from participants can help refine the program to better meet the needs of emerging leaders and enhance its impact on resilience development.

In the next chapter, we will dive deeper into these topics, exploring the nuances of mentorship and coaching in the context of resilience development. Through these discussions, we aim to provide a comprehensive overview of how organizations can leverage these relationships to cultivate a pipeline of resilient leaders.

Creating supportive organizational cultures that value and nurture resilience is essential for businesses aiming to thrive in an ever-changing and challenging environment. Such cultures empower employees to adapt to changes, overcome obstacles, and emerge stronger from adversities, thereby ensuring organizational sustainability and success. The foundation of a resilient organizational culture lies in the strategies leaders employ to model and encourage resilience across all levels of the organization.

At the heart of fostering a resilient culture is leadership by example. Leaders who demonstrate resilience in their actions, decisions, and communication set a powerful precedent for their teams. This involves openly facing challenges, acknowledging failures as learning opportunities, and showing adaptability in the face of change. By sharing their own experiences of navigating difficulties, leaders can instill a sense of possibility and strength among employees, encouraging them to approach their own challenges with a similar resilient mindset.

Encouraging open communication is another critical strategy for building a supportive culture. Leaders should foster an environment where team members feel comfortable sharing their ideas, concerns, and experiences without fear of reprisal. This openness not only helps in identifying and addressing potential issues early but also promotes a sense of belonging and support among employees, which is crucial for resilience.

Providing access to resources and training focused on developing resilience skills is a tangible way leaders can support their teams. Workshops on stress management, adaptability, and emotional intelligence can equip employees with the tools they need to navigate the complexities of their roles and the wider organizational landscape. Additionally, offering mental health support and resources demonstrates an organization's commitment to the well-being of its employees, further reinforcing a culture of resilience.

Recognition and appreciation play a significant role in encouraging resilience. Celebrating successes, acknowledging efforts to overcome challenges, and valuing the lessons learned from failures reinforce the importance of resilience and innovation within the organization. This recognition can take many forms, from formal awards and acknowledgments in company communications to informal praise in team meetings.

Creating collaborative and supportive team environments is also key to fostering resilience. Encouraging teamwork and collaboration not only leverages diverse perspectives for problem-solving but also builds a network of support that employees can rely on during challenging times. Leaders can facilitate this by promoting team-building activities and encouraging cross-departmental projects that foster a sense of unity and collective purpose.

Embedding resilience into the organizational values and practices ensures that it becomes an integral part of the company's identity. This might involve revising mission statements, setting resilience-related goals, and incorporating resilience into performance metrics. Such integration helps to sustain a culture of resilience over the long term, making it a defining characteristic of the organization.

Creating a supportive organizational culture that values resilience requires a multifaceted approach from leaders. By modeling resilience, fostering open communication, providing resources for resilience development, recognizing efforts, promoting teamwork, and embedding resilience into the organizational fabric, leaders can cultivate an environment where employees and the organization at large are better equipped to face the challenges of today and tomorrow.

Empowering leaders to face challenges is a critical aspect of building resilience within an organization. This empowerment involves creating an environment that encourages risk-taking and views learning from failure as an integral part of the resilience-building process. By fostering such a culture, organizations can ensure their leaders are equipped to navigate the complexities and uncertainties of the business world with confidence and adaptability.

Encouraging risk-taking is essential for innovation and growth, yet it often involves stepping into the unknown and facing the possibility of failure. Organizations can cultivate a culture of smart risk-taking by defining clear boundaries within which leaders are encouraged to experiment and explore new ideas. This clarity helps mitigate undue risks while allowing leaders the freedom to innovate. Additionally, providing leaders with the necessary resources and support to pursue these risks can further encourage them to take the initiative.

Learning from failure is equally important in the process of empowering leaders. Organizations should emphasize that setbacks and failures are not just acceptable but are valuable learning opportunities. This perspective can be fostered by debriefing sessions where leaders can reflect on what went wrong, what was learned, and how similar challenges can be approached differently in the future. Such reflective practices not only enhance learning but also help to destigmatize failure, making it easier for leaders to embrace challenges with an open mind.

Providing opportunities for leaders to navigate real-world challenges is another crucial element of empowerment. This can be achieved through leadership development programs that include simulations, case studies, and project-based learning experiences. These programs should be designed to mimic the complexities and ambiguities of real-life situations, allowing leaders to practice decision-making, problem-solving, and adaptability in a controlled yet realistic setting.

Mentorship and coaching also play a vital role in preparing leaders to face challenges. Experienced mentors and coaches can offer guidance, share insights from their own experiences, and provide feedback that helps emerging leaders refine their approach to tackling difficulties. These relationships not only support the development of resilience but also provide a sounding board for leaders as they navigate the challenges of their roles.

Recognizing and celebrating instances where leaders successfully navigate challenges or take calculated risks, even if the outcomes are not as expected, reinforces the value of these behaviors. Public acknowledgment of such efforts can inspire confidence and motivate other leaders within the organization to embrace challenges with a similar sense of courage and resilience.

Empowering leaders to face challenges is about creating an environment that values risk-taking, learns from failure, and provides ample opportunities for real-world application. Through supportive practices, mentorship, and recognition, organizations can develop leaders who are not only resilient but are also capable of guiding their teams through the uncertainties and opportunities of the future.

Implementing a feedback system that focuses on resilience improvement is pivotal in fostering a culture of continuous learning and development among leaders. This system enables leaders to receive constructive insights into their performance, particularly in how they navigate challenges, manage stress, and adapt to change. By integrating feedback mechanisms that specifically target resilience, organizations can encourage leaders to reflect on their experiences, identify areas for growth, and develop strategies to enhance their adaptability and perseverance.

Creating a culture of continuous learning and development in leadership necessitates a multi-faceted approach. It begins with establishing clear communication channels where feedback is not only welcomed but also sought after regularly. These channels might include formal processes like 360-degree reviews, where leaders receive feedback from their superiors, peers, and direct reports, as well as more informal methods like one-on-one meetings and reflection sessions. The key is to ensure that feedback is timely, specific, and actionable, providing leaders with concrete areas for improvement and suggestions on how to advance their resilience skills.

To further embed continuous learning and development into the leadership culture, organizations should provide ample opportunities for leaders to engage in professional development activities. This could involve access to training programs focused on resilience-building topics such as emotional intelligence, stress management, and adaptive leadership. Workshops, webinars, and coaching sessions can offer leaders the tools and knowledge they need to enhance their resilience, while also encouraging a mindset of lifelong learning.

Creating a supportive environment that encourages experimentation and learning from failure is essential. Leaders should be encouraged to view setbacks not as impediments but as integral to their development journey. By fostering an organizational culture that celebrates learning and growth from challenges, leaders are more likely to take calculated risks and innovate, knowing that their efforts to build resilience are recognized and valued.

Peer learning groups and communities of practice within the organization can also support continuous improvement in leadership. These groups provide a forum for leaders to share experiences, discuss challenges, and collaboratively develop solutions. The collective wisdom and diverse perspectives within these groups can be a rich resource for learning and development, further reinforcing the culture of resilience.

Monitoring and evaluating the effectiveness of the feedback system and continuous learning initiatives are crucial. Regular assessments can help organizations determine the impact of their efforts on leadership resilience and identify areas where adjustments may be needed. This ongoing evaluation ensures that the development of resilience remains a dynamic and responsive process, aligned with the evolving needs of leaders and the organization.

Fostering a culture of feedback and continuous improvement is vital for developing resilient leaders. By implementing structured feedback systems, providing development opportunities, encouraging a positive outlook on challenges, and facilitating peer learning, organizations can cultivate leaders who are not only equipped to handle adversity but are also committed to lifelong learning and adaptation.

Monitoring and evaluating the progress of resilience development in leaders is essential for ensuring that resilience-building initiatives are effective and meet the organization's strategic objectives. This process involves employing a variety of methods to track leaders' growth in resilience over time and to assess the impact of specific development programs and strategies.

One effective method for tracking resilience development is through regular self-assessment tools and surveys. These instruments can measure changes in leaders' perceptions of their resilience, including their ability to handle stress, adapt to change, and recover from setbacks. By administering these assessments at regular intervals, organizations can gather longitudinal data that reflects individual and collective progress in resilience development.

Another approach is the use of behavioral observations and feedback. This can be done through 360-degree feedback mechanisms where peers, supervisors, and direct reports provide input on a leader's behaviors related to resilience, such as adaptability, perseverance, and emotional regulation. Such feedback can offer valuable insights into how leaders' resilience manifests in the workplace and how it evolves over time.

Performance metrics and outcomes can also serve as indicators of resilience development. For example, tracking leaders' performance in managing projects through challenges, leading teams during periods of change, or achieving objectives under adverse conditions can provide concrete evidence of resilience in action. Changes in these metrics over time can signal improvements in resilience and the effectiveness of development initiatives.

In addition to these individual-focused methods, organizations should evaluate the overall impact of resilience-building programs and initiatives. This can involve analyzing participation rates, satisfaction scores, and perceived value of training sessions, workshops, and mentoring programs dedicated to resilience. Gathering feedback on these programs can help identify strengths, areas for improvement, and the overall contribution to the organization's resilience culture.

Assessing the effectiveness of resilience-building initiatives also requires considering the broader organizational outcomes. This might include evaluating changes in employee engagement, turnover rates, and organizational performance during and after periods of adversity. Positive trends in these areas can indicate that leaders' increased resilience is having a beneficial impact on the organization as a whole.

Qualitative methods such as interviews and focus groups can provide deeper insights into the subjective experiences of leaders undergoing resilience development. These discussions can reveal the personal and professional growth leaders attribute to resilience-building efforts, offering rich, narrative data that complement quantitative measures.

To ensure comprehensive monitoring and evaluation, organizations should integrate these various methods into a cohesive assessment strategy. This strategy should align with the organization's goals for resilience development, allowing for adjustments and enhancements to resilience-building initiatives based on empirical evidence and feedback. By systematically tracking and evaluating the progress of resilience development in leaders, organizations can ensure they are effectively cultivating a leadership cadre equipped to navigate the complexities of the modern business environment with strength and adaptability.

Building a resilient leadership succession plan involves strategically incorporating resilience as a core criterion in the identification, development, and selection of future leaders. This approach ensures that the organization is prepared to navigate future challenges, adapt to change, and sustain growth over the long term. By prioritizing resilience in succession planning, organizations can cultivate a pipeline of leaders equipped not only with the necessary technical skills and experience but also with the adaptability, emotional intelligence, and innovative thinking required for effective leadership in an unpredictable business environment.

The first step in incorporating resilience into leadership succession planning is to define what resilience means within the context of the organization's leadership needs. This definition should encompass the ability to handle stress and adversity, adaptability to change, emotional intelligence, and the capacity for innovative problem-solving. With a clear understanding of these attributes, organizations can identify potential leaders who exhibit these qualities, even in non-leadership roles, and begin grooming them for future leadership positions.

Developing a resilient leadership pipeline requires a multi-faceted approach to talent development. This includes offering targeted training and development programs focused on building resilience skills, such as stress management, adaptive leadership, and strategic decision-making under uncertainty. Providing emerging leaders with opportunities to lead projects, navigate real-world challenges, and learn from failures in a supportive environment is crucial for applying and strengthening these skills.

Mentorship and coaching play a pivotal role in developing resilient leaders. Pairing emerging leaders with experienced mentors who can share insights, offer guidance, and model resilient behaviors is invaluable. These relationships help to reinforce the importance of resilience, provide real-life examples of resilience in action, and offer personalized support and feedback.

Incorporating resilience into the evaluation and selection process for leadership positions ensures that the organization's future leaders are well-equipped to handle the demands of their roles. This might involve revising leadership competency models to include resilience as a key attribute, incorporating resilience-focused criteria into performance evaluations, and using behavioral interviews and assessments to gauge candidates' resilience capabilities.

To ensure the sustainability of the leadership pipeline, organizations should regularly review and update their succession planning processes to reflect changes in the business environment, organizational strategy, and leadership needs. This includes reassessing the criteria for leadership potential, monitoring the development progress of individuals within the pipeline, and adjusting development initiatives to address emerging challenges and opportunities.

Fostering a culture that values and supports resilience across the organization reinforces the importance of resilient leadership and encourages all employees to develop these critical skills. By embedding resilience into the fabric of the organization, businesses can ensure a continuous supply of leaders who are prepared to lead through complexity, drive innovation, and secure the organization's future success.

Building a resilient leadership succession plan is a strategic imperative that requires careful planning, targeted development efforts, and a commitment to cultivating the qualities of resilience across all levels of the organization. By prioritizing resilience in their succession planning, organizations can ensure they are well-positioned to meet the challenges of the future with a cadre of strong, adaptable, and innovative leaders.

The development of resilient leaders is paramount in today's ever-evolving and often unpredictable business landscape. The chapters have underscored the multifaceted nature of resilience in leadership, highlighting its critical role in enabling leaders to navigate adversity, embrace change, and emerge stronger from challenges. As organizations face an array of external pressures—from rapid technological advancements to global economic uncertainties—the need for leaders who can adapt, innovate, and guide their teams through turbulent times has never been more acute.

The journey to cultivating resilience within the leadership ranks is ongoing and requires a deliberate, strategic approach. It involves identifying potential leaders who exhibit resilience traits, providing them with opportunities to develop and strengthen these qualities, and embedding resilience into the organizational culture. This process is not only about preparing leaders to manage crises but also about empowering them to seize opportunities for growth and innovation that arise from adversity.

Training and development programs, mentorship and coaching, and supportive organizational cultures have been identified as key elements in fostering resilience. These initiatives must be carefully designed and implemented to ensure they effectively contribute to building the resilience capabilities of leaders at all levels. Moreover, embedding resilience into leadership succession planning ensures a continuous pipeline of resilient leaders ready to take on future challenges.

Encouraging an ongoing commitment to fostering resilience is crucial. Organizations must recognize that developing resilient leaders is not a one-time effort but a continuous process that requires regular reflection, adaptation, and reinforcement. Leaders themselves play a vital role in this process, not only by participating in their own resilience development but also by modeling resilient behaviors, supporting their teams in building resilience, and promoting a culture that values adaptability, learning, and innovation.

The benefits of investing in resilient leadership extend beyond the individual leaders to the organization as a whole. Resilient leaders are better equipped to maintain high levels of performance under pressure, inspire and motivate their teams, and drive organizational success in the face of challenges. They contribute to creating a robust, agile organization that can not only withstand adversity but also thrive in an increasingly complex and uncertain world.

The importance of developing resilient leaders cannot be overstated. As organizations look to the future, a sustained commitment to cultivating resilience at all levels of leadership will be a key determinant of their ability to navigate change, overcome challenges, and achieve long-term success. It is through fostering resilience that organizations can ensure they are prepared to meet the demands of the modern business environment, today and in the years to come.

Mentoring and Coaching for Future Leadership

The chapter on "Mentoring and Coaching for Future Leadership" researches the critical role that mentorship and coaching play in the development of the next generation of leaders. As organizations navigate an increasingly complex and dynamic business environment, the need for leaders equipped with a broad range of skills, competencies, and a resilient mindset has never been more pronounced. Mentorship and coaching emerge as pivotal strategies for nurturing these qualities, offering personalized guidance and support that can significantly accelerate leadership growth.

Understanding the distinction between mentoring and coaching is essential for leveraging their full potential in leadership development. While both are invaluable, they serve different purposes and approaches. Mentoring typically involves a more experienced individual guiding a less experienced mentee, focusing on long-term professional development and career growth. In contrast, coaching is often more focused on developing specific skills or competencies and achieving defined objectives within a shorter timeframe. Recognizing these differences allows organizations to employ both strategies effectively to support their leaders' development journey.

The role of mentors in leadership growth cannot be overstated. Mentors provide not just guidance and knowledge sharing but also serve as role models, offering insights drawn from their experiences to help mentees navigate their own leadership paths. The characteristics of effective mentors and the dynamics of successful mentoring relationships are crucial for ensuring that the mentorship experience is enriching and impactful for both mentors and mentees.

Coaching, on the other hand, plays a pivotal role in enhancing leadership skills and competencies. Through a structured process that includes goal setting, personalized feedback, and accountability, coaching helps leaders identify their strengths and areas for improvement, fostering personal and professional growth. The impact of coaching on emerging leaders is profound, influencing their leadership styles, enhancing decision-making capabilities, and refining problem-solving skills.

Designing mentorship and coaching programs that are effective and aligned with organizational goals requires careful planning and consideration. This includes structuring these programs to address both the organization's needs and the individual development needs of leaders, ensuring that they are equipped to meet current and future challenges.

The process of matching mentors and mentees is a critical component of successful mentorship programs. Effective matching strategies that consider personality, professional goals, and skills can significantly enhance the mentoring relationship's value, leading to more meaningful and productive outcomes.

The chapter further explores the impact of coaching on emerging leaders, highlighting how targeted coaching interventions can transform leadership potential into actual leadership effectiveness. Through case studies, the positive influence of coaching on leadership development is illustrated, showcasing real-world examples of how coaching has shaped successful leaders.

Feedback and reflection play integral roles in both mentorship and coaching, serving as tools for continuous learning and improvement. Effective feedback techniques that are constructive and forward-looking can facilitate growth, while reflective practices help leaders internalize lessons learned and apply them to their leadership approach.

Cultivating a mentoring culture within organizations is also addressed, emphasizing the importance of senior leadership's role in modeling, supporting, and participating in mentorship and coaching initiatives. This culture promotes an environment where continuous learning, development, and growth are valued and encouraged.

The chapter concludes by examining common challenges in mentorship and coaching relationships and offering solutions to overcome these obstacles. Additionally, it discusses methods for evaluating the effectiveness of mentorship and coaching programs, ensuring they deliver the desired outcomes in leadership development.

"Mentoring and Coaching for Future Leadership" underscores the indispensable role of mentorship and coaching in preparing leaders for the complexities of the modern business world. By fostering an ongoing commitment to these practices, organizations can ensure a robust pipeline of skilled, competent, and resilient leaders ready to take on future challenges.

Mentorship and coaching stand as cornerstone practices in the realm of leadership development, each playing a vital role in shaping the leaders of tomorrow. Their importance in the contemporary business environment cannot be overstated, as they provide the scaffolding for emerging leaders to grow, adapt, and thrive amidst the complexities and rapid changes characteristic of modern organizational life.

The essence of mentorship in leadership development lies in its capacity to offer guidance, wisdom, and support through the lens of personal experience. Mentors serve as navigators, helping mentees to chart their professional paths, make informed decisions, and avoid potential pitfalls. This relationship, often developed over a longer term, transcends mere professional advice, delving into the realms of career development, life choices, and personal growth. Mentors, with their wealth of experience, become invaluable sources of inspiration, encouragement, and sometimes, caution. They help inculcate in mentees a broader understanding of the organizational landscape, fostering a sense of belonging and purpose.

Coaching, while sharing some common ground with mentorship, is distinct in its focus and execution. Primarily concerned with enhancing specific leadership skills and competencies, coaching is more structured and goal-oriented. Coaches work with individuals to identify and achieve specific developmental objectives, leveraging a variety of techniques to foster self-awareness, accountability, and performance improvement. Unlike mentorship, coaching relationships are typically more short-term and focused, with clear metrics for success. Coaches do not necessarily draw from personal experiences but instead utilize questioning, feedback, and guided discovery to help leaders unlock their potential.

Differentiating between mentoring and coaching is crucial for effectively leveraging each in leadership development. While mentoring is characterized by its open-ended, holistic approach to professional growth, coaching is defined by its structured, targeted efforts to enhance leadership effectiveness. Both are integral to developing a well-rounded leader but serve different purposes at various stages of an individual's development.

Incorporating both mentorship and coaching into leadership development strategies ensures a comprehensive approach to nurturing future leaders. Mentorship provides the broader context and long-term perspective essential for career planning and personal development. In contrast, coaching offers the immediate, practical skills and behaviors leaders need to excel in their roles. Together, they create a dynamic, multifaceted development experience that prepares emerging leaders to navigate the challenges of leadership with confidence, resilience, and strategic acumen.

The role of mentors in leadership growth is pivotal, encompassing the provision of guidance, sharing of experiences, and facilitation of professional growth that collectively enrich the developmental journey of emerging leaders. Mentors, with their wealth of knowledge and experience, serve as invaluable resources, guiding mentees through the intricacies of leadership and the challenges of organizational dynamics. Their contributions are multi-faceted, offering not just professional insights but also personal wisdom that shapes the holistic growth of future leaders.

Mentors play a crucial role in providing guidance that is both strategic and practical. They help mentees navigate the complexities of their roles, offering advice on everything from decision-making and problem-solving to career advancement and network building. This guidance is grounded in the mentor's own experiences, lending authenticity and depth to their advice. By sharing their journey, including both successes and failures, mentors offer mentees a real-world perspective that textbooks and formal training programs often cannot provide. This sharing of experience fosters a learning environment that is rich in context and relevance, enabling mentees to draw parallels to their own situations and challenges.

Facilitating professional growth is another critical aspect of the mentor's role. Mentors identify potential in their mentees that the mentees themselves may not see, encouraging them to take on new challenges and stretch beyond their comfort zones. Through goal setting, action planning, and continuous feedback, mentors support mentees in achieving their professional objectives and in developing the skills and competencies required for effective leadership. This facilitation often involves opening doors to opportunities within the organization, such as high-visibility projects or connections with other leaders, which can accelerate the mentee's career progression.

The characteristics of effective mentors are foundational to the success of mentoring relationships. Effective mentors possess deep expertise and experience, but they also exhibit empathy, patience, and the ability to listen actively. They are committed to the mentee's development and are willing to invest their time and energy into the relationship. Trustworthiness and confidentiality are also critical, as these create a safe space for mentees to share their thoughts, fears, and aspirations openly.

Successful mentoring relationships are characterized by mutual respect, clear communication, and aligned expectations. They are built on a foundation of trust that allows for honest and open dialogue. Effective mentoring relationships are also dynamic, evolving according to the mentee's growth and changing needs. Setting clear goals and regularly reviewing progress towards these goals can help keep the mentoring relationship focused and productive. Additionally, a successful mentoring relationship benefits both mentor and mentee, offering mentors the opportunity to reflect on their own practices, learn new perspectives, and derive satisfaction from contributing to someone else's growth.

Mentors are indispensable to leadership growth, offering a blend of guidance, experiential sharing, and support that nurtures the development of future leaders. The effectiveness of mentoring in leadership development hinges on the characteristics of the mentor and the dynamics of the mentoring relationship. By fostering successful mentoring relationships, organizations can ensure a robust pipeline of leaders who are well-prepared to navigate the challenges of the modern business environment and lead with competence, vision, and integrity.

Coaching plays a crucial role in the enhancement of leadership skills and competencies, serving as a personalized and focused approach to development. Unlike other forms of professional development, coaching is highly individualized, addressing the specific needs, challenges, and goals of the leader. This tailored approach enables leaders to develop the precise skills and competencies required to navigate their unique organizational contexts and leadership roles effectively. It also helps in developing a wide range of leadership skills, from strategic thinking and decision-making to emotional intelligence and communication. It aids leaders in honing their ability to inspire and motivate teams, manage conflict, and drive organizational change. Through the coaching process, leaders gain insights into their leadership style, identifying both strengths to build upon and areas needing improvement. This awareness is crucial for personal and professional growth, providing a foundation upon which leaders can develop a more effective and adaptive leadership approach.

The process of coaching typically involves a series of structured sessions between the coach and the leader. These sessions are designed to facilitate self-reflection, exploration, and action planning. The coach uses techniques such as questioning, listening, and feedback to help the leader identify goals, challenge assumptions, and explore new perspectives. Coaches also support leaders in devising and implementing strategies to achieve their objectives, offering guidance and accountability throughout the process.

One of the key impacts of coaching on personal development is the enhancement of self-awareness. Leaders become more cognizant of their values, beliefs, and behaviors, understanding how these influence their leadership style and interactions with others. This heightened self-awareness enables leaders to make more conscious choices about their actions and responses, leading to more authentic and effective leadership.

Professionally, coaching facilitates the development of critical leadership competencies that are essential for success in complex and dynamic business environments. Leaders learn to better navigate organizational complexities, build resilient and high-performing teams, and foster innovation and agility. Coaching also supports leaders in developing a strategic vision for their teams and organizations, aligning resources and efforts to achieve long-term goals.

Coaching contributes to the building of a learning mindset, encouraging leaders to embrace continuous improvement and adaptability. This mindset is invaluable in today's rapidly changing business landscape, where leaders must continually evolve to meet new challenges and opportunities. It is a powerful tool for leadership skills enhancement, offering a customized approach that addresses the individual needs and goals of leaders. Through the coaching process, leaders develop not only specific leadership competencies but also a deeper understanding of themselves and their impact on others. The personal and professional growth facilitated by coaching equips leaders to navigate their roles with greater competence, confidence, and clarity, ultimately contributing to the success and sustainability of their organizations.

Designing and implementing effective mentorship and coaching programs within organizations require careful planning, clear objectives, and a deep understanding of both organizational goals and individual developmental needs. These programs are instrumental in fostering leadership skills, enhancing employee engagement, and driving organizational success. To ensure their effectiveness, several key considerations and best practices should be taken into account.

- Alignment with Organizational Goals: The design of mentorship and coaching programs should be closely aligned with the broader strategic objectives of the organization. This ensures that the programs contribute to achieving desired outcomes, such as leadership development, talent retention, and cultural transformation.

- Needs Assessment: Conducting a thorough needs assessment is critical to understanding the specific development needs of potential mentees and coachees. This assessment can help tailor the programs to address gaps in skills, knowledge, and leadership competencies, making them more relevant and effective.

- Selection of Mentors and Coaches: The success of these programs heavily relies on the quality of mentors and coaches. Criteria for selection should include not only expertise and experience but also the ability to inspire, empathize, and facilitate growth. Training for mentors and coaches can further enhance their effectiveness in these roles.

- Matching Process: Effective matching of mentors with mentees and coaches with coachees is vital. The matching process should consider personality fit, professional goals, and learning styles to foster productive and meaningful relationships.

- Program Structure: Determining the structure of the programs, including their duration, frequency of meetings, and format (e.g., face-to-face, virtual), is essential for meeting participants' needs and accommodating organizational realities. Setting clear expectations and guidelines for both parties involved can help maximize the benefits of the programs.

- Feedback and Evaluation: Incorporating mechanisms for ongoing feedback and evaluation allows for continuous improvement of the programs. Feedback from participants can provide insights into the programs' effectiveness and areas for enhancement, while formal evaluations can measure their impact on individual and organizational development.

Best Practices

- Clear Objectives and Outcomes: Define clear, measurable objectives and desired outcomes for the mentorship and coaching programs. This clarity helps in designing the programs to meet specific developmental needs and in evaluating their success.

- Comprehensive Support: Provide participants with the necessary resources and support to engage effectively in the programs. This could include training materials, access to learning platforms, and administrative support for scheduling and communication.

- Cultivating a Supportive Culture: Foster an organizational culture that values mentorship and coaching as key components of professional development. Leadership endorsement and participation can significantly contribute to this culture, signaling the organization's commitment to growth and development.

- Flexibility and Adaptability: Design the programs to be flexible and adaptable, allowing for adjustments based on feedback and changing needs. This flexibility can enhance the relevance and impact of the programs over time.

- Recognition and Reward: Recognize and reward the contributions of mentors and coaches. Acknowledging their efforts not only serves as a token of appreciation but also encourages a culture of mentorship and coaching within the organization.

By considering these key elements and best practices, organizations can design and implement mentorship and coaching programs that effectively support the development of their employees, nurture future leaders, and contribute to achieving strategic goals. These programs, when well-executed, can be powerful tools for personal and professional growth, enhancing the overall strength and resilience of the organization.

Effectively matching mentors and mentees is a critical component of a successful mentorship program. The matching process requires thoughtful consideration and a strategic approach to pair individuals in a way that maximizes the benefits of the mentorship experience for both parties. The success of a mentorship relationship often hinges on the compatibility of the mentor and mentee, making the matching process pivotal to the overall effectiveness of the program.

A key strategy for effective matching involves understanding the goals, preferences, and professional development needs of both mentors and mentees. This can be achieved through detailed applications or surveys that capture information about individuals' backgrounds, areas of expertise, learning objectives, and personal interests. Such information helps program coordinators identify potential pairs with complementary skills, experiences, and goals.

Criteria for successful pairings often include alignment of professional interests and goals, complementary personality traits, and mutual preferences for the mentorship relationship's structure and communication style. For example, a mentee seeking to develop leadership skills in a specific industry might be best paired with a mentor who has a proven track record of leadership within that sector. Similarly, pairing individuals with compatible personalities can enhance the likelihood of a productive and positive relationship.

The role of matching in the program's success cannot be overstated. A well-matched mentor and mentee are more likely to establish a strong, productive relationship based on mutual respect and understanding. This compatibility fosters an environment where mentees feel comfortable seeking advice, discussing challenges, and taking risks in their professional development. For mentors, a successful match provides an opportunity to impart wisdom and contribute to the growth of someone with shared interests or goals, which can be a deeply rewarding experience.

Beyond individual compatibility, successful matching also supports the broader objectives of the mentorship program. By facilitating effective learning and development relationships, matching helps ensure that the program meets its goals, whether they are to foster leadership development, enhance skill sets, or improve employee retention. Effective matches contribute to positive outcomes for participants, reinforcing the value of the mentorship program within the organization.

To further enhance the matching process, some programs incorporate initial meet-and-greet sessions or speed mentoring events where potential mentors and mentees can interact before formal pairings are made. This allows both parties to provide input on their preferred matches, adding another layer of personalization to the process.

The matching of mentors and mentees requires a deliberate and thoughtful approach that considers the goals, personalities, and preferences of participants. By prioritizing compatibility and alignment of objectives, organizations can create mentorship relationships that are both meaningful and effective, thereby maximizing the impact of their mentorship programs and supporting the professional growth of their employees.

Coaching has a profound impact on emerging leaders, significantly influencing their leadership styles, decision-making processes, and problem-solving abilities. Through personalized and focused interactions, coaching provides emerging leaders with the insights and skills necessary to navigate the complexities of leadership effectively. This section explores the transformative effect of coaching on emerging leaders and presents case studies that highlight the positive outcomes of coaching interventions.

Coaching's impact on leadership styles is one of its most significant benefits. By offering a mirror for leaders to reflect on their behaviors, attitudes, and impact on others, coaching encourages self-awareness and adaptability. Emerging leaders learn to evaluate their leadership approach critically and to adopt styles that are more inclusive, empathetic, and conducive to fostering high-performing teams. For instance, a coaching program focused on emotional intelligence can help leaders develop a more participative leadership style, enhancing team collaboration and engagement.

In terms of decision-making, coaching equips leaders with the tools and frameworks to make more strategic, informed decisions. Coaches guide leaders through the process of analyzing situations from multiple perspectives, weighing potential outcomes, and considering the broader implications of their decisions. This holistic approach to decision-making not only improves the quality of the decisions but also increases the leaders' confidence in their judgment. A case in point involves a coaching program for emerging leaders in a multinational corporation, which emphasized critical thinking and strategic analysis. Participants reported a marked improvement in their ability to make complex decisions under uncertainty, leading to more effective problem-solving and innovation within their teams.

Problem-solving abilities are also enhanced through coaching, as leaders learn to approach challenges with a solutions-focused mindset. Coaches encourage leaders to break down problems into manageable components, to leverage creative thinking, and to seek input from diverse sources. This methodical approach to problem-solving fosters resilience and resourcefulness, essential qualities for effective leadership. A notable example is a technology startup that implemented a coaching program for its leadership team. Through the program, leaders developed a more agile problem-solving approach, enabling the company to navigate rapid market changes successfully and maintain its competitive edge.

We present here several Case Studies Demonstrating the Impact of Coaching

In the financial services firm, the emerging leader embarked on a six-month coaching journey with a focus on cultivating leadership presence and enhancing their ability to influence effectively. The coaching sessions were designed to transition the leader from a predominantly directive style, characterized by top-down decision-making, to a more collaborative approach. This shift was facilitated through exercises that emphasized active listening, empowering team members to contribute ideas, and fostering a culture of shared responsibility for outcomes.

The coach employed techniques such as role-playing to simulate real-world scenarios, enabling the leader to practice new communication styles and leadership behaviors. Reflection sessions following these exercises allowed the leader to introspect on their natural tendencies and the impact of different styles on team dynamics. Additionally, the coach introduced the concept of emotional intelligence, guiding the leader to understand and manage their emotions and those of their team members more effectively.

The impact of the coaching program was profound. The leader's shift towards a collaborative style led to a notable improvement in team dynamics. Team members reported feeling more valued and engaged, contributing to a 20% increase in productivity. The team's enhanced cohesion and morale translated into improved performance metrics, underscoring the direct correlation between leadership style and team productivity.

During the COVID-19 pandemic, department heads in a healthcare organization faced unprecedented challenges in managing patient care and team coordination under crisis conditions. A targeted coaching intervention aimed to equip these leaders with enhanced decision-making and crisis management skills, focusing on areas such as stress management, effective communication during crises, and the implementation of innovative patient care strategies.

Coaches worked with the department heads to develop personalized action plans addressing the specific challenges of the pandemic, such as resource allocation, staff well-being, and adapting to rapidly changing health guidelines. Through scenario planning exercises, leaders were trained to anticipate potential crisis developments and prepare appropriate responses, thereby improving their agility and decision-making speed.

The coaching intervention led to significant improvements in how department heads managed stress and communicated during the crisis. By adopting a more composed and clear communication style, leaders were able to instill confidence and calm among their teams. Furthermore, the emphasis on innovative thinking prompted the development of new patient care protocols and team management strategies, enhancing the organization's ability to deliver care under challenging conditions.

A group coaching program was initiated for mid-level managers at a technology startup experiencing rapid growth and change. The program's objective was to develop adaptive leadership skills, enabling managers to navigate the startup's dynamic environment effectively. The coaching sessions covered strategic thinking, adaptability in leadership approaches, and fostering cross-functional collaboration.

The coaches introduced the managers to tools and frameworks for strategic analysis, encouraging them to think beyond immediate operational challenges and consider the long-term implications of their decisions. Group discussions and workshops facilitated the sharing of experiences and strategies among managers, enhancing their ability to collaborate across different functions of the startup.

Post-program evaluations highlighted several positive outcomes of the coaching intervention. Managers exhibited enhanced strategic thinking, enabling them to contribute more effectively to the startup's strategic planning processes. Their increased adaptability in leadership approaches allowed for more agile response to market changes and internal challenges. Improved cross-functional collaboration led to more integrated and cohesive efforts across the company, significantly contributing to its successful expansion into new markets.

These case studies underscore the transformative potential of coaching for emerging leaders. By developing self-awareness, strategic decision-making, and effective problem-solving skills, coaching enables leaders to navigate the challenges of their roles more effectively and to contribute more significantly to their organizations' success. The personalized nature of coaching ensures that these developments are closely aligned with the individual's needs and the organization's goals, making coaching an invaluable tool in the leadership development arsenal.

In the realm of mentorship, the practices of continuous feedback and reflection stand as critical pillars supporting the growth and development of mentees. These practices not only facilitate a deeper understanding of personal and professional progress but also reinforce the learning process, making the mentorship experience more impactful and meaningful.

The importance of continuous feedback in mentorship relationships cannot be overstated. It serves as a real-time guide for mentees, offering them insights into their strengths, areas for improvement, and progress towards their goals. Effective feedback, when delivered thoughtfully and constructively, encourages mentees to persevere through challenges and celebrate their achievements, fostering a positive mindset towards growth and learning. Moreover, feedback from mentees to mentors can enhance the mentoring relationship, making it a mutually beneficial and enriching experience.

Reflective practices complement feedback by encouraging mentees to introspect on their experiences, decisions, and the feedback received. Through reflection, mentees can gain a deeper understanding of their actions and their outcomes, enabling them to identify patterns, align their efforts with their goals, and make more informed choices in the future. Reflection also fosters self-awareness, a crucial component of personal and professional development, allowing mentees to recognize their values, motivations, and the impact they wish to have as leaders.

Several techniques can enhance the effectiveness of feedback and reflection in mentorship. One approach involves setting aside dedicated time during mentorship sessions for discussion and reflection on recent experiences, challenges faced, and lessons learned. This structured approach ensures that feedback and reflection are integral parts of the mentorship process, rather than afterthoughts.

Another technique is the use of specific, behavior-based feedback, which focuses on observable actions and their effects. This type of feedback is more actionable and less likely to be perceived as personal criticism, making it more effective in promoting growth and development. Additionally, encouraging mentees to set specific, measurable goals can provide a clear framework for feedback, making it easier to assess progress and identify areas for improvement.

Mentors can also employ open-ended questions to facilitate reflection, prompting mentees to think critically about their experiences and the feedback received. Questions such as "What did you learn from this experience?" or "How could this situation be handled differently in the future?" encourage deeper introspection and learning.

Creating a feedback-rich environment in which mentees feel safe to express their thoughts, concerns, and aspirations openly is crucial. Such an environment fosters trust and respect, essential components of a productive mentorship relationship.

Continuous feedback and reflective practices are foundational to the mentorship process, driving the growth and development of mentees. By employing effective techniques for feedback and fostering an environment conducive to reflection, mentors can significantly enhance the impact of their guidance, helping mentees to achieve their full potential as leaders.

Cultivating a mentoring culture within organizations is a strategic initiative that can yield significant benefits, including enhanced employee engagement, accelerated leadership development, and improved organizational performance. This culture is characterized by a shared commitment to growth, learning, and mutual support, where mentorship and coaching are recognized as key drivers of personal and professional development.

Fostering such a culture requires deliberate strategies that embed mentorship and coaching into the fabric of the organization. It starts with clear communication from the top, articulating the value of mentorship and coaching not just as tools for individual advancement but as essential components of the organization's strategy for success. By highlighting the direct link between these practices and the organization's goals, leadership can underscore their importance and encourage widespread participation.

The role of senior leadership in promoting and participating in mentorship programs is pivotal. When leaders themselves act as mentors, they not only provide invaluable guidance and support to their mentees but also signal to the rest of the organization that mentorship is both valued and rewarded. Senior leaders can further champion a mentoring culture by sharing their own experiences and successes with mentorship, both as mentors and mentees, thereby demystifying the process and showcasing its benefits.

Another strategy for cultivating a mentoring culture is to formalize mentorship and coaching programs, making them accessible to employees at all levels. This can involve developing structured programs with clear objectives, matching criteria, and support mechanisms. By institutionalizing mentorship and coaching, organizations can ensure these practices are not left to chance but are integrated into the career development pathway for all employees.

Providing training for mentors and coaches is also crucial. Effective mentorship and coaching require specific skills, such as active listening, providing constructive feedback, and facilitating goal setting. Training programs can equip potential mentors and coaches with these skills, enhancing the quality of the mentorship and coaching provided and contributing to a more positive experience for both parties.

Recognizing and rewarding effective mentorship and coaching is another key element. This can include acknowledging mentors and coaches in internal communications, celebrating mentoring successes, and incorporating mentorship and coaching effectiveness into performance evaluations. Recognition not only motivates current mentors and coaches but also encourages others to participate.

Creating opportunities for cross-functional and cross-level mentorship can further enrich the mentoring culture. By facilitating connections beyond immediate teams or hierarchical levels, organizations can foster a broader sense of community, enhance knowledge sharing, and break down silos.

Evaluating the impact of mentorship and coaching programs is essential for sustaining a mentoring culture. Regular assessment can help organizations understand the programs' effectiveness, identify areas for improvement, and adjust strategies to better meet the needs of employees and the organization.

Cultivating a mentoring culture requires a multi-faceted approach that involves clear communication, senior leadership involvement, formalized programs, training, recognition, cross-functional opportunities, and ongoing evaluation. By committing to these strategies, organizations can create an environment where mentorship and coaching thrive, contributing to the development of a robust, engaged, and skilled workforce.

Overcoming challenges in mentorship and coaching relationships is crucial for ensuring the effectiveness and sustainability of these programs within organizations. Common challenges include mismatched expectations, communication barriers, lack of commitment, and difficulties in measuring impact. Addressing these challenges requires thoughtful strategies and a commitment to continuous improvement.

Mismatched expectations between mentors and mentees or coaches and coachees can hinder the development process. Clear communication at the outset about the goals, roles, and responsibilities of each party is essential. Establishing a formal agreement or contract that outlines these aspects can help align expectations and provide a reference point for future discussions.

Communication barriers, such as differences in communication styles or a lack of open, honest dialogue, can also impede the effectiveness of mentorship and coaching relationships. Encouraging regular check-ins and providing training on effective communication techniques can enhance mutual understanding and foster a more productive relationship. Additionally, leveraging various communication platforms to suit the preferences of both parties can improve accessibility and engagement.

A lack of commitment, whether due to time constraints, competing priorities, or insufficient motivation, can undermine the success of mentorship and coaching initiatives. To address this challenge, organizations can emphasize the importance of these programs in career development, offering incentives for participation and recognizing the contributions of mentors and coaches. Ensuring that participants have adequate time allocated for these activities within their work schedules can also enhance commitment.

Measuring the impact of mentorship and coaching programs can be difficult, making it challenging to demonstrate their value and secure ongoing support. Implementing tools and methods for evaluation, such as feedback surveys, progress tracking, and goal attainment assessments, can help quantify the benefits. Sharing success stories and program outcomes with the broader organization can also highlight the positive impact of mentorship and coaching on individual and organizational growth.

Another challenge is ensuring the sustainability and relevance of mentorship and coaching programs. Regularly reviewing and updating the programs based on feedback and changing organizational needs can ensure they remain effective and aligned with participants' and the organization's goals.

Creating a supportive culture that values continuous learning and development is another key strategy. By embedding mentorship and coaching into the organizational culture, leaders can demonstrate their commitment to these practices, encouraging widespread participation and engagement.

While challenges in mentorship and coaching relationships are inevitable, they can be effectively addressed through strategic planning, clear communication, and a commitment to continuous improvement. By implementing solutions that enhance alignment, communication, commitment, and impact measurement, organizations can maximize the effectiveness of their mentorship and coaching programs, fostering a culture of growth, development, and mutual support.

Evaluating the effectiveness of mentorship and coaching programs is critical to understanding their impact on leadership development and identifying areas for improvement. This evaluation process involves a combination of qualitative and quantitative methods, tools, and metrics designed to provide a comprehensive view of the programs' success and influence on individual and organizational growth.

One effective method for evaluating the impact of these programs is through the use of pre-and post-program assessments. These assessments can measure changes in specific leadership competencies, skills, and behaviors that the programs aim to develop. By comparing data collected before and after participation in mentorship or coaching, organizations can gauge individual growth and development.

Feedback surveys from participants and their supervisors provide valuable insights into the perceived effectiveness of the programs. These surveys can cover aspects such as the quality of the mentorship or coaching relationship, the relevance of the content to the participants' development needs, and the application of learned skills in the workplace. Open-ended questions within these surveys can also elicit detailed feedback on program strengths and areas for improvement.

360-degree feedback, collected before and after the program, offers a holistic view of the participants' development from the perspectives of peers, supervisors, direct reports, and others. This feedback can highlight changes in leadership behavior and effectiveness, providing a multifaceted assessment of the programs' impact.

Another tool for evaluating program effectiveness is the tracking of specific, measurable goals set by the participants at the beginning of their mentorship or coaching engagement. Monitoring progress toward these goals can provide a clear indication of individual development and the extent to which the programs are meeting their objectives.

Case studies and success stories are qualitative methods that capture the personal experiences and outcomes of participants in mentorship and coaching programs. These narratives can provide in-depth insights into the transformative impact of the programs, showcasing examples of leadership growth, career advancement, and positive changes in leadership style.

In addition to these methods, organizations can employ metrics related to broader organizational outcomes, such as employee engagement scores, retention rates, and succession planning metrics. Increases in employee engagement and retention among program participants can suggest a positive impact on leadership development and organizational culture.

Continuous improvement sessions, where participants, mentors, coaches, and program administrators come together to discuss program outcomes and feedback, can further enhance the evaluation process. These sessions allow for real-time adjustments and the sharing of best practices, ensuring that the mentorship and coaching programs remain dynamic and responsive to participants' needs.

Evaluating the effectiveness of mentorship and coaching programs requires a thoughtful blend of methods, tools, and metrics. By implementing a comprehensive evaluation strategy, organizations can not only assess the impact of these programs on leadership development but also identify opportunities for enhancing their design and delivery, ultimately ensuring their continued success and relevance.

The significance of mentorship and coaching in the development of future leaders cannot be overstated. These practices stand as fundamental pillars in the architecture of leadership development, providing the personalized guidance, support, and learning opportunities necessary for emerging leaders to navigate the complexities of their roles and environments. Through mentorship, leaders gain access to the wisdom and experience of seasoned professionals, benefiting from their insights and perspectives. Coaching, with its focused and goal-oriented approach, offers leaders the tools and frameworks needed to enhance specific skills and competencies, driving personal and professional growth.

The journey of developing future leaders through mentorship and coaching is marked by transformation. Leaders emerge from these experiences not only with improved abilities but also with a deeper understanding of themselves and their potential to influence and inspire those around them. The impact of these practices extends beyond the individual, influencing team dynamics, organizational culture, and ultimately, the broader landscape of leadership across industries.

The ongoing commitment to mentorship and coaching is essential for sustained leadership growth. Organizations that prioritize and invest in these practices demonstrate a commitment to nurturing talent, fostering a culture of continuous learning, and building a resilient and adaptable leadership pipeline. This commitment requires a strategic approach, encompassing the careful design and implementation of programs, regular evaluation and adaptation, and the cultivation of an organizational environment that values and supports mentorship and coaching.

For mentorship and coaching to truly be effective, they must be embraced not only by HR departments or leadership development professionals but by the entire organization. Senior leaders, in particular, play a critical role in modeling the value of these practices, both by participating as mentors and coaches and by advocating for their importance. This top-down endorsement can help to embed mentorship and coaching into the fabric of the organization, making them integral components of the leadership development journey.

As we look to the future, the landscape of work and leadership continues to evolve, with new challenges and opportunities emerging at an unprecedented pace. In this dynamic context, the role of mentorship and coaching becomes even more critical. These practices equip leaders with the resilience, adaptability, and innovative thinking necessary to thrive in an ever-changing world. By committing to the ongoing development of leaders through mentorship and coaching, organizations can ensure they are prepared to meet the demands of tomorrow, fostering a legacy of strong, impactful leadership for generations to come.

The investment in mentorship and coaching is an investment in the future. It is a declaration of belief in the potential of emerging leaders and a commitment to their growth and success. As organizations continue to navigate the challenges and opportunities of the 21st century, let us reaffirm our commitment to these vital practices, ensuring that the leaders of tomorrow are equipped, inspired, and ready to lead.

Preparing for Unforeseen Challenges

In the forthcoming chapter, "Navigating Unforeseen Challenges," we investigate the critical imperative of preparing leaders to confront and navigate through the unexpected disruptions and challenges that are an inherent part of today's dynamic business landscape. This introduction sets the stage for a comprehensive exploration of the multifaceted nature of unforeseen challenges—ranging from economic upheavals, technological breakthroughs, to natural disasters—and their profound impact on organizations and the individuals who lead them.

The essence of leadership in the 21st century is not only defined by the ability to steer through the known but, perhaps more importantly, by the capacity to adapt and thrive amidst the unknown. The need for adaptability and resilience has never been more pronounced, as these qualities are paramount for leaders tasked with guiding their organizations through periods of uncertainty and abrupt change.

Understanding the nature of unforeseen challenges is the first step in preparing for them. These challenges can manifest in various forms, impacting organizations in wide-ranging and often unpredictable ways. By identifying the types of disruptions that can occur and understanding their potential impact on leadership roles and organizational dynamics, leaders can better prepare themselves for the inevitable uncertainties of the future.

Developing a proactive mindset is crucial for leaders to anticipate and mitigate the effects of unforeseen challenges. This chapter will explore strategies to cultivate such a mindset, emphasizing the importance of anticipatory thinking, strategic foresight, and the readiness to pivot when circumstances demand.

Risk assessment and management skills are indispensable tools for leaders, enabling them to identify potential threats and develop strategies to address them effectively. This chapter will provide insights into training leaders in these essential skills, integrating risk management into their regular leadership practices to ensure a robust response to potential challenges.

Flexibility in leadership and organizational structures can significantly enhance an organization's capacity to adapt to sudden changes. Through case studies, we will examine how organizations that have successfully navigated unexpected events did so by embracing flexible strategies and structures.

This chapter will cover the vital components of crisis management and response training, communication strategies during disruptions, and the critical role of emotional intelligence and stress management in leading through crises. These elements are foundational for maintaining team morale and ensuring organizational resilience in the face of adversity.

Learning from past disruptions is also key to preparing for future challenges. By analyzing previous events and incorporating the lessons learned into leadership training and development, organizations can strengthen their readiness for whatever lies ahead. Creating a culture of continuous learning and adaptability is essential for fostering an environment where leaders are not only equipped to handle current challenges but are also vigilant and responsive to emerging trends and potential disruptions.

This chapter aims to underscore the ongoing nature of readiness and adaptability in leadership. By summarizing the key aspects of preparing for unforeseen challenges, we emphasize the importance of a forward-looking approach that prioritizes resilience, adaptability, and proactive planning in the face of uncertainty.

The importance of preparing leaders for unexpected disruptions and challenges in today's fast-paced and increasingly interconnected world cannot be overstated. The ability of organizations to endure and thrive amid unforeseen events largely hinges on the readiness of their leaders to navigate through such uncertainties. These disruptions, which can range from global pandemics and economic recessions to rapid technological advancements and natural disasters, test the resilience and adaptability of leaders and their teams.

Adaptability and resilience have emerged as non-negotiable leadership qualities in this context. Adaptability, the ability to pivot and adjust strategies in response to changing circumstances, allows leaders to steer their organizations through turbulent times. It encompasses the foresight to anticipate changes, the agility to respond quickly to emerging challenges, and the creativity to find new opportunities within adversity.

Resilience, on the other hand, is the capacity to withstand and recover from difficulties. It involves maintaining focus and composure under pressure, sustaining morale among team members, and preserving the organization's core functions even in the face of disruptions. Together, adaptability and resilience enable leaders not only to survive unexpected challenges but also to emerge stronger and more prepared for the future.

The need for these qualities in leadership is further contextualized by the increasing frequency and intensity of global disruptions. As businesses operate in a more interconnected and digital landscape, the ripple effects of challenges in one part of the world can quickly impact organizations globally. Leaders must, therefore, be equipped with the skills to anticipate potential crises, manage risks proactively, and lead their organizations through periods of change with confidence and strategic insight.

Cultivating adaptability and resilience within leadership ranks has broader implications for organizational culture and performance. Leaders who embody these qualities set a powerful example for their teams, fostering a culture of flexibility, innovation, and resilience throughout the organization. This, in turn, enhances the organization's overall capacity to adapt to changes, seize new opportunities, and maintain competitive advantage in an unpredictable environment.

Preparing leaders for unexpected disruptions and challenges is a critical investment in the future sustainability and success of organizations. By emphasizing the development of adaptability and resilience, organizations can ensure that their leaders are not just equipped to handle the challenges of today but are also ready to embrace the opportunities and uncertainties of tomorrow.

Understanding the nature of unforeseen challenges is crucial for leaders aiming to navigate their organizations through turbulent times. These challenges can manifest in various forms, each with its unique set of implications for organizations and their leadership. Broadly categorized, unforeseen challenges include economic downturns, technological disruptions, and natural disasters, among others. Grasping the scope and potential impact of these disruptions helps leaders prepare more effectively and respond more adaptively.

Economic downturns, such as recessions, market crashes, or financial crises, pose significant challenges to organizational stability and growth. These periods are characterized by reduced consumer spending, tightening credit markets, and overall economic uncertainty. The impact on organizations can be profound, affecting everything from revenue and profitability to workforce morale and operational viability. Leaders must navigate these economic challenges with strategic foresight, making difficult decisions about cost management, resource allocation, and strategic investments to ensure the organization's survival and future growth.

Technological disruptions are another category of unforeseen challenges that can have a transformative impact on industries and organizations. Advances in technology, while offering opportunities for innovation and efficiency, can also render existing business models obsolete, disrupt market dynamics, and introduce new competitive pressures. The rapid pace of technological change demands that leaders remain vigilant and adaptable, ready to embrace new technologies, invest in digital transformation, and foster a culture of continuous learning and innovation within their organizations.

Natural disasters, including hurricanes, earthquakes, floods, and pandemics, present immediate and often severe challenges to organizational operations and employee safety. The direct impact of these events can range from physical damage to facilities and supply chain disruptions to significant shifts in market demand. Beyond the immediate response to ensure safety and continuity of operations, leaders must also manage the long-term recovery process, balancing the need for operational resilience with the well-being of employees and communities.

The impact of such unforeseen challenges on organizations and leadership roles is multifaceted. Leaders must not only address the immediate operational and financial implications of these disruptions but also consider their long-term impact on organizational strategy, culture, and stakeholder relations. This requires a balance of tactical decision-making to navigate the immediate crisis and strategic vision to position the organization for recovery and future success.

These challenges often test the personal resilience and adaptability of leaders themselves. Leading through uncertainty demands emotional intelligence, clear communication, and the ability to maintain team morale in the face of adversity. It also underscores the importance of building a resilient organizational culture, where teams are empowered to respond flexibly and creatively to challenges.

Understanding the nature of unforeseen challenges is a critical aspect of effective leadership. By identifying the types of disruptions that may impact their organizations and assessing their potential implications, leaders can develop more robust strategies for risk management, resilience, and adaptation. This preparation enables leaders and their organizations not just to survive unforeseen challenges but to emerge stronger and more prepared for the future.

Developing a proactive mindset among leaders is essential for navigating the complexities of modern organizational challenges. A proactive mindset shifts the focus from merely reacting to events as they occur to anticipating future trends, preparing for potential disruptions, and seizing opportunities for innovation and growth. Cultivating this mindset involves several strategic approaches aimed at enhancing leaders' capacity for anticipatory thinking and strategic foresight.

One effective strategy is to foster a culture of continuous learning and curiosity within the organization. Leaders should be encouraged to stay informed about global trends, industry developments, and emerging technologies that could impact their organization. This can be facilitated through regular knowledge-sharing sessions, participation in industry forums, and access to educational resources. A culture that values learning promotes an environment where leaders are naturally inclined to look ahead and consider the broader implications of today's decisions on tomorrow's outcomes.

Another key approach is to integrate scenario planning into the strategic planning process. Scenario planning involves developing a range of plausible future scenarios, each based on different assumptions about how current trends could evolve. By considering various potential futures, leaders can better anticipate changes, prepare for different outcomes, and develop flexible strategies that can be adapted as circumstances change. This practice not only enhances strategic foresight but also reduces the risk of being caught off-guard by unforeseen events.

Encouraging cross-functional collaboration is also crucial in developing a proactive mindset. Bringing together diverse perspectives from across the organization can uncover insights and opportunities that might not be apparent from a single vantage point. Cross-functional teams can work together to identify emerging threats and opportunities, develop innovative solutions, and implement proactive strategies. This collaborative approach fosters a sense of shared responsibility for the organization's future, reinforcing the importance of proactive thinking at all levels.

Implementing a system of early warning signals can help leaders identify potential disruptions before they fully materialize. This involves monitoring key indicators that could signal changes in the market, technology, regulatory environment, or other relevant areas. By establishing mechanisms to track these signals and assess their implications, leaders can take preemptive action to mitigate risks or capitalize on emerging opportunities.

Cultivating resilience and adaptability is fundamental to a proactive mindset. Leaders should be trained to embrace change as an inevitable and potentially beneficial aspect of the business landscape. Developing skills in adaptive leadership, stress management, and creative problem-solving can prepare leaders to navigate uncertainty with confidence and agility. This resilience ensures that leaders not only anticipate future challenges but are also equipped to respond effectively, whatever the future holds.

Developing a proactive mindset among leaders requires a deliberate and multifaceted approach. By fostering continuous learning, engaging in scenario planning, encouraging cross-functional collaboration, monitoring early warning signals, and cultivating resilience, organizations can equip their leaders with the tools needed to think ahead, prepare for the future, and lead with strategic foresight. This proactive approach positions organizations to navigate the uncertainties of the business environment more effectively and seize the opportunities that arise from change.

Training leaders in risk assessment and management techniques is crucial for equipping them with the skills necessary to identify, evaluate, and mitigate risks that could impact their organization's objectives. Integrating these techniques into regular leadership practices enables leaders to proactively address potential threats, ensure operational resilience, and capitalize on opportunities that align with their strategic goals.

To effectively train leaders in risk assessment and management, organizations can adopt a structured approach that includes both theoretical knowledge and practical application. This training might cover fundamental concepts of risk management, including the processes of risk identification, risk analysis, risk evaluation, and risk treatment. Leaders learn to distinguish between different types of risks—strategic, operational, financial, and compliance—and understand the methodologies for assessing and prioritizing these risks based on their likelihood and impact.

One effective technique is scenario analysis, which allows leaders to explore various risk scenarios and their potential effects on the organization. This helps in developing strategic responses and contingency plans for different risk outcomes. Additionally, training can introduce leaders to tools and frameworks such as SWOT analysis (Strengths, Weaknesses, Opportunities, Threats), PESTLE analysis (Political, Economic, Social, Technological, Legal, Environmental), and risk heat maps, enhancing their ability to analyze and visualize risks comprehensively.

Incorporating risk management into regular leadership practices involves creating a culture where risk awareness is part of the decision-making process. Leaders should be encouraged to routinely assess risks as part of their strategic planning, project management, and operational activities. This ongoing risk assessment enables organizations to remain agile and responsive to changes in their internal and external environments.

Organizations can also foster a risk-informed culture by establishing clear communication channels for discussing risks and sharing risk information across different levels of the organization. This transparency ensures that risk considerations are integrated into broader organizational strategies and that all team members are aware of and prepared to manage risks relevant to their roles.

To reinforce the practical application of risk management skills, organizations can conduct regular risk management workshops and simulations. These hands-on exercises allow leaders to practice identifying and responding to risks in a controlled environment, building their confidence and competence in managing real-world challenges.

Integrating risk management metrics and indicators into performance evaluations can motivate leaders to consistently apply risk management practices in their work. By recognizing and rewarding effective risk management, organizations can highlight its value and encourage a proactive approach to identifying and mitigating risks.

Training leaders in risk assessment and management skills and incorporating these practices into regular leadership activities are essential for building organizational resilience and strategic agility. Through structured training, practical exercises, and a culture that values risk awareness, leaders can better navigate the complexities of the business landscape, ensuring their organization's sustainability and success in the face of potential threats and uncertainties.

Building flexibility into leadership and organizational structures is increasingly recognized as a critical strategy for navigating the rapid pace of change in today's business environment. This flexibility allows organizations to respond swiftly and effectively to sudden changes, whether they arise from market dynamics, technological advancements, regulatory shifts, or global events. By cultivating flexible strategies and structures, organizations can ensure resilience, maintain continuity, and seize opportunities in the face of unpredictability.

Flexibility in leadership involves the capacity to adjust leadership style and approach based on the situation at hand. Adaptive leaders are those who can pivot their strategies in response to new information or changing circumstances, demonstrating versatility in their problem-solving and decision-making processes. This adaptability is crucial not only for managing crises but also for fostering innovation and growth. Leaders who embrace flexibility encourage a culture of experimentation and learning, where risk-taking is supported, and failure is viewed as a step toward success.

At the organizational level, flexibility is embodied in structures and processes that are designed to be dynamic rather than rigid. Traditional hierarchical models are giving way to more fluid structures that promote agility and faster decision-making. These might include cross-functional teams, decentralized authority, and project-based work that transcends conventional departmental boundaries. Such structures empower employees at all levels, enabling quicker responses to challenges and opportunities alike.

Implementing flexible strategies also means embracing a forward-looking approach to planning that accommodates multiple scenarios. Rather than relying solely on long-term plans set in stone, organizations benefit from developing a range of strategic options that can be activated as needed. This strategic flexibility ensures that the organization can pivot its focus and resources efficiently, minimizing disruptions and capitalizing on emergent trends.

Technology plays a pivotal role in enhancing organizational flexibility. Investing in digital tools and platforms that facilitate communication, collaboration, and data analysis can support more agile ways of working. Digital technologies enable remote work, streamline operations, and provide leaders with real-time insights needed to make informed decisions quickly.

Cultivating a mindset of continuous learning and adaptability among employees is essential for building flexibility into the organizational DNA. Training programs, learning opportunities, and policies that encourage innovation contribute to a workforce that is not only skilled but also resilient and open to change.

However, building flexibility into leadership and organizational structures does not come without challenges. It requires a delicate balance between providing enough structure to ensure coherence and direction while allowing enough freedom to adapt and innovate. Leaders must navigate this balance, fostering an environment where flexibility is seen as a strategic asset.

The importance of flexible strategies and structures cannot be overstated in the current business landscape. Organizations that prioritize flexibility in their leadership and organizational design are better positioned to navigate the uncertainties of the modern world. They can adapt to sudden changes more effectively, ensuring their long-term sustainability and success in an ever-evolving global market. Let's explore four case studies here that provide real-life explanations of organizations that have thrived after a crisis.

Case Study 1: LEGO's Strategic Pivot During the Financial Crisis

Background: In the early 2000s, LEGO faced a dire financial crisis, with 2003 marking one of its biggest losses in history. The company was struggling due to overexpansion into markets and products that diluted its core business.

Adaptation: In response to the crisis, LEGO underwent a significant strategic overhaul. The company refocused on its core product lines, improving efficiency and reducing costs. It also embraced digital innovation, developing online communities and digital platforms for LEGO enthusiasts. Additionally, LEGO expanded its licensing agreements, capitalizing on partnerships with blockbuster franchises like Star Wars and Harry Potter.

Outcome: These strategic pivots not only helped LEGO survive the financial crisis but also set the stage for unprecedented growth. By 2015, LEGO had become the world's largest toy company by revenue, demonstrating the power of adaptability and strategic focus.

Case Study 2: Netflix's Evolution from DVD Rentals to Streaming Giant

Background: Netflix started as a DVD rental service by mail in the late 1990s. However, the founders foresaw the potential impact of digital streaming on the entertainment industry.
Adaptation: In 2007, ahead of significant market demand, Netflix launched its streaming service, allowing subscribers to watch

television shows and movies on their computers. This move required a complete transformation of the company's business model, from logistics and distribution of DVDs to investing in digital infrastructure and content licensing for streaming.

Outcome: The shift to streaming positioned Netflix as a leader in the entertainment industry, significantly disrupting traditional television and film distribution. Today, Netflix is a dominant force in media, producing its own content and expanding globally, showcasing the importance of foresight and flexibility in corporate strategy.

Case Study 3: Toyota's Response to the 2011 Earthquake and Tsunami

Background: The 2011 earthquake and tsunami in Japan severely disrupted Toyota's supply chain, halting production due to shortages of parts and materials.

Adaptation: Toyota responded by overhauling its supply chain management approach. It developed a risk assessment tool that mapped the supply chain network, identifying critical vulnerabilities. Toyota also diversified its supplier base and increased its inventory of critical components. Furthermore, the company invested in disaster response strategies and business continuity planning to better manage future crises.

Outcome: These adaptations made Toyota's supply chain more resilient to disruptions. The company's swift recovery and subsequent measures to mitigate similar risks in the future have been widely regarded as a benchmark in supply chain risk management, emphasizing the importance of preparedness and adaptability in the face of natural disasters.

Case Study 4: Airbnb's Strategy Shift During the COVID-19 Pandemic

Background: The COVID-19 pandemic hit the travel industry hard, with Airbnb experiencing a significant drop in bookings due to global travel restrictions.

Adaptation: Airbnb quickly adapted by shifting its focus towards "staycations" and local travel experiences, catering to the changing behavior of travelers seeking escapes close to home. The company also introduced enhanced cleaning protocols to address health and safety concerns and offered more flexible cancellation policies to accommodate the uncertainty faced by travelers.

Outcome: These strategic shifts allowed Airbnb to recover more quickly than many traditional travel and hospitality businesses. The company successfully went public in December 2020, amidst the pandemic, showcasing resilience and the ability to pivot in response to global events.

These case studies underscore the critical importance of adaptability, strategic foresight, and resilience in navigating unexpected events. Organizations that can swiftly pivot their strategies, reassess their business models, and innovate in the face of challenges are better positioned to thrive in an ever-changing global landscape.

Crisis management and response training equip leaders with the essential skills and knowledge needed to navigate their organizations through unexpected and potentially disruptive events. Effective crisis management involves more than just damage control; it requires a proactive approach to identifying potential crises, planning responses, and leading teams with confidence and clarity under pressure. Incorporating role-playing and simulation exercises into this training can significantly enhance leaders' preparedness for real-world crisis scenarios.

- Essential Skills and Knowledge for Effective Crisis Management
- Strategic Decision-Making: Leaders must be able to make quick, informed decisions during a crisis. This involves assessing the situation accurately, considering the short-term

and long-term implications of different actions, and choosing a course that minimizes harm and supports recovery.

- Communication: Clear, transparent, and timely communication is crucial during a crisis. Leaders need to know how to effectively communicate with internal stakeholders, such as employees and board members, as well as external stakeholders, including customers, regulators, and the media.

- Emotional Intelligence: The ability to manage one's emotions and understand and influence the emotions of others is particularly important during a crisis. Leaders with high emotional intelligence can maintain composure, inspire confidence in their teams, and navigate the emotional complexities of crisis situations.

- Adaptability: Crises are often unpredictable, requiring leaders to be flexible in their approach. Adaptability allows leaders to pivot strategies as new information emerges and to find innovative solutions to challenges.

- Team Leadership: Effective crisis management often requires a coordinated team effort. Leaders must be able to rally their teams, delegate responsibilities clearly, and maintain morale in the face of adversity.

Role-Playing and Simulation Exercises

- Scenario-Based Role-Playing: This involves creating realistic crisis scenarios based on potential risks the organization might face, such as a cybersecurity breach, a product recall, or a natural disaster. Leaders are then guided through role-playing exercises where they must navigate the crisis, make decisions, and communicate with stakeholders. This hands-on approach helps leaders practice their response strategies and refine their decision-making and communication skills in a safe environment.

- Crisis Simulation Exercises: These exercises take role-playing a step further by simulating the dynamics of a real-life crisis in real-time. Participants may be divided into teams, each responsible for different aspects of the crisis response, such as operations, communications, and logistics. The simulation can include unexpected developments and challenges, forcing leaders to adapt their strategies and work together under pressure. Simulations often conclude with a debriefing session, where participants can reflect on their actions, discuss what went well, and identify areas for improvement.

- Tabletop Exercises: Tabletop exercises are discussion-based sessions where leaders gather to walk through a specific crisis scenario step-by-step. This format encourages open discussion about the organization's response plan, roles and responsibilities, and potential challenges. It's an effective way to identify gaps in the crisis response plan and to ensure that all team members understand their roles.

Incorporating these role-playing and simulation exercises into crisis management and response training not only enhances leaders' skills but also tests and improves the organization's overall preparedness for crises. By simulating the pressures and complexities of real-world scenarios, leaders can develop a deeper understanding of what effective crisis management entails and build the confidence needed to lead their organizations through challenging times.

Developing effective communication strategies during disruptions is a cornerstone of successful crisis management, ensuring that both internal and external stakeholders remain informed, engaged, and reassured. Crafting and executing these communication plans requires a nuanced understanding of the crisis at hand, the needs and concerns of different stakeholder groups, and the channels most effective for reaching them. A well-thought-out communication strategy not only helps to mitigate the immediate impacts of a crisis but also plays a crucial role in preserving the organization's reputation and trust over the long term.

For internal stakeholders, such as employees, clear and transparent communication is vital for maintaining morale and ensuring continuity of operations. Leaders should prioritize regular updates about the situation, the steps the organization is taking in response, and what is expected of employees during this time. Providing a forum for employees to ask questions and express concerns can also foster a sense of community and support. Importantly, internal communication should be empathetic, acknowledging the challenges and uncertainties employees may face and offering resources or support where possible.

External stakeholder communication, including customers, partners, investors, and the broader public, requires a similarly strategic approach. The focus should be on conveying how the organization is addressing the disruption, the implications for stakeholders, and any changes to operations or services. Transparency is key; being upfront about the challenges and uncertainties, while also highlighting the steps being taken to manage the situation, can help maintain trust and confidence. Tailoring the message to the specific concerns and needs of each external stakeholder group, and choosing the appropriate channels to reach them, whether through social media, press releases, or direct communication, is essential for effective outreach.

In all communication during a crisis, maintaining clarity and consistency is crucial. Mixed messages or conflicting information can exacerbate confusion and erode trust. Organizations should designate official spokespersons and ensure all communications are coordinated and consistent across different channels and platforms. This unified approach helps to reinforce the organization's message and maintain a single, reliable source of information for stakeholders.

Listening and responding to stakeholder feedback during a crisis can provide valuable insights into their concerns and perceptions, allowing the organization to adjust its communication and response strategies as needed. Monitoring social media, customer inquiries, and media coverage can offer a real-time gauge of stakeholder sentiment and identify areas where additional communication or clarification may be required.

Effective communication strategies during disruptions involve a balance of transparency, empathy, clarity, and responsiveness. By developing comprehensive communication plans that address the needs and concerns of both internal and external stakeholders, organizations can navigate the challenges of a crisis more smoothly, maintain stakeholder trust, and lay the groundwork for recovery and future resilience.

The role of emotional intelligence in leading through crises is paramount, as it equips leaders with the ability to understand and manage their own emotions as well as those of their team members. Emotional intelligence involves self-awareness, self-regulation, empathy, social skills, and motivation—all crucial for navigating the heightened tensions and uncertainties inherent in crisis situations. Leaders with high emotional intelligence can maintain their composure, make reasoned decisions under pressure, and communicate effectively, fostering a sense of stability and confidence among their teams.

In the context of a crisis, emotional intelligence allows leaders to recognize and address the emotional needs and concerns of their team members. By demonstrating empathy and understanding, leaders can build trust and loyalty, essential components for maintaining team morale and cohesion during challenging times. Additionally, emotional intelligence enables leaders to provide support and encouragement tailored to individual team members' needs, promoting resilience and a positive outlook even in the face of adversity.

Managing stress is another critical aspect of leading effectively through crises. Techniques for stress management are vital for both leaders and their teams to prevent burnout, maintain productivity, and ensure well-being. One effective technique is promoting open communication about stress and well-being. Creating an environment where team members feel comfortable discussing their stressors and seeking support can help leaders identify and address issues before they escalate.

Mindfulness and relaxation techniques, such as deep breathing exercises, meditation, or yoga, can also be beneficial for managing stress. These practices can help individuals remain centered and calm, improving their ability to think clearly and respond to challenges more effectively. Encouraging regular breaks and time off, even during busy periods, can also help prevent burnout and maintain physical and mental health. Physical activity is another powerful stress management tool. Encouraging team members to engage in regular exercise, whether through organized team activities or individual workouts, can help reduce stress levels, improve mood, and boost overall well-being.

Setting realistic goals and priorities can help manage workload and reduce stress. Leaders can work with their teams to identify critical tasks, delegate responsibilities, and set achievable deadlines. This approach helps to ensure that team members are not overwhelmed and that efforts are focused on the most important objectives.

Providing resources and support for professional development and personal growth can also contribute to stress management. Opportunities for learning and development can offer team members a sense of progress and achievement, even in difficult times, boosting morale and engagement.

Emotional intelligence and effective stress management are crucial for leading through crises. By understanding and addressing the emotional needs of their teams, promoting open communication, and employing techniques to manage stress, leaders can maintain team morale, foster resilience, and navigate their organizations through challenging times with compassion and clarity.

Learning from past disruptions is a crucial process for organizations aiming to enhance their resilience and adaptability. This process involves a thorough analysis of previous unexpected events, extracting valuable lessons, and then integrating these insights into leadership training and development programs. Such an approach not only prepares leaders for future challenges but also strengthens the organization's overall capacity to respond to and recover from disruptions.

The first step in learning from past disruptions is to conduct a comprehensive review of the events, focusing on the sequence of events, the decisions made, and their outcomes. This review should include both internal disruptions, such as operational failures or leadership crises, and external ones, like natural disasters, economic downturns, or technological shifts. The goal is to identify what worked well, what didn't, and why, to uncover valuable insights into the organization's response capabilities and resilience.

From this analysis, organizations can distill key lessons on various fronts, including crisis management, decision-making under pressure, communication strategies, and the importance of flexibility and adaptability in leadership and organizational structures. These lessons then become foundational elements in designing leadership training and development initiatives, ensuring that future leaders are equipped with the knowledge and skills to navigate similar challenges.

Incorporating lessons learned into leadership training involves more than just sharing knowledge; it requires integrating these insights into the curriculum in a way that promotes understanding, reflection, and application. This can be achieved through various methods:

- Case Studies: Developing case studies based on past disruptions allows leaders to analyze the situation, evaluate decision-making processes, and discuss alternative strategies in a structured learning environment.

- Simulation Exercises: Simulating crisis scenarios based on previous disruptions enables leaders to practice their response in a controlled, risk-free setting, enhancing their problem-solving and decision-making skills under pressure.

- Reflective Exercises: Encouraging leaders to reflect on their experiences with past disruptions, either personally or within their organizations, helps to internalize the lessons learned and apply them to future situations.

- Mentoring and Coaching: Incorporating discussions about past disruptions and the lessons learned into mentoring and coaching sessions provides a more personalized learning experience, allowing leaders to explore how these insights apply to their specific context and leadership style.

Furthermore, embedding a culture of continuous learning and adaptability within the organization ensures that the lessons learned from past disruptions are not forgotten but remain a living part of the organization's collective memory. This can be facilitated by maintaining an accessible repository of case studies, best practices, and key learnings, as well as regularly revisiting and updating these resources as new challenges and disruptions arise.

Learning from past disruptions and incorporating these lessons into leadership training and development is an ongoing cycle of reflection, learning, and application. By systematically analyzing previous unexpected events, extracting and sharing lessons learned, and integrating these insights into leadership development efforts, organizations can better prepare their leaders for the uncertainties of the future, fostering a culture of resilience and proactive adaptation.

Creating a culture of continuous learning and adaptability within an organization is pivotal for staying relevant and resilient in today's ever-evolving business landscape. Such a culture not only equips individuals and teams to respond effectively to changes and challenges but also fosters an environment of innovation and growth. This dynamic culture is characterized by an openness to new ideas, a commitment to personal and professional development, and a proactive stance toward anticipating and adapting to future trends and disruptions.

To foster this culture, organizations must prioritize learning and adaptability at every level, from top leadership down to entry-level employees. This begins with embedding continuous learning into the organization's core values and strategic objectives. By doing so, learning and adaptability become integral to the organizational identity, influencing decision-making, strategy, and daily operations.

Leaders play a crucial role in championing and modeling this culture. They must demonstrate a commitment to their own continuous learning, staying abreast of industry trends, technological advancements, and shifts in the global business environment. Leaders can share insights and learnings with their teams, encourage open dialogue about changes and challenges, and inspire others by showing how adaptability has positively impacted their leadership and the organization.

Encouraging leaders to stay informed about emerging trends and potential disruptions involves creating formal and informal mechanisms for knowledge sharing and trend analysis. This could include subscribing to industry journals, participating in professional networks, attending conferences and webinars, and leveraging social media and other digital platforms to gather and disseminate information. Organizations might also establish internal forums or regular meetings where leaders can discuss trends, share insights, and collaboratively explore implications for the organization.

To truly embed continuous learning and adaptability into the organizational fabric, it's essential to provide accessible learning resources and opportunities for all employees. This could involve developing in-house training programs, offering access to online courses and workshops, supporting participation in external professional development activities, and encouraging cross-functional project involvement. By making learning resources widely available, organizations empower their employees to take ownership of their development and adapt more readily to change.

Fostering a culture of experimentation and tolerance for failure is key to promoting adaptability. Organizations should encourage calculated risk-taking, viewing failures as opportunities for learning and growth. Celebrating successes, as well as constructive examination of failures, reinforces the value of experimentation and adaptability.

Feedback mechanisms and performance metrics can also reinforce a culture of continuous learning and adaptability. By incorporating measures of learning, innovation, and adaptability into performance evaluations, organizations can signal their importance and encourage behaviors that support this culture.

Creating a culture of continuous learning and adaptability is a strategic imperative that requires commitment, leadership, and structured support. By valuing and encouraging continuous learning, staying informed about emerging trends, providing accessible development opportunities, fostering an environment of experimentation, and reinforcing these values through feedback and recognition, organizations can navigate the complexities of the modern business environment with agility and resilience.

Preparing for unforeseen challenges is an essential facet of effective leadership and organizational resilience. The preceding discussion has illuminated the multifaceted approach required to navigate the unpredictable terrain of today's business landscape. At the heart of this preparedness lies the cultivation of adaptability and resilience, qualities that empower leaders and organizations to face unexpected disruptions head-on and emerge stronger.

The exploration of various strategies—from developing a proactive mindset and enhancing risk assessment skills to fostering a culture of continuous learning—underscores the complexity of readiness. It is not a static state but a dynamic process that evolves in response to new information, challenges, and opportunities. Leaders play a critical role in this process, not only by embodying these qualities themselves but also by instilling them within their teams and throughout their organizations.

Adaptability, the ability to pivot in response to changing circumstances, and resilience, the capacity to endure and recover from setbacks, have emerged as indispensable attributes of successful leadership. These qualities are supported by a foundation of continuous learning, which ensures that leaders and their teams are always expanding their knowledge base, refining their skills, and staying abreast of emerging trends and potential disruptions.

The incorporation of lessons learned from past disruptions into leadership training and development programs is another key aspect of preparedness. By analyzing previous challenges and integrating these insights into ongoing learning initiatives, organizations can equip their leaders with the wisdom and foresight needed to navigate future crises more effectively.

Creating a culture that values adaptability and continuous learning is essential for sustaining organizational resilience. This culture encourages an openness to change, supports innovation, and fosters a collective ability to respond to unforeseen challenges with agility and confidence.

Readiness and adaptability in leadership are ongoing endeavors. They require a commitment to continuous improvement, a willingness to embrace change, and a proactive approach to identifying and addressing potential challenges. As organizations look to the future, it is clear that the ability to prepare for and adapt to unforeseen challenges will be a defining characteristic of successful leadership.

Emphasizing the ongoing nature of readiness and adaptability, this chapter concludes with a call to action for leaders at all levels to cultivate these essential qualities. By doing so, they not only enhance their own effectiveness and resilience but also contribute to the creation of organizations that are robust, agile, and capable of thriving in an ever-changing global environment. The journey toward preparedness is perpetual, and it is through embracing this journey that leaders can ensure the long-term success and sustainability of their organizations.

Conclusion

Reflecting on the leadership journey post-pandemic offers a profound opportunity to consider the lasting impacts of a global crisis on the essence and execution of leadership. The COVID-19 pandemic, an unprecedented event in modern history, has not only challenged leaders across sectors but also catalyzed a reevaluation of leadership values, strategies, and the very skills deemed necessary for effective leadership in a rapidly changing world.

This period of disruption has underscored the resilience of leaders and organizations, pushing them to navigate through uncertainty, adapt to new ways of working, and lead with empathy and flexibility. The pandemic has accelerated digital transformation, necessitated the adoption of remote and hybrid work models, and highlighted the importance of mental health and well-being in the workplace. These shifts have expanded the leadership playbook, requiring leaders to cultivate new skills and adapt existing ones to meet the demands of a transformed work environment.

Adaptability has emerged as a paramount leadership quality. The ability to pivot quickly in response to changing circumstances, to rethink business models, and to innovate in the face of challenges has distinguished successful leaders during the pandemic. This adaptability extends beyond strategic flexibility to include emotional adaptability—nurturing resilience, maintaining team morale, and supporting employees through personal and professional upheavals.

Digital literacy has also been propelled to the forefront of essential leadership skills. As organizations have leaned more heavily on technology for operations, communication, and collaboration, leaders have needed to champion digital initiatives, ensuring their teams are equipped to thrive in a digital-first environment.

The pandemic has highlighted the critical role of emotional intelligence in leadership. The crisis brought personal and professional challenges into sharp focus, requiring leaders to lead with empathy, understanding, and compassion. The ability to connect with and support employees through difficult times has been vital for maintaining engagement and productivity.

Crisis management, always a component of leadership, took on new dimensions during the pandemic. Leaders had to make rapid decisions with limited information, manage the immediate impacts on their operations, and plan for an uncertain future. This experience has reinforced the importance of preparing for unforeseen challenges, emphasizing the need for leaders to develop a proactive and resilient mindset.

The journey through and beyond the pandemic has also reinforced the necessity for continuous learning and development in leadership. The fast-paced changes in the business environment demand that leaders remain lifelong learners, constantly acquiring new knowledge and skills to navigate the complexities of the modern world.

As we reflect on the leadership journey post-pandemic, it becomes clear that the challenges encountered have also presented opportunities for growth, innovation, and strengthened leadership. The lessons learned during this time will undoubtedly shape the future of leadership, emphasizing the need for adaptability, digital proficiency, emotional intelligence, and a steadfast commitment to continuous improvement. The post-pandemic world calls for leaders who are not only prepared to face ongoing uncertainties but who can also inspire and guide their organizations toward a future marked by resilience, agility, and enduring success.

As we approach the concluding reflections of our exploration into leadership in the aftermath of the COVID-19 pandemic, it becomes crucial to pause and assimilate the profound transformations and enduring lessons this period has imparted on the realm of leadership. The pandemic has irrevocably altered the contours of leadership, presenting both formidable challenges and unprecedented opportunities that demanded a reimagining of leadership practices. This closing chapter aims to encapsulate the major themes and insights that have surfaced throughout our discussion, offering a reflective synthesis on how the landscape of leadership has been reshaped in response to the pandemic.

Our journey has underscored the indispensable skills and competencies leaders must embrace to navigate the complexities of a post-pandemic world. Adaptability, digital literacy, emotional intelligence, and crisis management emerged as the cornerstones of effective leadership, essential for steering organizations through turbulent waters and into realms of innovation and growth. These skills, as we've discovered, are not just transient necessities but enduring requisites in the evolving business environment.

The narrative consistently highlighted the critical need for leaders to embody flexibility and adaptiveness. In an era marked by continuous flux, the ability of leaders to pivot their strategies and maintain organizational agility stands as a definitive factor in achieving resilience and seizing the momentum for change.

The shift towards remote and hybrid working models accentuated the importance of mastering communication and collaboration within geographically dispersed teams. Our exploration into best practices for managing such teams revealed the intricacies of fostering connectivity, clarity, and cohesion in virtual workspaces.

Drawing inspiration from case studies and real-world examples, we explore the narratives of leadership success amidst the pandemic. These stories illuminated the paths of leaders who navigated their organizations through crises with ingenuity and steadfastness, offering valuable lessons in resilience and adaptability.

A recurring theme has been the vital role of resilience and innovation in sustaining organizations through adversity. We explored strategies to nurture a culture that champions these qualities, recognizing their significance in driving long-term organizational vitality.

The discourse on mentorship and coaching underlined the importance of cultivating future leaders, prepared to face the uncertainties of tomorrow. The invaluable role of experienced leaders in mentoring and guiding emerging talents was emphasized as a cornerstone of sustainable leadership development.

A forward-looking perspective on leadership preparedness for unforeseen challenges highlighted the necessity of fostering a mindset geared towards continuous learning and adaptability, ensuring leaders are equipped to meet future disruptions with resilience and strategic foresight. Encouraging leaders to adopt a forward-thinking mindset emerged as a pivotal call to action. The importance of relentless personal and professional development was stressed as a means to thrive in the dynamic landscape of future leadership.

As we conclude this book, it is a call to action for today's leaders to harness the insights and strategies discussed, to not only navigate the post-pandemic world with confidence but also to be catalysts of positive transformation within their organizations and the broader community. Looking forward, we anticipate the future of leadership with optimism, recognizing the boundless potential for growth and innovation in the evolving narrative of leadership. This concluding chapter, therefore, serves not as an end but as an invitation to leaders to continue their journey of learning, adaptation, and visionary leadership.

In the new era of leadership that has unfolded in the aftermath of the global pandemic, certain key skills and competencies have emerged as critical for leaders seeking to navigate the complexities of the modern business landscape. These skills—adaptability, digital literacy, emotional intelligence, and crisis management—form the cornerstone of effective leadership, enabling leaders to respond to challenges with agility, lead their teams with empathy and understanding, and steer their organizations toward sustainable success.

Adaptability, the ability to pivot and respond swiftly to changing circumstances, has proven indispensable. The rapid pace of change in today's world, accelerated by the pandemic, demands that leaders remain flexible in their strategies and open to new approaches. This agility allows leaders to seize opportunities in the midst of uncertainty and guide their organizations through transitions with foresight and resilience.

Digital literacy has also taken center stage as businesses have increasingly moved online, leveraging technology for operations, communication, and service delivery. Leaders must now be proficient in digital tools and platforms, understanding how to harness technology to drive innovation, improve efficiency, and engage with stakeholders. This digital acumen is essential not only for navigating the present but also for shaping the future of organizations in an increasingly digital world.

Emotional intelligence, the capacity to be aware of, control, and express one's emotions, and to handle interpersonal relationships judiciously and empathetically, has always been a valuable leadership trait. However, its importance has been magnified in the context of the pandemic's challenges. Leaders with high emotional intelligence can support their teams through crises, manage stress and conflict effectively, and foster a positive, inclusive work environment. This skill is vital for building and maintaining trust, engagement, and morale among team members.

Crisis management, while always a component of leadership, has gained new significance. The unpredictability of recent events has underscored the need for leaders to be prepared for emergencies, capable of making quick decisions under pressure, and adept at navigating their organizations through periods of disruption. Effective crisis management involves not just addressing the immediate challenges but also anticipating potential impacts and preparing the organization for recovery and growth.

These essential skills—adaptability, digital literacy, emotional intelligence, and crisis management—are not merely responses to the current moment; they are indicative of the broader shifts in the business environment and society at large. As such, their importance will only continue to grow, shaping the contours of leadership in the years to come. Leaders who cultivate these competencies will be well-equipped to lead their organizations into the future, embracing change, driving innovation, and creating value in an ever-evolving world.

The imperative of flexible leadership in today's fast-paced and uncertain world cannot be overstated. As organizations navigate through continuous change—be it technological advancements, shifting market dynamics, or global disruptions—the ability of leaders to adapt their leadership styles in response to evolving circumstances becomes crucial. This adaptability ensures not only the survival but also the thriving of organizations in the face of adversity and opportunity alike.

Flexible leadership is characterized by an openness to change, a willingness to revise strategies in light of new information, and the capacity to lead with agility across various situations and challenges. Leaders who embody this flexibility are better positioned to respond to unexpected events, pivot their approaches when original plans are thwarted, and seize new opportunities as they arise. This agility enables organizations to stay ahead of the curve, maintaining relevance and competitive advantage in a constantly evolving world.

The benefits of adopting flexible and adaptive leadership styles are manifold. Firstly, it fosters a culture of innovation within the organization. When leaders are open to change and willing to experiment, it encourages a similar mindset among team members, cultivating an environment where innovation flourishes. This can lead to breakthroughs in products, services, and processes that drive organizational growth and success.

Secondly, flexible leadership enhances organizational resilience. Leaders who can quickly adapt to changing circumstances and guide their teams through transitions with confidence and clarity are instrumental in building resilience. This ability to bounce back from setbacks and navigate through uncertainty ensures that the organization can withstand disruptions and emerge stronger on the other side.

Flexible leadership is crucial for effective crisis management. In times of crisis, rigid leadership approaches can exacerbate challenges, whereas adaptive leaders can swiftly assess situations, make informed decisions, and communicate clearly with stakeholders. This agility in crisis situations helps to mitigate risks, protect the organization's reputation, and lead the organization toward recovery and stabilization.

Being agile and adaptive in leadership fosters employee engagement and retention. Leaders who demonstrate flexibility and support their teams through change positively impact team morale and job satisfaction. This not only enhances productivity but also attracts and retains top talent, who are drawn to dynamic and supportive work environments.

The imperative of flexible leadership in the current and future business environment is clear. As the pace of change accelerates and the nature of work continues to evolve, leaders must embrace flexibility and adaptability as core components of their leadership approach. By doing so, they can navigate the complexities of the modern business landscape with agility, driving their organizations forward in the face of continuous change and uncertainty.

Leading remote and hybrid teams successfully has become an essential skill for leaders in today's increasingly digital and flexible work environment. The shift toward remote and hybrid work models, accelerated by the COVID-19 pandemic, has highlighted the need for leaders to adapt their management styles to effectively support and engage teams that are not physically co-located. Key to this adaptation are the principles of communication and collaboration, which serve as the foundation for high-performing remote and hybrid teams.

Effective communication is paramount in remote and hybrid settings, where the lack of face-to-face interactions can lead to misunderstandings and a sense of isolation among team members. Leaders must prioritize clear, consistent, and open communication channels that facilitate not only the exchange of information but also the expression of ideas, concerns, and feedback. This involves regular check-ins with team members, the use of various communication tools to suit different needs, and the establishment of clear guidelines on communication norms and expectations. By ensuring that all team members feel heard and informed, leaders can foster a sense of inclusivity and belonging, critical components of team cohesion and morale.

Collaboration is equally important in dispersed team settings, where the physical distance can hinder the natural collaborative dynamics found in traditional office environments. Leaders must leverage technology to create virtual spaces that encourage teamwork, creativity, and innovation. This might include adopting collaboration platforms that allow for seamless project management, document sharing, and real-time communication. Additionally, fostering a culture that values collaborative achievement over individual success is crucial. Encouraging team members to share knowledge, support one another, and work together toward common goals can enhance productivity and drive better outcomes.

Successfully leading remote and hybrid teams involves acknowledging and addressing the unique challenges these work models present. This includes recognizing the potential for work-life balance issues and taking steps to encourage healthy boundaries between work and personal time. Leaders should also be attuned to the signs of remote work burnout and proactively offer support and resources to those struggling to adapt to remote work dynamics.

Another best practice involves fostering a strong team identity and culture, even in the absence of a shared physical workspace. Celebrating team achievements, facilitating virtual team-building activities, and creating opportunities for informal interactions can help build relationships and strengthen the team's collective sense of purpose and belonging.

Leading remote and hybrid teams successfully requires a deliberate focus on communication and collaboration, underpinned by a deep understanding of the unique challenges and opportunities presented by these work models. By embracing best practices that promote clear communication, seamless collaboration, work-life balance, and a strong team culture, leaders can ensure their remote and hybrid teams are engaged, productive, and poised for success in the evolving world of work.

Reflecting on real-world adaptations during the pandemic provides invaluable insights into successful leadership strategies under crisis conditions. The global spread of COVID-19 forced leaders across industries to rapidly adjust their approaches, demonstrating resilience, innovation, and the ability to pivot in response to unprecedented challenges. These case studies and examples highlight not just the necessity of swift adaptation but also the potential for such periods of disruption to catalyze positive transformation and growth.

One notable adaptation observed was the shift to remote work, which required leaders to rethink communication, collaboration, and team engagement strategies. Successful leaders navigated this transition by leveraging technology to maintain connectivity, fostering a culture of trust and accountability, and prioritizing employee well-being in the face of blurred work-life boundaries. The experience underscored the importance of flexibility and empathy in leadership, with many organizations discovering unforeseen benefits of remote work, including increased productivity and employee satisfaction.

Another significant adaptation involved organizational pivots to meet changing market demands and societal needs. For example, manufacturing companies retooled production lines to produce personal protective equipment, and distilleries shifted to making hand sanitizer, demonstrating agility and a commitment to social responsibility. These adaptations not only helped address critical shortages but also opened new business avenues and enhanced brand reputation.

Leaders in the healthcare sector faced the daunting task of managing frontline responses to the pandemic. Effective leadership in this context involved not only operational adaptations, such as expanding capacity and implementing telehealth services but also emotional support for overwhelmed staff. Leaders who communicated transparently, acknowledged the hardships faced by their teams, and provided psychological support emerged as pillars of strength, enhancing organizational resilience.

The education sector also witnessed remarkable adaptations, with institutions transitioning to online learning platforms. Leaders in education had to ensure technological access, adapt curricula for virtual delivery, and support teachers, students, and parents through the transition. Success in this area highlighted the importance of innovation in teaching methods and the need to consider equity and accessibility in remote education.

Reflecting on these real-world adaptations, several key lessons emerge for leaders navigating crises. First, the ability to adapt quickly to changing circumstances while maintaining a clear vision is crucial. Second, crises present opportunities for innovation and can serve as catalysts for long-term positive change. Third, leadership during crises requires not only strategic acumen but also a deep sense of empathy and commitment to the well-being of teams and communities.

The pandemic has been a powerful reminder of the capacity for human ingenuity and resilience in the face of adversity. The leadership adaptations witnessed across the globe during this period serve as testament to the potential for organizations to not only survive but thrive, by embracing change, fostering innovation, and leading with empathy and clarity. These real-world examples offer rich insights and inspiration for leaders seeking to navigate future challenges with agility and strength.

The crucial role of resilience and innovation in sustaining organizations through challenging times cannot be understated. Resilience, the ability to withstand and bounce back from adversity, and innovation, the capacity to create novel solutions in response to evolving challenges, are foundational qualities that enable organizations to navigate uncertainty and emerge stronger. Building a culture that supports these qualities involves a multifaceted strategy that permeates every level of the organization.

Creating an environment where resilience is valued starts with leadership. Leaders must model resilience by demonstrating a positive outlook in the face of challenges, showing a commitment to overcoming obstacles, and maintaining a focus on long-term goals despite short-term setbacks. This sets a tone that resilience is not just encouraged but expected, inspiring teams to adopt a similar mindset.

To foster innovation, organizations must cultivate a culture of curiosity and openness to new ideas. This involves encouraging experimentation and being receptive to unconventional solutions. Creating safe spaces for brainstorming, where all ideas are welcomed and considered, can spark creativity and lead to breakthrough innovations. Recognizing and rewarding innovative efforts, even when they don't always lead to success, reinforces the value placed on thinking outside the box and taking calculated risks.

Embedding resilience and innovation into the organizational fabric also requires a commitment to continuous learning. Providing opportunities for professional development, whether through formal training programs, workshops, or access to learning resources, empowers employees to expand their skill sets and adapt to new challenges. This commitment to growth ensures that the organization and its people are always evolving, making it more resilient and innovative over time.

Another strategy is leveraging diversity and inclusion. Diverse teams bring a range of perspectives, experiences, and ideas to the table, enriching the brainstorming process and increasing the likelihood of innovative solutions. Ensuring that all voices are heard and valued not only enhances creativity but also strengthens the sense of belonging and resilience among team members.

Transparent communication plays a pivotal role in building resilience and fostering innovation. Keeping teams informed about organizational challenges, changes, and successes creates a shared sense of purpose and alignment. Open channels of communication also encourage feedback and idea sharing, which are essential for continuous improvement and innovation.

Organizations can foster resilience and innovation by investing in technology and infrastructure that support flexible and agile work practices. This not only prepares the organization to adapt to unforeseen challenges but also enables teams to collaborate more effectively, regardless of physical location, enhancing their ability to innovate.

Building resilience and fostering innovation requires a deliberate approach that involves modeling resilience at the leadership level, encouraging curiosity and openness to new ideas, committing to continuous learning, leveraging diversity, maintaining transparent communication, and investing in supportive technology and infrastructure. By embedding these strategies into the organizational culture, leaders can ensure their teams are equipped to withstand adversity and capitalize on new opportunities, driving sustained success even in the face of challenges.

Mentorship and coaching stand as pivotal components in the development of future-ready leaders, underscoring the importance of passing on wisdom, experience, and guidance from seasoned leaders to emerging talents. This transfer of knowledge and skills is critical in preparing the next generation to navigate the complexities of modern leadership challenges, fostering a continuum of leadership excellence that sustains organizational growth and innovation.

The essence of mentorship lies in the personal, often long-term, relationships established between experienced leaders and their mentees. Through these relationships, mentees gain invaluable insights into the nuances of leadership, from strategic decision-making and problem-solving to navigating organizational politics and building resilient teams. Mentors act as role models, advisors, and sounding boards, offering not just advice but also support and encouragement, helping mentees to identify and achieve their professional goals. This one-on-one guidance is instrumental in accelerating the development of emerging leaders, equipping them with the confidence and competencies needed to assume leadership roles.

Coaching, while sometimes used interchangeably with mentorship, offers a more structured and goal-oriented approach to leadership development. Coaches work with individuals to develop specific leadership skills and competencies, address performance challenges, and unlock their potential. Unlike mentorship, which may evolve organically and cover a broad range of leadership aspects, coaching is typically more focused, with clear objectives and timelines. This focused development is crucial for honing the specific abilities leaders need to be effective in their roles, from communication and emotional intelligence to strategic thinking and crisis management.

Experienced leaders play a crucial role in guiding emerging talents through both mentorship and coaching. By sharing their experiences, challenges, and lessons learned, they provide a roadmap for navigating the path to successful leadership. This guidance is invaluable in helping future leaders understand the realities of leadership, anticipate challenges, and develop strategies for overcoming them. Furthermore, experienced leaders can offer critical feedback, helping mentees and coachees to refine their leadership styles, improve their decision-making, and enhance their overall effectiveness.

Mentorship and coaching contribute to the creation of a learning culture within organizations, where continuous personal and professional development is valued and supported. This culture not only benefits the individual leaders but also enhances the organization's capacity for innovation, resilience, and adaptability. By investing in the development of future-ready leaders, organizations ensure a pipeline of talented individuals prepared to lead with vision, empathy, and agility.

In conclusion, mentorship and coaching are essential for developing the next generation of leaders, providing them with the tools, knowledge, and confidence to face the challenges of the future. The role of experienced leaders in guiding emerging talents cannot be overstated, as their insights and support are fundamental to nurturing leadership capabilities. By prioritizing mentorship and coaching, organizations can cultivate a robust leadership pipeline, ensuring their continued success and relevance in an ever-evolving business landscape.

Preparing for the unpredictable underscores the need for leaders to cultivate resilience and foresight, ensuring they and their organizations can navigate through unforeseen challenges with agility and strength. The essence of leadership in today's rapidly changing environment is not just about steering through known obstacles but also about anticipating the unknown and being equipped to handle it when it arises. This necessitates a mindset shift towards continuous learning and adaptability, foundational qualities that enable leaders to respond to changes and disruptions effectively.

The unpredictability of the business landscape, marked by rapid technological advancements, economic fluctuations, and global events like the COVID-19 pandemic, illustrates the critical importance of being prepared for unforeseen challenges. These challenges test the resilience of organizations and demand a proactive rather than reactive approach to leadership. Leaders who cultivate the ability to anticipate potential disruptions, adapt their strategies accordingly, and lead their teams through uncertainty can better protect their organizations and seize opportunities that arise from such situations.

Encouraging a mindset of continuous learning is paramount in this context. Leaders who commit to lifelong learning, staying abreast of industry trends, emerging technologies, and global developments, position themselves to anticipate changes more accurately and prepare their organizations for the future. This learning extends beyond formal education to include experiential learning, reflection on past experiences, and learning from the successes and failures of others. By fostering a culture of curiosity and openness to new ideas, leaders can encourage their teams to embrace change and innovation, further enhancing the organization's adaptability.

Adaptability, in turn, requires flexibility in thought and action. It involves being open to revising plans and strategies in light of new information, experimenting with different approaches, and being willing to pivot when necessary. Leaders who demonstrate adaptability show their teams that change is not only expected but can be beneficial, fostering an organizational culture that is resilient in the face of unpredictability. This culture supports rapid decision-making, encourages innovation, and enables the organization to respond dynamically to challenges and opportunities alike.

Preparing for the unpredictable involves building robust systems and processes that can withstand disruptions. This includes diversifying supply chains, investing in technology infrastructure, developing contingency plans, and ensuring clear communication channels are in place. By taking these proactive steps, leaders can ensure their organizations are better equipped to manage unforeseen challenges when they arise.

The unpredictable nature of the modern business environment necessitates that leaders be ever-vigilant and prepared. Cultivating a mindset of continuous learning and adaptability is not just beneficial but essential for navigating the complexities of leadership today. By embracing these qualities, leaders can guide their organizations through uncertainty, leverage opportunities for growth, and build resilience against future disruptions.

Cultivating a leadership mindset for the future involves encouraging leaders to embrace a forward-thinking approach, characterized by an anticipation of future trends and challenges, as well as a commitment to ongoing personal and professional development. In an era marked by rapid technological advancements, evolving market dynamics, and increasing global interconnectedness, leaders who possess a forward-thinking mindset are better equipped to navigate the complexities of the modern world and steer their organizations toward long-term success.

Embracing a forward-thinking mindset requires leaders to look beyond the immediate challenges and opportunities, to envision what the future could hold for their industry, their organization, and their team. This involves staying informed about emerging technologies, societal shifts, and global economic trends, and considering how these could impact their business. Leaders must cultivate the ability to think strategically about the future, identifying potential risks and opportunities, and planning accordingly. This proactive approach to leadership not only prepares organizations to adapt to change but also positions them to shape the future of their industry.

The importance of ongoing personal and professional development in cultivating a future-ready leadership mindset cannot be overstated. The landscape of leadership is constantly evolving, with new theories, tools, and technologies emerging all the time. Leaders must, therefore, commit to a process of lifelong learning, actively seeking out opportunities to expand their knowledge, skills, and competencies. This could involve formal education, such as advanced degrees or professional certifications, as well as informal learning opportunities, such as attending conferences, participating in workshops, or engaging in self-directed study.

Personal development plays a critical role in enhancing a leader's effectiveness. This includes cultivating emotional intelligence, developing resilience, and honing critical thinking and decision-making skills. Leaders should also seek feedback from peers, mentors, and team members to gain insights into their leadership style and identify areas for improvement. By continuously working on their personal and professional growth, leaders can enhance their ability to inspire and motivate their teams, navigate complex challenges, and drive organizational success.

Encouraging leaders to embrace a forward-thinking mindset and commit to ongoing development also involves creating a supportive environment that values and rewards innovation, creativity, and strategic thinking. Organizations can foster this environment by providing resources for learning and development, recognizing and celebrating achievements in innovation and leadership, and encouraging risk-taking within the context of informed strategic planning.

Cultivating a leadership mindset for the future is essential for navigating the uncertainties and seizing the opportunities of the 21st century. By encouraging leaders to embrace a forward-thinking approach and commit to ongoing personal and professional development, organizations can prepare themselves to meet the challenges of the future, drive innovation, and achieve sustained success. This mindset not only benefits the leaders themselves but also serves as a model for their teams, promoting a culture of continuous learning and adaptability across the organization.

This book serves as a clarion call to action for today's leaders, urging them to absorb the insights shared and actively incorporate them into their leadership journey. In an era characterized by rapid change and complexity, the role of a leader transcends mere management and strategy. Leaders are called upon to be visionaries, catalysts for innovation, and architects of a future that is sustainable, inclusive, and resilient. The insights presented are not just theoretical constructs but practical guideposts designed to navigate the intricate landscape of modern leadership.

Leaders are encouraged to reflect deeply on the lessons drawn from real-world adaptations, the imperatives of flexible leadership, and the strategies for fostering resilience and innovation. These lessons provide a roadmap for leading with agility, empathy, and foresight. By embracing adaptability, digital literacy, emotional intelligence, and effective crisis management, leaders can elevate their capacity to guide their teams through uncertainties, leveraging challenges as opportunities for growth and development.

This call to action emphasizes the importance of leaders becoming agents of positive change within their organizations and broader communities. Leadership, in its essence, is about making an impact—shaping the culture of organizations, influencing the direction of industries, and contributing to the well-being of society. Leaders are urged to view their roles through the lens of service and stewardship, recognizing the profound influence they wield in creating environments where people can thrive, innovation can flourish, and sustainable growth can be achieved.

The journey of leadership is ongoing, marked by continuous learning, self-reflection, and adaptation. Leaders are encouraged to commit to their personal and professional development, seeking out new knowledge, challenging their assumptions, and expanding their perspectives. This commitment to growth not only enhances individual leadership effectiveness but also inspires others to pursue their own journey of learning and development.

Leaders are also called upon to mentor and coach the next generation, passing on their knowledge, experience, and insights to emerging talents. By investing in the development of future leaders, today's leaders can ensure the continuity of visionary and effective leadership that is capable of navigating the challenges and opportunities of the future.

This book's call to action for today's leaders is a reminder of the significant role leadership plays in shaping the future. Leaders are encouraged to take the insights from this book and apply them with intention and conviction. By doing so, they can become catalysts for positive change, driving their organizations toward success and making a lasting impact on their communities and the world at large. The path of leadership is both a privilege and a responsibility, and by embracing this path with courage, curiosity, and compassion, leaders can forge a legacy of transformation and achievement.

As we look forward to the future of leadership in a post-pandemic world, it is clear that the role of leaders is more critical than ever. The COVID-19 pandemic has irrevocably changed the global landscape, presenting both unprecedented challenges and unique opportunities for growth and innovation. As organizations and societies navigate the complexities of recovery and transformation, the evolving nature of leadership stands at the forefront of this journey, shaping the path forward.

The future of leadership calls for a blend of resilience, adaptability, and visionary thinking. Leaders will need to continue navigating the uncertainties of a world that has been fundamentally altered by the pandemic, leveraging the lessons learned to build stronger, more agile, and more innovative organizations. The ability to anticipate and respond to rapid changes in the environment, technology, and societal expectations will define the effectiveness of leaders in this new era.

The pandemic has underscored the importance of empathy, inclusivity, and sustainability in leadership. The leaders of tomorrow must not only drive economic success but also champion social responsibility, environmental stewardship, and the well-being of their teams and communities. This holistic approach to leadership reflects a growing recognition of the interconnectedness of business success with societal health and environmental sustainability.

The potential for growth and innovation in the post-pandemic world is immense. Leaders who embrace a forward-thinking mindset, who are committed to continuous learning, and who foster a culture of innovation within their organizations will be well-positioned to capitalize on new opportunities. The challenges of the pandemic have sparked innovations in technology, work practices, and business models that will continue to influence the landscape of leadership and organizational development.

As we close this exploration of leadership in a post-pandemic world, it is evident that the nature of leadership is continuously evolving. The qualities that define effective leadership today may be expanded or transformed as we confront the challenges and opportunities of tomorrow. Yet, the essence of leadership remains rooted in the ability to inspire and guide others towards a shared vision, to navigate through adversity with courage and insight, and to drive positive change within organizations and society at large.

In this moment of reflection, leaders are invited to consider their role in shaping the future. The journey ahead is both a challenge and an opportunity—an opportunity to redefine leadership for a new era, to contribute to the resilience and prosperity of organizations and communities, and to leave a lasting impact on the world. As we look forward, let us embrace the potential for growth and innovation with optimism and determination, guided by the enduring principles of visionary leadership and a steadfast commitment to making a difference.